Romani Writing

The Roma (commonly known as "Gypsies") have largely been depicted in writings and in popular culture as an illiterate group. However, as this book demonstrates, the Roma have a deep understanding of literacy and its implications, and use writing for a range of different purposes. While some Romani writers adopt an "oral" use of the written medium, which aims at opposing and deconstructing anti-Gypsy stereotypes, other Romani authors use writing for purposes of identity-building. Writing is for Romani activists and intellectuals a key factor in establishing a shared identity and introducing a common language that transcends linguistic and geographical boundaries between different Romani groups. Romani authors, acting in-between different cultures and communication systems, regard writing as an act of cultural mediation through which they are able to rewrite Gypsy images and negotiate their identity while retaining their ethnic specificity. Indeed, *Romani Writing* shows how Romani authors have started to create self-images in which the Roma are no longer portrayed as "objects", but become "subjects" of written representation.

Paola Toninato is a Research Fellow at the University of Warwick, UK. Her publications include *The Creolization Reader*, co-edited with Robin Cohen, and *Differences on Stage*, co-edited with Alessandra De Martino and Paolo Puppa.

Routledge Research in Literacy

EDITED BY DAVID BARTON, *Lancaster University, UK.*

1 **Women, Literacy and Development**
Edited by Anna Robinson-Pant

2 **Literacy and Globalization**
Reading and Writing in Times of
Social and Cultural Change
Uta Papen

3 **Popular Culture and Representations of Literacy**
Bronwyn T. Williams and Amy A. Zenger

4 **Romani Writing**
Literacy, Literature and Identity
Politics
Paola Toninato

Romani Writing
Literacy, Literature and Identity Politics

Paola Toninato

NEW YORK AND LONDON

First published 2014
by Routledge
711 Third Avenue, New York, NY 10017, USA

and by Routledge
2 Park Square, Milton Park, Abingdon, Oxfordshire OX14 4RN

First issued in paperback 2016

*Routledge is an imprint of the Taylor & Francis Group,
an informa business*

Library of Congress Cataloging-in-Publication Data
Toninato, Paola.
   Romani writing : literacy, literature and identity politics / by Paola Toninato.
      pages cm. — (Routledge Research in Literacy ; 4)
   Includes bibliographical references and index.
 1. Romani language—History. 2. Romanies—Education. 3. Romani literature—History and criticism. 4. Literacy—Social aspects. I. Title.
   PK2896.T66 2013
   491.4'97—dc23
   2013021500

ISBN 13: 978-1-138-28675-7 (pbk)
ISBN 13: 978-0-415-80590-2 (hbk)

Typeset in Sabon
by IBT Global.

For Alexander

Contents

List of Figures   ix

List of Tables   xi

Foreword   xiii
PROFESSOR JUDITH OKELY

Acknowledgements   xvii

Introduction: A People without Writing?   1

PART I
Romani Literacies

1   Writing and the Gypsies   7

2   Educating the Gypsies   25

3   Education and Literacy Acquisition from a Romani Perspective   42

PART II
The Rise of Romani Literature

4   The Rise of Romani Writing: An Overview   71

5   Roma Writing Themselves   92

6   Theorising Romani Literature: Literary Categories and
    Textual Strategies   114

PART III
The Politics of Romani Writing

7   The Political Use of Romani Writing and the Rise of an
    International Romani Intelligentsia   139

8   **The Mediating Role of Romani Literacy**   161

Notes   181
Bibliography   201
Index   227

Figures

1.1   A dark-skinned Gypsy.   12

1.2   A tent of Zapari—"wild" Turkish Gypsies.   17

1.3   German sign warning off Gypsies.   21

1.4–1.6   No parking signs specifically aimed at "nomads" and
Roma/Gypsies.   22

3.1   Trail signs.   57

3.2   Trail signs:
a) Harp-shaped drawings. b) A pile of three stones.   58

3.3   Advertisement.   63

3.4   Business card.   63

3.5   Roma/non-Roma communicative situations.   66

3.6   Romani writing: main functions and uses.   66

8.1   Nursery rhyme in Romani.   175

8.2   Teaching maths to Romani pupils.   178

Tables

3.1   "Tragi" Signs   58
3.2   Chine Signs   60
8.1   Romani Chib: The Romani Language   176

Foreword

Professor Judith Okely

This is a meticulously detailed overview of key historical and current controversies concerning the most stigmatised minority throughout Europe and especially focusing on the ambiguous role of literacy. This can be perceived as a weapon against difference but eventually as a means to self-assertion and the elaboration of identity. The reader is confronted by the earliest negative treatment of Roma or Romanies since they were first recorded centuries ago. They have been a unique type of nomad who inter-related with the dominant political economy. Unlike other nomads, they were never self-sufficient. Thus as service nomads, they had to know the non-Roma or *Gaje*, whether as customer or enemy.

Toninato argues convincingly, despite the popular misrepresentations, that Roma or Romanies were ever aware of the power of writing and indeed resorted early on to letters of approval from key power brokers to gain acceptance first as pilgrims. Such a reason for movement was valued in the dominant religious hegemony. Subsequently, these travelling individuals and groups were separated out as stigmatised nomads in opposition to the approved pilgrim category. More threateningly, written laws were instigated against them. The power of the written word was no route to enlightenment but the enforcement of the brutal dispersal if not near genocide. Roma were thus never ignorant of this mode of communication but instead learned of its use as the outsiders' weapon against difference.

We are reminded that the Roma, like groups and cultures around the world, have alternative if not additional means of communication, such as signs left on the pathways and landscape. What this text recognises as patrin is thus part of the Romani history. Toninato, with the support of key theoreticians such as Brian Street, challenges the simplistic divisions between literacy and non-literacy. It is mistaken, indeed arrogant to presume that so-called "traditional" societies lack scientific and rational thought.

I recall being informed by the English Gypsies, with whom I lived in the 1970s, how they would leave seemingly non-visible markings on gates and posts of house-dwellers indicating their welcome or hostility to Gypsy hawkers. Other times, non-motorised pedestrian Gypsy women left marks showing kin and allies their routes. A sympathetic solicitor in the area was told there was a very positive mark near her door, although she said she herself never found it.

For over a century or more anthropologists have challenged the notion of the so-called "primitive" with allegedly limited intellectual attributes. As this delicately written text reveals, in a culture where oral learning is prioritised, there are different ways of understanding the world, but no less sophisticated. Toninato distinguishes different ways of learning through childhood: "The Roma's informal and intergenerational approach to education" is different from "the Western formal educational system". In the latter, verbal communication and direct instruction dominates, whereas in Romani society knowledge is transmitted through observation and mimesis.

Again I recall being given travel directions by my non-literate Gypsy site neighbour to a locality some miles away. He described in minute visual detail, how the road curved at a specific tree and adjoined a house with red doors. Some miles on, I was to look out for certain hedges and some large grey building, whose details I immediately forgot. Then there would be a gate on the side of the road where I should turn. My book-trained mind was lost after just two of the visual images. I was schooled to look for road numbers and written signposts. My oral and visual memory, unprepared for this form of direction, could not compete. I marvelled at this hitherto unknown mental memory.

As Toninato poignantly describes, literacy as official writing has been associated with the persecuting dominant society which has wished to control, outlaw if not destroy a people with contrasting values. In other contexts, non-literacy has been used as justification for compulsory schooling; something the Romanies have rightly recognised as enforced assimilation disguised as benevolence. During my fieldwork, I soon learned how the very appearance of writing implements was perceived as a menacing signal. Gypsy site residents, who perhaps had one occasional literate inhabitant married into the community, informed me how they would always recognise a policeman in disguise, as soon as the individual brought out a notebook and pen from his inner jacket. Writing was thus associated with persecution. They did not mind the occasional and then rare tape recorder because they claimed their speech and testimony could not be distorted. The justifiable terror of an outsider, literate official was inculcated through the equivalent of bedtime stories, not read to them, but recounted as oral narrative. The children described to me how the devil was "a man with a briefcase". They were not deluded. Such persons, armed with papers, had ruthless power to "kidnap".

As Toninato documents, there has been a long and scandalous history of the seizure of Gypsy/Roma children from their parents. When policies of seemingly benevolent or enforced assimilation through compulsory schooling failed, brutal alternatives were implemented. This was the placing of the children into "homes", orphanages or subject to compulsory non-Roma adoption. Such practices, to be compared to the children "stolen" from

Australian Aboriginals, have been found throughout Europe. In my field area, one Gypsy family living in a comfortable tent, described how they had to be passively polite to a stranger insisting on inspection of their living conditions, for fear of seizure. Random outsiders could pose as officials. The Gypsies could not tell, let alone ask for paper identification. Indeed one leading UK Gypsy activist was taken into care, decades ago. He did acquire literacy during his compulsory incarceration but cultural assimilation failed in the long run. As soon as he was released as "free adult", he sought out his people and rejoined his community. From then on, he used that enforced insider knowledge of the dominant society to argue effectively in wider arenas and the media for the recognition of the Gypsies' cultural heritage and right to travel.

This carefully researched book explains how literacy has been historically associated with policies of assimilation, not intellectual liberation. There are descriptions of the contrast between the forms of socialisation among travelling Roma/Gypsies and those enforced among children of the dominant society. We read that greater autonomy is encouraged among Gypsy children in contrast to the rigid disciplinary school regime. Educationalists and others often have been unable to make sense of this alternative way of being. From infancy, Gypsies or Roma learn to be independent, resourceful and thus innovative. They also learn different linguistic communications. Romani languages or vocabulary interspersed within the dominant discourse are used to confirm solidarity and separation from non-Roma or *Gaje*.

I recall with wonder watching the children always being the first to run out to greet strangers entering the site. Dismissing them as helpless infants, the outsider would naively answer questions and explain his purpose. This was immediately conveyed back to the adults secluded in the caravans. In these and other ways, children were politicised from the outset. But the authorities, and especially educationalists, were oblivious to such sophistication. Autonomous behaviour by Gypsy children in any school classroom was perceived merely as undisciplined and chaotic. This study documents the practice of segregating Roma children, sometimes in classes, if not separate schools, for those labelled subnormal.

In the name of benevolence, Gypsy children have been victims of ethnocentric and ignorant assessments. A 1960s educational report cited by Toninato, declared that Gypsy children were the "most deprived" of all children in the UK. I recall the report's added observation that the children had "no toys" and engaged in "auto-destructive behaviour". Instead, I noted their imaginative use of surrounding objects and innovative play. Their alleged destructive behaviour was learning to break up metal and discarded objects in imitation of their parents' re-cycling work. They learned to distinguish different metals from a pre-school age. All this is consistent with Toninato's detailed but simultaneously generalised observations and evidence from across time and space through Europe.

The second half of this book explores the dramatic transformations in the Roma's use of writing. There have indeed been star Gypsy authors but today the number is increasing. In recent years, I have had the joy of supervising a Bulgarian Roma masters student and the doctorate of a Scottish Traveller. Both have used these qualifications to highlight their heritage, rather than "pass" as *Gaje*. Such invisibility was the defensive strategy in the past.

Toninato outlines the defining features of "polycentrism and linguistic hybridity". She reveals how intellectuals, artists and political activists are emerging alongside the rise in literacy. Romani writing can be a means of "bearing witness", a way to trace hitherto hidden histories. Toninato has for long engaged with Romani women authors and again we are offered more precious insights and examples. As argued by Paulo Freire long ago, literacy and writing can be a means to liberation and empowerment, not brutal domestication by the powerful alien. The political use of writing can be a way of talking back to dominant groups. Writing opens the routes to intercultural understanding and the celebration of the full range of human alternatives. In these current times of political and economic uncertainty, when Roma or Gypsies are scapegoated if not demonised in the mass media, it is a delight that they are not merely fighting but writing back.

Acknowledgements

The author would like to thank the following for granting permission to reproduce copyright material:

Franco Angeli for permission to reprint Figure 8.2, from Ignazi, Sabrina, and Monica Napoli, eds. *L'inserimento scolastico dei bambini rom e sinti*. Milan: Franco Angeli, 2004.

Archive Stadtmuseum Nördlingen for permission to reprint Figure 1.3.

Simon Evans for permission to reprint Figure 1.6, from Evans, Simon. *Stopping Places. A Gypsy history of South London and Kent*. Hatfield: University of Hertfordshire Press, 2005.

Aldo Francisci for permission to reprint extracts of the following poems in English translation: "Senza diritti né umanità" and "Senza speranza" by Mansueto Levacovich, originally published in: Levacovich, Mansueto. *Popolo mio dei Rom*. Abano Terme: Francisci, 1991.

Grafo—Igb Group and Leonardo Piasere for permission to reprint Figure 3.2, from Piasere, Leonardo. "I segni 'segreti' degli Zingari". *Ricerca Folklorica* 31 (1995): 83–105.

Damian Le Bas, for permission to print the poem "Words I Like".

Ronald Lee for permission to reprint his English translation of the Romani anthem *"Djélem djélem"*, originally published in: Lee, Ronald. *Learn Romani: Das-duma Rromanes*. Hatfield: University of Hertfordshire Press, 2005.

Sandra Jayat for permission to reprint extracts of the following poems in English translation: "The blue eagle" and "Not born to follow", originally published in: Jayat, Sandra. *Nomads Moons*. St Albans: Brentham Press, 1995.

Gerald Kurdoğlu Nitsche, Emirgan Yayinlari Editions, for permission to reprint extracts of Ceija Stojka's poems originally published in: Stojka, Ceija. *Meine Wahl zu schreiben—ich kann es nicht/O fallo de isgiri—me tschschanaf les: Gedichte und Bilder*. Landeck: Emigan Yayinlari Editions, 2003.

PEN American Center for permission to reprint extracts of the poems "The long road" and "I was born in black suffering" by Iliaz Šaban; "Without House or Grave" by Rajko Djurić; "The raid" by Santino Spinelli, originally published in: Hancock, Ian, Siobhan Dowd, and Rajko Djurić, eds. *The Roads of the Roma*. Hatfield: University of Hertfordshire Press, 1998.

Jack R. Rollwagen, Matt T. Salo and Sheila Salo for permission to reprint Figure 3.3, from Salo, Matt T., and Sheila Salo. "Romnichel Economic and Social Organization in Urban New England, 1850–1930". *Urban Anthropology* 11, nos. 3–4 (1982): 273–313.

Santino Spinelli for permission to reprint extracts of the following poems in English translation: "So ći ȝanàvas me" by Jorge M.F. Bernal; "Phir" and "Giuvli Romani" by Nada Braidic, originally published in: Spinelli, Santino, ed. *Baxtalo Drom/Felice Cammino*. Pescara: Tracce, 1995–1996; "Ćori kali morći" and "Av te ğav" by Ilija Jovanovic, originally published in: Spinelli, Santino, ed. *Baxtalo Drom/Felice Cammino*. Pescara: Tracce, 1995; "Auschwitz" by Santino Spinelli, originally published in Spinelli, Santino. *Gilí Romaní/Canto Zingaro*. Rome: Lacio Drom, 1988; "Figli del vento", "Kusibbè Romano", "Rodm" and "Meribbè" by Santino Spinelli, originally published in: Spinelli, Santino. *Romanipè/Ziganità*. Chieti: Solfanelli, 1993.

Giorgio Viaggio and Mirella Karpati, for permission to reprint extracts of the following poems in English translation: "Bistardi Laida" by Paula Schöpf, and "Destino" by Pučo, originally published in: Karpati, Mirella, ed. *Zingari ieri e oggi*. Rome: Lacio Drom, 1993.

Cecilia Woloch, for permission to reprint an extract from her poem "Tsigan: The Gypsy Poem", originally published in: Woloch, Cecilia. *Tsigan: The Gypsy Poem*. Los Angeles: Cahuenga Press, 2002.

Every effort has been made to trace the copyright holders and to seek authors' consent. If any have been inadvertently overlooked, at the first opportunity, the publisher will be pleased to make the necessary arrangements.

Introduction
A People without Writing?

This book addresses the complex understanding of literacy and writing among Roma, Sinti and Travellers,[1] groups that have long been arbitrarily labelled as people "without writing" (Toninato 1997). Such a negative definition, apparently confirmed by official low literacy rates among Roma, is ultimately based on two basic assumptions: that "true" writing coincides with alphabetic writing, and that the Roma are an exclusively oral culture with no knowledge of the written medium. This study challenges both assumptions.

Sweeping statements about the Roma's "illiteracy"[2] have a long and influential legacy (Graff 1991). They follow from a theoretical paradigm according to which a "Great Divide" (Horton and Finnegan 1973; Goody 1977) separates literate and non-literate peoples. The belief in the existence of such a divide has given rise to the idea of an alleged gap between traditional societies, dominated by "primitive" or "pre-logical" modes of thinking, and "modern" cultures, characterised by the dominance of logical and scientific thought (Lévy-Bruhl 1922). Yet anthropological evidence points to different conclusions: that Western literate societies have no monopoly over scientific thought (Lévi-Strauss 1962), and that there is no binary opposition between oral and literate cultures. As Ruth Finnegan states, "a degree of literacy has been a feature of human culture in most parts of the world for millennia". Although this "has rarely meant mass literacy", explains Finnegan, it has nevertheless entailed "a measure of influence from the written word and literatures even in cultures often dubbed 'oral'" (Finnegan 1977, 23). Romani groups are clearly no exception to this phenomenon.

As this study shows, the Roma were aware of the existence of writing and of its socio-political implications from a very early stage. The Roma appeared in Europe in the first half of the fifteenth century, around the time printing was invented (Williams 1986, 21; Piasere 1995, 83). At that time, although it had not yet become a mass phenomenon, literacy fulfilled a number of administrative and official purposes. To a certain extent, the Roma were able to use the written medium to their own advantage, as confirmed by the widespread use of "letters of protection" by Romani groups across Europe (see Chapter 1). However, despite their awareness of writing and literacy, ethnographic evidence suggests that the Roma have long eluded the dominant group's approach to literacy. Far from being symptomatic of "illiteracy" *tout court*, the Roma's traditional avoidance of writing constituted an ethnic strategy aimed at minimising the acculturative effects associated with schooled literacy. This study shows how this strategy has evolved through time in response to socio-economic changes: whereas in the past a pattern of restricted literacy acted as an effective barrier against assimilation, it is no longer regarded by all Roma as economically and politically viable. As a result, over the past few decades a new Romani approach towards writing has begun to emerge.

Chapter 1 investigates the deployment of writing as a hegemonic tool to assimilate the Romani population into mainstream society and culture at a representational and practical level. It distinguishes between an "official" use of writing by police and public authorities, whose main purpose was to control the Gypsies and restrict their movements, and the use of writing in a range of historic, literary and academic texts that played a crucial part in the narrative construction and essentialisation of the Gypsies' difference. By focusing on the first written records of the encounter between Romani groups and Western European populations, the chapter shows how textual renditions of "Gypsies" were instrumental in categorising their ethno-cultural difference in negative terms, thus marking out their behaviour as deviant and potentially dangerous. It discusses the socio-legal implications of the textual constructions of the "Gypsy", and argues that such narratives played a crucial role in establishing the Gypsy as the "ultimate alien" (Lucassen 1998, 61) in European society. The emphasis is on textual images that would greatly influence later stereotypical views of Gypsies, particularly the stereotypes based on their allegedly "deviant" and "savage" nature.

Chapter 2 uncovers the main social and cultural dynamics that explain the high official illiteracy rate among the Roma. The chapter provides an overview of the main educational initiatives aimed at the Roma, Gypsies and Travellers at EU level, and identifies the possible reasons for the overall failure of Gypsy school provision. It explains that the relationship between the Roma, Gypsies and Travellers and the school system has been fraught with difficulties and tensions from the beginning. Furthermore, it demonstrates that the field of Gypsy education is inextricably linked to the historical context of asymmetrical power relations between the Roma and non-Roma, and focuses on the official educational policies adopted towards Gypsies in previous centuries. In particular, the policies implemented by Maria Theresa of Austria and the attempts at educating the Gypsies by nineteenth-century missionaries are seen as representative of the assimilative orientation of the Western education system towards the Roma. The policy of assimilation through education carried out by political and religious authorities has left a permanent mark on the collective memory of several Romani and Sinti groups, and is the ultimate reason why education has been historically viewed as a threat by the Roma.

Chapter 3 illustrates the main features of the Romani approach to education vis-à-vis the non-Romani school system. While the Romani approach is informal and closely connected to the daily life of the group, the non-Romani model is decontextualised and considered as preparatory to "real" life. In addition, the two educational systems rely on different communication systems: the Romani system on the oral mode and the formal school system almost exclusively on written communication. Failure to acknowledge the specific differences between the two systems has led to the tension and incomprehension that together form another major obstacle to adequate education provision for Romani children. Yet despite their difficult relationship with the formal school system, the Roma appreciate that schooling can provide them with an invaluable tool: literacy. What the Roma mean by "literacy", however, does not correspond to the dominant view of this phenomenon.

Contrary to common opinion, the Roma have a deep understanding of literacy and its implications. The Romani approach does not narrowly focus on alphabetic writing, but is highly diversified and comprises a range of alphabetic and non-alphabetic writing systems with important socio-economic functions. Non-alphabetic writing includes early Romani writing systems such as the trail signs and graphic codes used by nomadic Western European Roma. Meanwhile, the Roma's contemporary use of alphabetic writing systems is often characterised by a mixture of oral and written modes of communication and instances of instrumental uses of alphabetic writing. In view of the instrumental and socially "situated" nature of the Romani approach towards education and literacy, it is imperative that literacy provision for Romani children suits their socio-economic environment.

Chapter 4 traces the history of the rise of Romani written literature in Europe and discusses its defining features: polycentrism and linguistic hybridity. Romani literature is characterised by a varied corpus and encompasses a wide variety of genres. It includes the works of professional authors and those of intellectuals, artists and political activists. The chapter identifies the enabling factors in the development of Romani literature, such as the steady rise in literacy levels among the Roma, the recent standardisation of the Romani language and its use in inter-ethnic communication.

Chapter 5 provides an overview of key themes and tropes in Romani literature. It argues that Romani authors regard writing as an ethical activity and as a vehicle for cross-cultural communication. This understanding of writing is what motivates them to tackle issues shrouded in controversy and misunderstanding, particularly the Romani Holocaust, and themes such as forced nomadism, racial discrimination, violence and social marginalisation. Specific attention is devoted to the work of Romani women authors, whose texts are characterised by a strong need to express an alternative point of view on their male-dominated society, and an acute self-awareness of the possibilities and implications of the act of writing. The chapter shows that, through the creation of powerful images in which the Roma are no longer portrayed as literary "objects", Romani authors succeed in reappropriating their literary self.

Chapter 6 explores the applicability of theoretical approaches centred on "ethnic", "migrant" and "minor" paradigms to the study of Romani literature. In addition, the chapter explores the usefulness, at the textual level, of notions of linguistic deterritorialisation, hybridity, and intertextuality. The concept of hybridity, due to its emphasis on processes of cross-cultural exchange and creative "borrowing", is regarded as particularly appropriate to describe the key textual features of Romani literature, which, as it arises from the syncretic encounter among various literary traditions, can be defined as a "literary hybrid".

The rise and development of a written literature among Romani groups points to a crucial change in the Roma's attitude towards literacy and reflects a positive view of Romani education. This change marks an unprecedented shift from the traditional strategy of restricted literacy to a perception of literacy as a tool to preserve and revitalise the Roma's linguistic and cultural heritage. It is not surprising, then, that the rise of Romani writing has been accompanied by a certain level of political mobilisation.

The crucial link between the rise of Romani literacy and the emergence of the Roma as a political subject is examined in Chapter 7. This chapter investigates how Romani activists and academics have successfully reappropriated the field of Romani studies. Their texts have enhanced the credibility of Romani writing within the academic community and provided a major source of legitimation for the Roma's political struggle. Furthermore, the political use of writing by Romani writers provides a means to talk back to the dominant group and reclaim ownership of an identity that in their view has been colonised by the non-Roma (Lee 2004). Finally, Romani writing plays a major role in current identity-building processes by helping establish a sense of shared cultural identity that transcends linguistic and geographical boundaries, as current attempts at building a transnational Romani nation demonstrate.

Chapter 8 examines how literacy has been appropriated by the Roma not only as a tool of cultural resistance, but also as an instrument to overcome tension and conflict both within Romani communities and in relation to the non-Roma. In particular, this concluding chapter discusses the potential of Romani writing as an instrument to establish proper forms of inter-group communication to facilitate mutual understanding between the Roma and non-Roma. The mediating potential of Romani writing is discussed in relation to two domains—the literary sphere and intercultural education—within which hybrid literacy practices provide a site of cross-cultural dialogue. Cases of good practice in these areas are evaluated and it is recommended that they serve as the foundation for a new understanding of the Roma/non-Roma relationship.

Part I
Romani Literacies

1   Writing and the Gypsies

The history of the relationship between the Roma and non-Roma is intricately linked to the alphabetic practices of the dominant group. This relationship has largely been defined by the public and official writings about Gypsies that started to appear in Western Europe during the fifteenth century. The chapter demonstrates how this relationship has evolved through time and how these stereotypes contributed to the politics of marginalisation, exclusion and, later, assimilation enacted against the Romani population in Europe.

The appearance of Gypsies in Europe coincides with the creation of a corpus of textual representations and written records about their presence in Western sedentary societies. These texts, it should be emphasised, were often based on generalisations rather than first-hand experience or direct contact with the Roma. As such, they generally fail to provide a reliable source of information about the Roma and their culture. This is not to say that textual renditions of "Gypsy" identity should simply be dismissed as misleading and biased. They should instead be approached and assessed for what they are: representations—that is, narrative constructions—formulated by the dominant group in a specific context of power relations. From this perspective, these narratives are of some importance as instances of the (usually hostile) reaction of the settled population vis-à-vis the Roma. More specifically, the dominant representations of the Gypsies are manifestations of the role played by literacy practices in "colonising" the Gypsy image through dominant representational paradigms. Finally, written representations focusing on the Gypsies' primitive and deviant behaviour contributed to the creation of criminal categories (the "Egyptian", the "vagrant" and so on) that were targeted for special repression and persecution.

The chapter argues that the textual construction of Gypsy identities can be seen as part of a wider attempt, on the part of the non-Roma, to monitor and discipline the Roma and come to terms with their most puzzling and unsettling ethno-cultural traits: their swarthy appearances, their itinerant and unconventional occupations, their apparent lack of origins, and their primitive way of life. More specifically, these texts constitute a set of narratives written by the literate dominant group with the aim of constructing the Gypsies' difference in negative terms: that is, interpreting their ethnic specificity from within the dominant cultural framework while at the same time deliberately marking out their behaviour as deviant and dangerous. Such narratives played a fundamental role in defining the Gypsy as the "ultimate alien" (Lucassen 1998, 61) in European society.

As Michel Foucault emphasises, "knowledge" and "power" are closely intertwined (Foucault 1977, 1980). The main aim of the texts discussed here was to create a particular kind of knowledge about the Gypsies: that is, to portray the Gypsies as an "object" of knowledge. The fact that these texts are written is crucial, as it reveals that non-Gypsy authorities had an understanding of the written code as a source of authority and a tool to control and discipline the Gypsies.

It is possible to detect two main uses of non-Romani writing about Gypsies. The first is an "official" or "legalistic" use of writing by the police and other public and/or legal actors, whose main purpose was to control the Roma or exclude them from so-called civilised society. The second use is found in historic, literary and academic texts—which Judith Okely (1983, 1) subsumes under the category of the "exotic"—that played a crucial part in the narrative construction and essentialisation of Gypsies' difference. In both cases, I argue, writing has been deployed as a hegemonic strategy to assimilate the Romani people into mainstream society and culture either at a representational or practical level. On their part, the Roma showed an acute awareness of the implications—both positive and negative—of the hegemonic uses of writing in non-Romani society, as demonstrated for example by the numerous "letters of protection" carried by Romani leaders while crossing Western Europe in the Late Middle Ages.

The chapter opens with a discussion of the first written records of the encounter between Romani groups and Western European populations, focusing both on the initial reactions of the settled group and the adaptation strategies pursued by the Roma. The central section of the chapter deals with crucial instances of textual construction of the "Gypsy", analysing the emergence of textual images that would greatly influence later stereotypical views of Gypsies, such as that of the "savage Gypsy". Finally, the chapter discusses the socio-legal implications of these textual constructions, focusing on representative examples of early anti-Gypsy legislation issued in a number of Western European countries.

EARLY ENCOUNTERS

Written records of the Gypsy presence in Western Europe date back to the early fifteenth century. These recorded the arrival of bands of "Egyptians"[1] in Germany (1417), France (1419), and Italy (1422). These groups of Gypsies were met with a mixed reception. On the one hand, they were feared because their behaviour challenged the social and cultural conventions of the majority group. In medieval times, itinerancy was regarded with suspicion by the settled population. As Bronisław Geremek emphasised, during this time being in exile (that is, living far from one's place of origin)[2] was perceived as an "unnatural" condition (Geremek 1990, 348). As a result, the general perception of the sedentary population towards itinerancy and nomadism was generally not favourable. Yet medieval society was far from static and in fact was characterised by continuous flows of migrants such as day workers, beggars, and pilgrims, and the itinerancy of these marginal subjects was largely tolerated. The itinerant way of life of pilgrims and hermits in particular was considered socially and culturally acceptable, as they embodied the ideal of the *homo viator* (Ladner 1967). Pilgrims were helped and received with good grace, and their peripatetic way of life regarded as a means of achieving moral elevation. A possible reason for this is that, within a medieval *Weltanschauung*, nomadism was not yet appreciated as a condition *per se*, but was rather perceived as a temporary, exceptional state that could only be justified and conceptualised in religious terms.[3] And it was as pilgrims, not migrants or nomads, that these strange-looking foreigners introduced themselves.

From an early stage, the Roma were arguably aware of the popular and religious beliefs surrounding pilgrimage. We can safely assume, then, that the main reason why they claimed to be penitents and pilgrims was that they endeavoured to receive a warm welcome in their host societies. Fraser refers to this as "the great trick" (*xonxanó baró*) and interprets it as "a strategy for exploiting [the religious environment of the time] and enhancing the prospects of survival" (Fraser 1995, 62). Shortly after their first appearance in medieval chronicles, the Roma were thus already taking part in an official narrative—one connected to pilgrimage and devotional practices—that presupposes a clear understanding not only of the sociohistorical and cultural context within which they moved, but also of the role of writing in the official sphere.

The existence of Gypsy safe-conducts,[4] recorded in several medieval texts, seems to confirm this. According to O. van Kappen (1965), one of the oldest safe-conducts granted to Gypsies was issued in 1442 by Frederick III during his stay at Seefeld, Austria. In it, the Emperor grants Michael (a "Gypsy Count") and his people the right to wander safely through his empire. He also recommends that the Gypsies should not be harassed or treated unlawfully. Hermann Cornerus (1723) mentions that as early as 1417 bands of Gypsies, led by chiefs (who appear to be "dukes" or "counts") and travelling through northern Germany, were carrying official letters of recommendation with them. Such letters enabled them to wander freely in foreign lands and "to be admitted and kindly treated by states, princes, fortified places, towns, bishops and prelates to whom they turned".[5] An imperial document carried by Gypsies is also cited by Sebastian Münster (1550), who reports having seen a copy of a letter that some Gypsies near Heidelberg had received from Sigismund at Lindau,[6] on Lake Constance, which granted them free passage. Like Cornerus, Münster was told by some Gypsies that their ancestors, having abandoned and subsequently re-embraced the Christian faith, were sent into exile and condemned to travel the world for several years.

A certain "Duke Michael of Egypt" was also reported to have exhibited, upon his arrival in Basel on 16 July 1422, a letter of safe-conduct granted by the Pope. The letter stated that the Gypsies were atoning for their sins by performing a seven-year journey through foreign lands, and it enjoined local authorities to grant them free passage through their territory. Pontifical letters were also allegedly exhibited by Gypsy leaders at Paris and Amiens in 1427, at Douai, Rotterdam and Utrecht in 1429 and at Fermo, in Italy, in 1430 (Fraser 1995, 73).

A poignant example of a letter of protection exhibited by Gypsies is that recorded on 23 April 1423 by Andreas, a priest from Ratisbon (now Regensburg), in his *Diarium Sexennale*. The letter, carried by a group of *Cigani* led by voivoda[7] Ladislaus, was originally obtained from King Sigismund:

> Our faithful Ladislaus voivoda of the Gypsies [*waynoda Ciganorum*][8] and others pertaining to him came in person into our presence, and tendered their very humble supplications to us, here in Zips [*in Scepus*] before us [. . .]. In consequence we, being persuaded by their supplication, have thought proper to grant them this liberty: therefore at whatever time that the said voivoda Ladislaus and his people shall come into our said domains, be it cities or market towns, from that time we strictly entrust and order to your present fidelities that you should without any hindrance or trouble support and sustain the said voivoda Ladislaus and the Cigani who are subject to him, and indeed that you shall please to preserve them from any impediments or vexations.[9]

The Roma's handling of official safe-conducts is a typical example of their approach to writing, which is characterised from the outset by an instrumental attitude that seems confined to their relationship with the non-Roma.[10] It can also be viewed as an early example of "camouflage" and "mimicry" (Bhabha 1994) on the part of the Roma, that is, of their apparent ability to embrace stereotypes and categories belonging to the dominant group—in this case, the category of the pilgrim—while at the same time managing to retain their status as a separate ethnic group.

THE TEXTUAL CONSTRUCTION
OF THE GYPSY AS OTHER

As we have seen, the Roma displayed from an early stage a good understanding of the role of writing among the non-Roma. In particular, they were aware that in non-Romani society writing was a source of authority and an instrument of power. For a time, the Roma were able to benefit from this knowledge, as shown by their successful use of safe-conducts granting them freedom of movement. Through their insightful use of writing, the Roma were thus able to coexist in a relatively peaceful manner with the non-Roma. However, this situation was doomed not to last.

As centralised states began to emerge, governments increasingly relied on writing for a number of administrative and policing tasks, such as restricting the movements of their citizens and especially those of potentially dangerous groups or individuals. This shift towards an institutional, official use of writing coincides with the rise of a body of written texts documenting the appearance and customs of the Gypsies in Europe. These texts had two main functions. The first was recording and monitoring their arrival in and movements across Europe. The second aim was more subtle, that of highlighting, and largely constructing, their cultural difference by focusing on essentialist traits such as skin colour and the supposedly "savage" and "deviant" Gypsy nature.

The "Ugliest People Ever Seen"

A typical example of official writing about Gypsies can be found in the *Chronica Bononiensis*, which is one of the earliest accounts of Gypsies in Western Europe. It describes the arrival of a group of Egyptians in the city of Bologna on 18 July 1422. These Egyptians claimed that they had gone into exile for a seven-year period for religious reasons. They were led by Andrew, "Duke of Little Egypt", and carried with them a letter of protection from King Sigismund that granted them free passage. By virtue of this safe-conduct they were authorised to wander "throughout the world for seven years". They "had a decree of the King of Hungary allowing them to steal with impunity during these seven years, wherever they may go, without having to be brought to justice" (Muratori 1730, 611).

The anonymous author of the *Chronica* describes the Gypsies as the "ugliest people ever seen around here" (*la più brutta genìa che mai fosse in queste parti*).[11] Later in the same passage, the author provides further descriptions of their appearances: they were "skinny and black", it was reported, and they "ate like pigs" (*erano magri e negri e mangiavano come porci*).[12] Such a stark essentialisation of Gypsy identity seems to be a recurrent textual pattern within medieval chronicles portraying Gypsies. For example, the already-mentioned text of Cornerus recorded the passage of a "strange, wandering horde of people" through northern Germany in 1417. According to Cornerus, these people were "very ugly" and "as black as Tartars".[13] The anonymous writer of the *Journal d'un bourgeois de Paris* summed up this less-than-flattering portrait by describing in the following terms the Gypsies who arrived at La Chapelle, near Paris, on 17 August 1427:

[T]heir children—almost all of them—had their ears pierced and wore a silver ring in each ear, or two rings in each [. . .]. The men were very dark, with curly hair; the women were the ugliest you ever saw and the darkest, all with scarred faces and hair as black as a horse's tail.[14]

A stereotypical image thus began to take shape, that of a dark-skinned character with dark hair, a slender physique and a magnetic gaze: an image that went on to capture the European imagination for centuries to come.

In early modern times, colour perception was associated with a complex set of symbols and popular beliefs. A clear link was established between inner qualities and outward appearances, and physical appearances were thought to be reflections of an inner state. As Roger Bastide explained, "colours are not important in themselves as optical phenomena, but rather

Figure 1.1   A dark-skinned Gypsy (Colocci 1899, 129).

as bearers of a message" (Bastide 1967, 312). The darkness of the Gypsies is therefore more than a physical quality: it amounts to a metaphorical darkness that refers not only to their skin but also their "dark" side—"a kind of outlaw savagery", as Toby Sonneman puts it (Sonneman 1999, 122).[15] The dark side of the Gypsy, imagined and constructed as mysterious and dangerous by the dominant group, is precisely what seems to repel (yet simultaneously attract) the non-Gypsies.

While the colour white was thought to be indicative of virtue and inner harmony, the colour black was associated with evil and considered a manifestation of the diabolical. Due to their dark skin colour, Gypsies were often depicted as mysterious creatures connected to the mythological world of the underground. They were thought to be the offspring of deities such as Mercury and Vulcan (the Roman god of fire), or even demons from hell. By virtue of this association with demonic entities, they were attributed the power to curse, cast spells and foretell the future, and the fact that they practised the art of divination seemed to confirm these beliefs. In short, they were portrayed as cunning characters capable of *maleficia* (sorcery).[16]

The belief in the evil nature of the Gypsies was reinforced by the conviction that they were the victims of a biblical curse. A number of legends began to emerge during the Late Middle Ages concerning Gypsies. They were thought to be the descendants of Cush, son of Ham (sometimes spelled "Cham"), one of the three sons of Noah, cursed by his father[17] and condemned to wander the earth due to the original curse put upon their fratricidal ancestor.[18] There were also legends according to which the Gypsies were under a curse for having denied shelter to the Holy Family on their flight from Egypt and for suggesting to Judas that he betray Christ. They were even associated with the massacre of the children of Bethlehem, and were accused (together with the Jews) of having forged the nails of the Cross (Kenrick and Puxon 1972).[19] Later, the biblical curse hanging over the Gypsies came to be reinterpreted by non-Gypsy authorities in terms of deviance, and used to stigmatise their entire way of life.

The Deviant Gypsy

Early chronicles and textual descriptions of Gypsies focus not only on their physical appearance and nomadic way of life, but also provide important clues as to which activities and occupations the Roma were engaged in. These seem to have ranged from metalworking to fortune telling, and from entertaining to horse dealing and door-to-door selling.[20] Some of the skills and services offered by the Roma as craftsmen, traders, seasonal workers and entertainers constituted an independent economic niche within preindustrial societies (Mayall 1988). Services provided by Romani artists and musicians were particularly appreciated by the aristocracy and the rich gentry, who welcomed the Roma and often gave them shelter in defiance of expulsion orders.[21]

Rather than dealing with such positive aspects, however, most written records seem to dwell purposely upon some of the least accepted of the Roma's socio-economic practices. As the sixteenth century progressed, fewer authorities were prepared to give credit to the Gypsies' narrative of pilgrimage, as testified by the use of terms such as "pagan", "heathen" and "Saracen" (i.e., non-Christian) in coeval European chronicles and legal texts concerning Gypsies (Fraser 1995). The Roma's socio-economic practices were thus progressively demonised in both the official and popular spheres, with a range of different factors contributing to this attitude change.

During the Late Middle Ages, the religious climate in Europe began to change (culminating in the Reformation and the Catholic Counter-Reformation), and so did the attitude towards pilgrims and the wandering poor (Geremek 1980, 71). Toward the end of the fifteenth century, which has been defined as "the Golden Age" for mendicants (Schreiber 1839), pauperism was perceived as a problem of public order and a threat to Christian religious values. A distinction began to emerge between the so-called "deserving" poor (the old, the sick and so forth), who were deemed worthy of assistance, and the "undeserving" poor (also referred to as "false" or "sturdy beggars" and as "vagabonds") who, it was believed, could work but instead chose to lead an unproductive way of life. Individuals included in the latter category became the target of increasing stigmatisation and harsh legislation. In the *Liber vagatorum*, Martin Luther warned the German population against the tricks of such "false beggars". It was in this category that public authorities placed the Gypsies, accusing them of turning mendicity from a state of real need into "a sort of free art" with its own secret language, the beggars' cant (Luther 1528).[22] Like church mendicants, vagabonds and rogues, Gypsies were accused of being "idle"[23] and dishonest, and frequently accused of theft.

A number of occupations carried out by Gypsies, such as forging, entertaining and fortune telling, were included among the so-called *negotia illicita*.[24] In particular, the itinerant condition associated with their trades was perceived as a potential threat to the social order since it enabled them to encounter a whole class of "marginal" subjects: beggars, vagrants, peddlers, disenfranchised soldiers and students, whose mobility was initially tolerated by public authorities but who were later overtly criminalised. From the sixteenth century onwards, Gypsy nomadism was in itself sufficient grounds for punishment. As a magistrate from Strasbourg wrote of Gypsies at the beginning of the nineteenth century: "I have no evidence of criminal acts committed by these people, but their situation is such that they must of necessity be tempted to commit them if the occasion presents itself ... [T]hey cannot but be dangerous".[25] Gradually, Gypsy occupations became the target of repressive legislation by both religious and secular authorities.

The Church was particularly anxious to put an end to magic practices among Gypsies and, in particular, to the immoral conduct of the "*fallax Cinganorum genus*" (Nicolini 1987, 21). After the Council of Trent (1563), a number of decrees included Gypsies in the same category as magicians, fortune-tellers and diviners: that is, people held responsible for promoting superstition and false beliefs among the population.[26] Such decrees were aimed against the magic arts carried out mostly by Gypsy women. Practices such as divination through palmistry (chiromancy) and tarot cards, and astrology, oneiromancy, hydromancy and sorcery, were all mentioned in the proceedings of the Synods of Milan (1565), Messina (1589), Palermo (1586), Salerno (1596), Amalfi (1597) and Siracusa (1651). These practices smacked of heresy and were particularly likely to attract witchcraft allegations.[27]

The increasingly negative attitude of religious authorities towards the Gypsies seems to suggest that the Church—at that time concerned with restoring the unity of the Catholic Church after the Reformation—considered the ambiguous status of Gypsies as potentially disruptive for the system it endorsed. It also indicates that the metamorphosis of the Gypsies from pilgrims worthy of assistance to dangerous and socially deviant subjects was well under way.

The Savage Gypsy

The image of the savage has played an important role in European folklore and art since at least the Middle Ages (Bernheimer 1952; Hodgen 1964; Boas 1997). The savage derived from the medieval figure of the wild man, which was initially associated with a condition of wildness that stood in opposition to Christianity and civilisation (White 1978).[28] Due to their nomadic way of life and their closeness to nature, the Gypsies were perceived as quintessentially "wild". In the *Chronica Bononiensis* quoted above, Gypsies were described as unclean, savage creatures whose behaviour was closer to that of animals than humans ("they ate as pigs"). In a coeval text, the *Chronicon fratris Hieronymi de Forlivio*, we find the following description of a group of Gypsies who, the chronicler noted incidentally, were said to have come from India:

> [In 1422] arrived in Forlì some people, sent by the Emperor, who were eager to receive our faith. They arrived in Forlì on August the 7th. And, as I heard, some said that they were from India. They stayed here for two days, and were not moderate people, but [behaved] almost like wild and ferocious beasts. There were almost two hundred of them, and were going to the Pope in Rome: men, women and children. (Quoted in Muratori 1731, 890; my translation)

Gypsies were portrayed in this text as "immoderate people" (*gentes non multum morigeratae*), behaving almost like "beasts" and "wild animals" (*quasi bruta animalia et furentes*). This animal-like behaviour seemed to be a recurrent trope in contemporary historical accounts where Gypsies were variously depicted as the "scum of the nation" and as people who "lived like dogs" and had no religion. An article of the Register of the Deliberations of the town of Mâcon reported the arrival on 24 August 1419 of a group of Gypsies and described them as "people of formidable size, in person, in hair, as well as otherwise" (*gens de terrible stature, tant en personnes, en cheveux comme autrement*), who were lying in the fields "like beasts" (Bataillard 1888–1889, 325).

In the texts quoted above, Gypsies' appearances are explicitly associated with their allegedly savage and primitive nature. They testify to the birth of another powerful representational paradigm that has gone on to dominate representations of Gypsies in European literature and culture up to the present day:[29] that of the savage Gypsy, an image equally despised and idealised depending on the socio-historical circumstances. Fifteenth- and sixteenth-century records are characterised by an overwhelmingly negative view of the primitive qualities of the Gypsies, which seems to suggest that in early modern European society their primitive condition was interpreted negatively.[30] Conversely, in the nineteenth century, when the primitivism of the Gypsies was taken as a deliberate refusal of the comforts of urban life in the name of freedom and independence, the "savage" qualities of the Gypsy did not carry a negative connotation.

Despite their widely divergent perspectives, both positive and negative renditions of the savage Gypsy centred on the idea that the Gypsies, because of their closeness to the natural world, had somehow acquired animal features. Arthur Symons wrote in his famous essay "In Praise of Gypsies" that "the Gypsy represents nature before civilisation" and that "the Gypsies are nearer to the animals than any race known to us in Europe" (Symons 1908, 296), while Richard Jefferies defined the Gypsy as "a species of human wild animal" (quoted in Sampson 1930, 8).

Describing the Gypsies as "animal-like" equated to emphasising their irrational nature and their lack of control over their instincts: two central foundations of civilised society. It is not by chance, then, that attributes commonly attached by non-Gypsy authors to wild Gypsies centred on their alleged lawlessness, idleness, promiscuity, violence, moodiness, unpredictability, childishness, lack of hygiene, and ignorance.

According to Walter Simson, the Gypsies were "destitute of everything above the grossest of animal wants and propensities", and had a "savage and unsophisticated nature" (Simson 1866, 50). Adriano Colocci further emphasises that "the Gypsy is unable to resist his whims" (*lo Zingaro è incapace di resistere alle sue voglie*), and that Gypsies are exceptionally nervous and irascible people by nature (Colocci 1889, 150–151). This particular aspect of the Gypsies' "wild" disposition reappeared in the study of the archivist Francesco Predari (1841), who claimed Gypsies were lazy, canny, impulsive and quick-tempered: any attempt to improve their condition was doomed to be unsuccessful due to the features of their race. As with all peoples used to living in hot, arid climates, Predari explained, Gypsies lacked any aptitude for working the land. Their proverbial idleness made them only suitable for futile, fruitless occupations that did not require any durable effort or application.

Figure 1.2　A tent of Zapari—"wild" Turkish Gypsies (Colocci 1889, 185).

As in the case of other Gypsy textual stereotypes, the implications of labelling Gypsies as savages extended well beyond the field of textual representation. The belief in the primitive nature of the Gypsies brought serious consequences, including accusations of cannibalism during the eighteenth century (Fraser 1995, 195) and of child stealing, a false allegation that is still repeated today. Moreover, the paradigm of the Gypsy as "bad savage" inspired a large number of academic works based on the belief in Gypsies' in-born propensity to crime. This culminated in Lombroso's notion of Gypsy atavism (Lombroso 1897), which formed the basis of the persecution carried out against Gypsies during the twentieth century.

As Hayden White has emphasised, the notion of wildness does not simply describe "a specific condition or state of being", but acts as a cognitive device used to "confirm the value of [its] dialectical antithe[sis:] 'civilisation'" (White 1978, 151). Written texts labelling Gypsies as "wild" served as a powerful textual mechanism whereby the non-Gypsies were able to conceptualise the boundary between "us" and "them". By confining the Gypsies to a wild social space opposed to civilised society, the dominant group was able to mark out a symbolic boundary separating what they perceived as "socially acceptable" (white, good, civilised) from what was "socially unacceptable" (black, evil, uncivilised), thereby stigmatising Gypsies as "deviant". Dehumanising Gypsies through the attribution of wild or animal traits was a powerful justification of their active exclusion from mainstream society (Mayall 1988). It also paved the way for later attempts at "humanising" and "reforming" the Gypsies through education (see Chapter 2).

THE EMERGENCE OF THE VAGRANT PARADIGM

As previously mentioned, the beginning of the modern era in Europe brought a significant change in the official attitude towards itinerant occupations and mobility in general, and signalled the start of a period of growing intolerance against Gypsies. At a time when European nation-states began to take shape, Gypsies and other ethnic minorities such as Jews and Moors found themselves in an increasingly difficult position, and were perceived as a potential source of disorder and destabilisation. To attain political unity and bureaucratic centralisation, governmental authorities pursued policies reinforcing cultural and political cohesiveness and strived to separate what lay inside and outside the border of the nation-state: in other words, to identify and label those who should be considered part of mainstream society and those who lay outside it. Like other marginal groups, Gypsies were excluded from the nation-building process at different levels. First, the demarcation of national borders was achieved through the banishment of transnational, non-territorial minorities (such as the Gypsies). Second, the creation of a unified administrative system entailed stricter control over its citizens, including their movements, economic activities and social status. Third, the rise of modern nation-states brought with it the need to introduce taxes to raise money (to fund the functioning of the state, the army, etc.). The Gypsies, because of their nomadic habits and itinerant activities, were able to eschew any form of centralised control. Their failure to fit into the new socio-political order ultimately led to their inclusion in the "dangerous classes" category.[31] This is clear given the sharp rise in anti-Gypsy legislation that swept across Western Europe between the late fifteenth century and the eighteenth century. The aim of such legislation was to rid European states of an unwelcome Gypsy presence and, during this period, official writings concerning Gypsies were widely used to enforce a policy of exclusion. It was at this time that pre-existing stereotypes and symbolic markers of the "otherness" of Gypsies (especially those stigmatising their primitive and canny nature) were reactivated and deployed in the legal domain in an attempt to eradicate their way of life.

The sheer volume of anti-Gypsy bans and edicts that emerged around the same time indicates that they were being implemented throughout Western Europe, a point also made by Fraser, who remarks that "there is a depressing uniformity about the response of most European powers to the presence of Gypsies" (Fraser 1995, 129). It is thus clear that state authorities were concerned about the great geographical mobility of their Gypsy population and were anxious to bring it under control. They tried to achieve this by either forbidding Gypsies from entering European countries, or charging them to leave under threat of incarceration and corporal punishment.[32]

From Pilgrims to Dangerous Vagrants

The first signs of the "turning of the tide" against the Gypsies (Fraser 1995) were evident in 1416 in the German states, which were among the first to issue anti-Roma legislation. In 1498, the Diet of the Holy Roman Empire accused the Gypsies of being spies for the Turks and it ordered their expulsion based on this allegation. In 1500, the Diet renewed the 1498 decree and ordered the Gypsies to leave the country within three months. The text of the decree established the view that "whoever harms a Gypsy commits no crime" (*Wer Zigeuner schädigt, frevelt nicht*).[33] Fifty years later, the German chronicler Aventinus (Johann Georg Thurmaier, 1477–1534) revealed that the so-called *Zigeni* falsely claimed to come from Egypt (*ex Aegypto se esse mentiuntur*) and "shamelessly pretend" to have been sent on a seven-year-long exile (*septem annorum exilio expiare impudentissime confingunt*) for having refused to shelter the Virgin Mary and baby Jesus (Thurmaier 1554, 792). Münster denounced as "mere fables" the Gypsies' account of their pilgrimage as having started in Little Egypt (Münster 1550).

As the sixteenth century progressed, French authorities also displayed a high degree of scepticism towards these alleged pilgrims. In 1539, the French sovereign Francis I took repressive measures against "certain unknown persons" calling themselves "Bohemians", who travelled across his kingdom "under the guise of a simulated religion or of a certain penitence which they claim to be making through the world".[34] In 1593, an act of the Scottish Parliament defined the Gypsies as "the counterfeit idle rogues and harlots falsely calling themselves Egyptians", who were in fact "nothing else but thieves, witches and abusers of the people".[35]

Clearly, the itinerant way of life of the Gypsies was regarded as a potential source of social unrest and the reason why they became the target of growing legislation against vagabondage. A new legal category of the vagrant was created to outlaw them. Vagrants were characterised by five main traits: poverty, fitness to work, lack of work due to idleness, rootlessness, and lawlessness (Beier 1985, 4). As A. L. Beier explains, "vagrants were no ordinary criminals: they were actually menaces to society" (Ibid., 6). Ultimately, the vagrants' marginality and their apparent lawlessness determined their categorisation as dangerous.[36]

Although Gypsies were different from vagrants and rogues given that they constituted a separate ethnic group, the legislation that covered them did not substantially differ from general anti-vagrant legislation. In early modern times, the image of the Gypsy and that of the vagrant tended to overlap. Both Gypsies and vagrants led itinerant, masterless lives, and in some cases vagrants ended up adopting the language and attire of the Gypsies. The difficulty in determining Gypsies and vagrants was particularly evident in sixteenth-century England (Ribton-Turner 1887).

In the English legal discourse, the Gypsies were associated from an early stage with other vagrants such as rogues, vagabonds and "sturdy beggars", and charged with similar offences such as stealing and cheating (Beier 1985, 62).[37] The enactment against the Gypsies issued under Queen Elizabeth I in 1562 was entitled, significantly, "An Act for the Punishment of Vagabonds Calling Themselves Egyptians". This act aimed to discipline not only Gypsies, but also others found in their company (Ribton-Turner

1972, 490, 679). Thomas Harman in his *Caveat, or Warning for Common Cursetors, Vulgarly Called Vagabonds* defined them as "the wretched, wily, *wandering vagabonds* calling and naming themselves Egiptians [*sic*]" (Harman 1814, vi; my emphasis). Interestingly, Harman's text portrayed the Gypsies first as "vagabonds" and only in the second instance as "Egyptians" (a term adopted due to self-ascription). In other words the author, rather than dwelling on (or even acknowledging) the ethnic specificity of the Gypsies, emphasised their closeness to other social deviants.

The criminalisation of the vagrant-Gypsy coincided with the depenalisation of anti-Gypsy violence and persecution, which in turn led to a situation whereby authorities were entitled to persecute or even execute Gypsies without trial. An example of this can be found in France, where the first royal decree against Gypsies was issued by Louis XII in 1504 (Vaux de Foletier 2003, 88; Fraser 1995, 94). In it, the king ordered the expulsion of Gypsies from Rouen even though they were holding a safe-conduct: a measure extended to all Gypsies in France six years later. An even more harsh royal decree, the "Déclaration contre les Bohémiens ou Égyptiens", was issued by Louis XIV in 1682 to target *Bohémiens* (Gypsies) simply because of what they were called. This decree was widely observed throughout France (Fraser 1995, 144).[38]

In Italy, a large number of edicts against Gypsies (variously named by local authorities as *zingani*, *Cingani* or *Cingari*) began to appear at the end of the fifteenth century. An edict issued in April 1493 under the rule of Ludovico il Moro in the State of Milan ordered them to leave immediately and threatened that they would be hanged if they refused to do so (Arlati 1989, 4). In 1570, an edict issued in the Duchy of Modena went as far as inciting the local population to incarcerate the *Cingari*, to rob them and beat them (Spinelli 1978, 35). A further edict issued in Milan on 11 July 1657 referred to the *Cingari* as the "most dangerous people who ha[d] ever entered the state", and ordered them to leave the territory in three days' time, under pain of imprisonment for five years for men and of public flogging for women.[39] Extreme anti-Gypsy measures were also enacted in the Republic of Venice. For example, a resolution issued in 1558 by the Council of the Pregadi established that, "considering the evil disposition of the Gypsies, and the annoyance, damages, and manifold troubles that our faithful subjects sustain from their intercourse" (*considerando la mala qualità dei Cingani, e la molestia, danni e molti disturbi, che ricevono li fedeli nostri dalla loro practica*), they should be expelled at once from the territory of the Republic. Crucially, this edict established that "the said Gypsies, both men and women, found in our territories, may be with impunity slain, without the perpetrators of such murders to incur any penalty whatever".[40]

In addition to written bans and expulsion orders, non-Gypsy authorities displayed explicit visual warnings and special signs in an attempt to eradicate the Gypsy presence. Such warnings were placed at strategic locations such as road crossings, city gates, town halls, church doors, taverns and other public places (Opfermann 2007, 141). They usually included both an inscription and a visual representation of the punishment for criminals and transgressors to convey more effectively their message to a non-literate readership, particularly the Gypsies.

Figure 1.3 is an example of a *Zigeunerwarntafel* (visual warning for Gypsies) from eighteenth-century Bavaria, aimed at preventing Gypsies and rogues from entering the country. The wooden panel shows a gallows on which hangs a Gypsy, while in the foreground a man and a woman are being flogged. As in the case of written texts, the *Zigeunerwarntafeln* targeted Gypsies based on their ethnicity and officially outlawed their nomadic practices.

Similar anti-Gypsy warnings are still in use today. They can be observed at the entrance to cities and are used to demarcate so-called "anti-Gypsy territories" (Piasere 2005, 164–174), that is, territories declared off-limits to the Roma by non-Gypsy authorities (Figure 1.4–1.6).

Figure 1.3 German sign warning off Gypsies (Archive Stadtmuseum Nördlingen).

Figures 1.4–1.6   No parking signs specifically aimed at "nomads" and Roma/Gypsies (Figures 1.4–1.5 from http://sucardromimmagini.blogspot.co.uk/2008/03/discriminazioni-di-stato.html; Figure 1.6: photo by Simon Evans (2005, 155)).

Unlike the *Zigeunerwarntafeln*, contemporary warning signs are almost exclusively written, which is why non-literate Roma may not be able to understand them. Although their content is less extreme than that found on *Zigeunerwarntafeln*, their ultimate goal is remarkably similar: to prevent the Gypsies from entering a protected territory.

CONCLUSIONS

In this chapter we have seen how, at least from the beginning of the fifteenth century, the Roma displayed a certain awareness of the role of literacy practices in the official sphere, as demonstrated by their use of safe-conducts and letters of protection. For a time they were able to use this knowledge to their advantage but, after this initial phase, the Roma were confronted with a disciplinary use of writing on the part of non-Romani authorities.

Literacy practices aimed at controlling the Roma operated at the level of cultural representation and at the legal and policy level. Textual representations of Gypsies were used to brand them symbolically as Other. They helped to establish a cluster of stereotypes of remarkable endurance: from the stereotype of the Gypsy as vagrant to that of the Gypsy as primitive and savage, giving rise to a Gypsy persona with no empirical referent but nevertheless regarded by public authorities as real. Such textual representations had serious repercussions at the policy level, as they fostered the inclusion of Gypsies into criminal categories targeted by repressive legislation.

Labelled as deviant and dangerous by state authorities, the Gypsies were forced either to abandon nomadism and "forget" their language and culture, or to leave their host countries. Many decided to leave, and their decision triggered a sort of chain reaction whereby the Gypsies embarked on a circular journey in the hopeless search for more favourable living conditions.[41] They also discovered that, to survive as a separate ethnic group, they somehow had to become invisible to the eyes of the majority society. The main result of this process was that the Gypsies, who had already been constructed as deviant subjects within the imaginary geography of the dominant group, were increasingly confined to peripheral landscapes on the edge of dominant society, what David Sibley describes as "residual" or exclusionary spaces (Sibley 1995, 68). Using a contemporary terminology, we can say that the policies of exclusion targeting Gypsies reinforced their "pariah" status within the settled society (Barth 1969; Hancock 1987).

Despite their severity, exclusionary policies did not succeed in eradicating the "Gypsy problem". In fact, the Gypsies' spatial and social marginalisation largely suited their socio-economic practices, which entailed the provision of goods and services to non-Gypsies in an itinerant fashion. Once the authorities realised the ineffectiveness of their banishing methods, it became increasingly clear that a radical change in approach was necessary. This led to a major shift in official policies over the ensuing centuries:

policies of exclusion of the Gypsy population were gradually supplanted by policies of forced inclusion, which ultimately aimed to assimilate the Gypsies into mainstream society. It is in this context that existing stereotypes of Gypsy primitivism were re-enacted to validate the official use of education as a tool to "reform" and "civilise" them. The use of educational institutions as a means of assimilation played a major role in shaping the Romani approach to literacy and education, which will be explored further in Chapter 2 and Chapter 3.

2   Educating the Gypsies

I am afraid of sending [my children] to school, because I don't know how they will be treated. I could not stand it if someone mistreated them and made them cry or made them feel inferior because we are Gypsies.

They consider us bad, they keep us at a distance. I want my little girl to be respected, I don't want them to consider her like a gypsy. The *gage* has his own life and he does not value that of a *sinto* [*sic*]. But a *sinto* has many things he can be proud of . . . (Gypsy parents' views on school, in Karpati 1982, 7)

What I don't understand is why, if kids want to get on at school, why they're getting kept back . . . why sit you in a corner to doodle . . . The school [staff] are very nice when you go, but they think there is no problem. But there has to be a problem if I've been there and my wife has been, there has to be a problem . . . obviously they (the children) are going to have a bad attitude to it as well, because they are not being heard, they are not being heard. (Show Traveller father, in Lloyd, Stead and Jordan 1999, 13)

Walking past the primary schools where [Gypsy] children have been placed, one can meet the parents outside the school's courtyard. They are waiting to see their children during the break. The parents themselves explained to me that they do it in order to check that everything goes well. The thought that their child is away from the camp, in an environment that is so different from that of their family, urges them to spend hours outside the school building. (Tomasi 1999, 84)

One family where both spouses were illiterate and of the highest economic status refused to send their son to school while staying on a temporary site for several months. They stated they did not want their children brought up in a way which risked losing them. (Okely 1983, 162)

The above views of Gypsy parents were gathered during fieldwork among Roma and Sinti groups in Italy and Traveller-Gypsies in England. These groups view the schooling process as surrounded by an atmosphere of fear, anxiety and mistrust. Gypsy children and their parents perceive the school as a dangerous environment, a place where they are exposed to many risks. What quality of learning can possibly take place in such a situation? Are these fears justified? To answer these questions, it is first necessary to look at the long history of the relationship between the Roma, Gypsies and

Travellers and the school system. This chapter is an attempt to demonstrate how this relationship has been fraught with tensions and difficulties from the beginning. It argues that the field of Gypsy education is inextricably linked to the wider socio-political context, and must be studied in light of the official policies adopted towards Gypsies in previous centuries.

The chapter begins by looking at nineteenth-century and early twentieth-century portrayals of Gypsies as primitive, uncivilised and unable to impart any education on their children. It discusses in particular the educational policies introduced by Maria Theresa of Austria, attempts at "rescuing" the Gypsies through moral reformation and more recent efforts to save their culture "in crisis". In addition, it highlights the main principles of the educational philosophy underpinning these first attempts at educating the Gypsies, and shows how some of these principles survive today. In particular, the idea that Gypsy children are socially and culturally disadvantaged led to the creation of a specialised school provision that risks isolating and segregating them further.

Centrally, the chapter focuses on current issues concerning the education of Romani children in Western Europe and provides an overview of the main educational initiatives for the Roma at both EU and national levels over the past fifty years. As will be seen, school provision for Romani, Gypsy and Traveller children has thus far failed to achieve substantial results. The chapter attempts to identify the possible reasons for this failure by examining the historical and political context of Gypsy school provision, which is now widely regarded as a decisive aspect of Roma/non-Roma coexistence.

EARLY EDUCATIONAL POLICIES AIMED AT GYPSIES: FROM EXCLUSION TO FORCED INCLUSION

As noted in Chapter 1, the severe anti-Gypsy measures pursued by European states during the sixteenth and seventeenth centuries proved largely ineffective: banishment and indiscriminate violence did not succeed in eradicating the Gypsy population. When European authorities realised this, they started to pursue a different strategy in the effort to contain (i.e., to forcibly assimilate) their Gypsy population (Liégeois 1994, 137). In this context, education played a crucial role. What is meant by "education" here, however, should be clarified. As Enlightenment ideas spread through eighteenth-century Europe, education began to be regarded not only as the key to improving human nature, but also as a tool to maintain the existing social order. Essentially, the idea behind the education of the Gypsies was to eradicate their lack of conformity to dominant social norms. For an increasing number of reformers and enlightened sovereigns, education and vocational training became alternative tools with which to transform them into respectable and "useful" citizens. Schools, together with workhouses and prisons, were the main institutions within which the Gypsies could be practically disciplined and reformed.

As ever, textual representations played a crucial role in shaping public perceptions of the Gypsies, and therefore in influencing educational policies aimed at them. One book in particular proved highly influential in bringing to public attention the grave situation of the Gypsies and highlighting the urgent need to reform them: Heinrich Moritz Gottlieb Grellmann's dissertation *Die Zigeuner*. This text, originally published in Göttingen in 1783, was subsequently translated into English, French and Dutch and enjoyed a remarkable diffusion. Basing his analysis on linguistic evidence, Grellmann argued that the Gypsies were not simply vagrants, but in fact constituted a separate racial group of Indian origin with distinct cultural features.

Grellmann's book can be regarded as an example of an authoritative text on Gypsies (Willems 1997, 11). It was immediately received as a scientific and objective account of Gypsy society and retained its influence during the subsequent centuries. Most importantly, this text was used as a reference in designing governmental policies targeting Gypsies during the eighteenth and nineteenth centuries (Ibid., 72). Despite its chief merit (that of theorising an explicit link between the Romani language and the Indian origin of the Romani people), Grellmann's work seems to rehearse all-too-familiar tropes of Gypsy primitivism. It depicts Gypsies as a "people with a childish way of thinking", as "guided more by sense than reason" and exceedingly prone to anger and other violent emotions (Grellmann 1787, 66). According to Grellmann, the Gypsies were "idle", "canny" and "their volatile disposition and unsteadiness [did] not allow them to complete anything which requires perseverance of application" (69). This is why, according to Grellmann, they were not suitable to work in agriculture or for carrying out work that required patience and industry. Instead of being engaged in productive activities, the author continued, they preferred leading a life of begging and doing "mischief" (70).

Although the nomadic life of the Gypsies was actually idealised during the Romantic period, in the eighteenth century it was perceived as socially and culturally unacceptable.[1] At that time, all subjects (Gypsies included) were expected to contribute to the finances of the state. However, it seemed clear that, to become useful citizens, the Gypsies needed help. Grellmann's view (which was shared by many of his contemporaries) was that, if left to their own devices, the Gypsies would never learn anything, but would simply carry on living in filth, "wickedness and barbarity". They needed assistance particularly in raising their children, whom they spoiled by being too permissive: "The Gypsies, in common with uncivilised people, entertain unbounded love for their children" (Grellmann 1787, 65–66). The Gypsies' excessive love for their children, Samuel Augustini ab Hortis wrote, went as far as not sending them to school: they brought them up without imparting in them any sort of discipline, but allowing them to do whatever they liked (Augustini ab Hortis 1995[1775], 39).

Grellmann (unlike later authors such as Predari) believed that there remained hope for the emancipation of the uncivilised Gypsies. He considered their "uncommonly bad and pernicious qualities" (Grellmann 1787, 75) and their primitive habits mainly a result of their way of life. To reform the Gypsies it was thus necessary to force them to "quit their unsettled manner of life, by instruction and teaching" (82). In other words, Gypsies had to cease being Gypsies, and education was key to their "de-ethnicisation". Unsurprisingly, Grellmann was a great supporter of Maria Theresa of Austria and her policies—which he called "wise dispositions"—concerning the Gypsies in Hungary.

Civilising the Savage Gypsy through Education

The policies of Maria Theresa of Austria with regards Gypsies constitute an illustrative example of containment policies that deployed education as a tool for assimilation. After pursuing a harsh policy of exclusion, from 1758 onwards the sovereign issued several edicts aimed at reforming the Gypsies. This objective was to be achieved through a disciplined process of scholarisation, sedentarisation and productive work. Gypsies were supposed to leave behind all the "aberrant" features that had hitherto interfered with their full emancipation: in short, what formed their ethnic identity. In a move that closely recalled the *premática* of Philip IV, Maria Theresa ordered that the Gypsies living in her territories should "cease to behave like Gypsies". Under her rule, Gypsies' nomadic life was to stop at once, and they were required to "sell their horses and vehicles", live in "proper" houses (not huts or tents) and become good farmers. Restrictions on their movements were coupled with the compulsory registration of Gypsy families by local authorities, which from 1769 were required to keep a census of their Gypsy population (Fraser 1995). Furthermore, Maria Theresa's edicts enjoined that Gypsy traditional occupations should be abandoned, together with their characteristic clothes and eating habits. Gypsies were even forbidden to use the name *Cigáni*, and had to adopt instead denominations such as *Új Magyár* (new Hungarians), "new citizens", or *Neubauern* (new farmers).[2] They were also forbidden to speak their own language and had to adopt the language spoken in their host countries. Another radical measure aimed at assimilating the Gypsies was enacted in 1773, when marriage between Gypsies was prohibited by law, whereas mixed marriages were "rewarded" with a 50-florin grant (Liégeois 1994, 138).

Maria Theresa's enlightened policies were based on the premise that it was possible to reform the Gypsies by forcing them to abandon their "unsettled manner of life". They were also based on the belief that any hope of improving their condition ultimately lay in their successful education, which is why young Gypsies became the focus of special educational measures. All Gypsy children were to be forcibly removed from their parents at the age of five and entrusted to peasant families who were compensated by the authorities for their services. Young Gypsies had to join the army at age sixteen and learn a trade or find a master.

The policies adopted by Emperor Joseph II, successor to Maria Theresa and co-regent since 1765, were also allegedly aimed at the "betterment" of the Gypsies. To achieve this aim, however, the Emperor devised even more strict policies to assimilate Gypsies into mainstream society. In 1783[3] he issued an edict that remained in force until 1790, the year of his death, which imposed the following restrictions on Gypsies:

> No changing of names; houses to be numbered; monthly reports on way of life; nomadism forbidden; settled Gypsies allowed to visit fairs only in cases of special need; smithery banned except when certified as necessary by the authorities; numbers of musicians restricted; begging prohibited; Gypsies not to be settlers in their own right, but to be put into the service of others; Gypsy children, from the age of four upwards, to be distributed at least every two years among the neighbouring districts. (Fraser 1995, 159)

Consequently, many Gypsies were forced to abandon their nomadic way of life and cultivate the land, whilst many others decided to leave the country to avoid the effects of this policy of ethnic cleansing. As for the consequences of Joseph II's—and Maria Theresa's—policies on the dynamics of the Gypsy/non-Gypsy relationship, this is a crucial turning point. As Liégeois rightly observes:

> While simple rejection policies never need to confront the question of the existence or non-existence of Traveller culture, containment—a brutal first step or first stage towards assimilation—actively opposed the notion of Gypsy and Traveller culture, holding that one is not born Gypsy, but becomes so. (Liégeois 1994, 146)

Liégeois' insight can be taken a step further. The assimilationist policies mentioned above proved that the authorities did not even contemplate the notion of a Gypsy cultural distinctiveness. These policies indicated that the focus of public authorities had shifted from a strategy of control to a more proactive strategy aimed at suppressing Gypsy ethnic identity altogether.

To sum up, enlightened policies aimed at reforming Gypsies relied on forced education as one of its most powerful tools. In this period, educational policies for Gypsies were based on the following beliefs:

- Gypsies were "idle" and "work-shy", or otherwise engaged in occupations that were not seen as "useful";
- They lived in a natural, primitive state (of which nomadism was thought to be the major cause);

- They behaved "like children", and were unable to look after themselves and educate their offspring properly;
- They were "heathens", and this lack of religion was one of the main causes of their illiteracy.

The remedies used to tackle these issues were forced sedentarisation, manual work and physical punishment. Clearly, compulsory sedentarisation was primarily aimed at controlling nomadic Gypsies and deterring other Gypsies from entering the country. However, the ultimate goal was to assimilate them into mainstream society. To achieve this, state intervention was needed to ensure that Gypsy parents would send their children to school and to monitor school attendance.

What were Gypsy children to be taught at school? The teaching of literacy skills was certainly considered paramount, while some basic vocational training was also provided. Additionally, the teaching of religious principles was considered of great importance, and this is why, alongside the State, the main institution involved in Gypsy education was the Church.

Religious Reformation of the Gypsies

A clear example of the Church's concern for the education of Gypsy children is found in the work carried out by evangelical missionaries in England during the first half of the nineteenth century (Fraser 1995; Mayall 1988; Willems 1997). The Quaker John Hoyland in particular was a great supporter of policies of forced education of the Gypsies. Hoyland, whose ideas were influenced by Grellmann's work (as he himself admitted), was convinced that the Gypsies' itinerant condition was the root cause of their "depraved" and "savage" life. Despite his sympathetic attitude towards the Gypsies, Hoyland viewed negatively their nomadic way of life, their propensity to steal and their apparent lack of religion. For him, the only way to reform them was to take Gypsy children away from their parents, thus removing them from the negative influence of other Gypsies (Hoyland 1816, 69–70).

To support his views, Hoyland reported the words of Cooper, "a Gypsey [sic] at Chingford Green", who talked about the education of his children in the following manner: "It is a pity that they should be as ignorant as their fathers". Hoyland interpreted these words as a "cry for help":

This may be considered as the language of: "*help us*", accompanied with this acknowledgement, "*for we are unable to help ourselves*"; and certainly there is but too much reason to conclude it is strictly true, respecting the instruction of this forlorn and destitute race. (Hoyland 1816, 253–254; emphasis in original)

Hoyland considered charity schools as being best suited to the Gypsy population as they could provide "all that is requisite", and he advocated

Gypsy children being sent to charity school from the age of six until they turned fourteen. In their case, education ought to provide some basic working skills: Gypsy boys were expected to undertake some sort of full-time apprenticeship, and Gypsy girls to enter domestic work.

Hoyland was well aware that setting up this kind of school would be a costly enterprise, but he was convinced that it was absolutely necessary to elevate the moral tone of this "degraded" and "uncultivated" Eastern race that was affected by a "strange torpor and vileness" (Hoyland 1816, 256). He was also equally convinced that the State had a duty to take care of its Gypsy population because they were unable to look after themselves. To strengthen his point, Hoyland quoted Grellmann's "judicious observation": "If the Gypsey [*sic*] knows not how to make use of the faculties with which nature has intrusted him, let the State teach him, and keep him in leading strings till the end is attained" (Grellmann 1787, 255).

Another clergyman who devoted himself to the reformation of the Gypsies was the Methodist preacher Reverend James Crabb, author of a book on English Gypsies (Crabb 1832) and founder of the Southampton "Committee for the Amelioration of the Condition of the Gipsies". He called them "these poor English heathens" for whom he had "feelings of pity, mercy, love and zeal" (Crabb 1832, ix). His interest in the fate of the Gypsies began in March 1827, when he witnessed the trial of two men accused of horse stealing who were subsequently sentenced to death. One of these men was a young Gypsy with a wife and a young child, and Crabb was so moved by this case he later assumed custody of the child.

According to Crabb, the Gypsies were an "unhappy race" (Ibid.) and lived "in a most lamentably wretched state" (Ibid., 64). Yet their condition was not entirely hopeless, since they were, after all, "rational beings" who had "many feelings honourable to human nature" (Ibid.). Conversion to Christianity was key to their improvement, and many of them were "willing to receive instruction" (Ibid., 160). Unlike other religious reformers, Crabb did not believe in the policy of forced sedentarisation. However, he did believe that the Gypsies should be warned against the moral hazards of the nomadic way of life and would benefit from receiving a Christian education. For this reason, he regularly visited Gypsy camps, trying to persuade their inhabitants to send their children to school during the winter months.

The idea underpinning the charitable efforts of nineteenth-century missionaries was not simply to provide Gypsies with basic literacy skills and religious instruction, but specifically to persuade them to abandon their nomadic existence and embrace the moral and social order of civilised life. Once again, the forced integration of the Gypsies, albeit under the official cover of religious reformation, was the ultimate goal. In this respect, the rationale behind the missionaries' reforming attempts was similar to that of the education policies set out by enlightened sovereigns.

Early educational policies aimed at Gypsies proved largely unsuccessful. Their failure was partly a consequence of the unsystematic, sporadic nature of such policies, which were mainly dependent on charitable donations and the efforts of volunteers, and partly due to the refusal of local governments to allow Gypsies to settle (Willems 1997, 146). Most importantly, such policies were doomed to fail because, predictably, the Gypsies refused to abandon their way of life and be separated from their children. Nevertheless, the forced removal of Gypsy children from their parents continued during the twentieth century,[4] until as recently as the 1970s,[5] leaving a traumatic mark on the cultural memory of the Gypsies of central Europe (Tauber 2002, 108).

ROMA EDUCATION TODAY: AN OVERVIEW

What is the situation of Roma education today? Until the 1950s, the vast majority of Western European Roma had never attended school. This situation began to change in the following two decades, partly because of a widespread process of sedentarisation that had a profound effect on Romani nomadic practices. During the 1960s, examples of school provision specifically aimed at Romani children began to emerge. Such provision was originally delivered through isolated and uncoordinated initiatives, but in subsequent years some of these initiatives were implemented at a national level. From the late 1980s onwards, we witness the emergence of EU-wide educational policies. As Olivier De Schutter emphasised, the growing involvement of EU institutions in Roma issues is motivated by the "structural character" of anti-Roma discrimination, which simultaneously affects all "the different spheres of social life which are crucial to their social integration—education, employment, health and housing".[6] The right to education is one of the "seven pillars" included in the European Social Charter (adopted in 1961 and revised in 1996), and is also included in the Convention for the Protection of Human Rights and Fundamental Freedoms (1950) and a cornerstone of the EU Charter of Fundamental Rights (2000, article 14).[7]

At EU level, educational policies aimed at Romani and Traveller children should ensure "non-discriminatory access to quality education" (Recommendation CM/Rec [2009]4, adopted by the Committee of Ministers of the Council of Europe). Given the dispersion of Romani communities at the pan-European level, the Council regards the cooperation of all the countries of Europe as essential. The emergence of school provision for Roma, Gypsies and Travellers as a transnational issue enables us to outline a comparative analysis of the main concerns surrounding Romani education. As we shall see, this analysis reveals that the problems are remarkably similar throughout Western Europe. Given that the majority of the Gypsy population consists of children of school age, these problems are particularly pressing and should be addressed as a matter of priority. As Liégeois had cogently put it: "The future of Gypsy communities depends to a considerable extent upon the manner of their children's education" (Liégeois 1987b, 1).

Gypsy Educational Provision in the 1960s: The Paradigm of a Culture in Crisis

The scholar and educator Mirella Karpati was a key figure in early attempts to educate Gypsies in Italy. In the early 1960s she conducted research among the Sinti in Trentino Alto Adige, and published the results of her fieldwork in the book *Romano Them* (Karpati 1962).[8] Additionally, Karpati authored a number of articles for the journal *Lacio Drom*, of which she was the editor, and actively campaigned for the education of Gypsy children and adults as a way to improve their condition and overcome their "state of degeneration".[9] According to Karpati, Gypsy culture was "in deep crisis" (Karpati 1962, 189).[10] She conceded that, in theory, education should take into account one people's culture and inclinations. However, considering the state of abjection in which Gypsies lived, they should be offered "the means to overcome their static condition, making it possible to become adjusted to non-Gypsy culture" (Ibid.). Not unlike nineteenth-century scholars and Gypsiologists, she believed that Gypsy culture was frozen in a "timeless" dimension (Lucassen 1997; Mayall 2004), which emphasised their hopelessness and need to be "rescued".

According to Karpati, Gypsy children lived in a primitive state that had a direct impact on their cognitive "underdevelopment". She believed the Gypsies' primitive way of life also had major psychological implications, and she regarded them as "psychologically weak". In view of their cognitive and psychological weakness, they needed special assistance, especially regarding their children's education (Karpati 1979, 43).

Karpati was of the opinion that Gypsy parents indulged their offspring too much, and described Gypsy children as the "little rulers" of the family. Parents were willing to sacrifice everything for them, meaning the children grew up without rules, running around half naked and dirty, barefoot even in the snow, sleeping when they felt like it and eating when they were hungry (Karpati 1962, 65). They were only concerned with their immediate needs and possessed little abstract knowledge. Their primitivism was evident in their games, which Karpati summed up as a "disorderly tumbling, which recalls that of a nest of puppies", which soon degenerated into quarrels (Ibid., 66). Their activities were invariably characterised by a certain degree of aggression: they "hit each other, tear each others' hair, throw stones to each other, wallow in the mud and in the dirt for no reason" (Ibid.). Karpati contrasted their games with the "socialised playing" typical of children in "our civilisation" (Ibid.). To her, the complete lack of guidance and discipline, which characterised Gypsy childhood, was the root cause of the "fragmented and confused view of the world" of grown-up Gypsies and explained their lack of critical skills and logical reasoning.

She concluded that the problematic situation of the Gypsies was a matter of education, not just of instruction (Karpati 1962, 189), and in this respect school was seen as a civilising tool that played a crucial role alongside other educational institutions.

Karpati's insights into Gypsy education combined the missionary's zeal for a people in need of charitable help,[11] enlightened ideas of education as a means to improve human nature and the evolutionist paradigm of Gypsy culture as being in crisis. Unlike other educationalists, however, she did not argue for the complete assimilation of Gypsies into mainstream society. According to Karpati, Gypsy school provision could not and should not reproduce the features of non-Gypsy school provision, as Gypsies were not yet ready to attend so-called "normal classes" (Karpati 1962, 190). They should instead attend "special schools", that is, schools with a structure and contents more suitable to the particular features of Gypsy society, and specifically Gypsy nomadic practices. Rather than advocating the suppression of these practices, Karpati envisaged the creation of temporary settlement areas (*campi sosta*) to enable Gypsy children to attend school regularly. Such areas would constitute a point of reference for nomadic Gypsy groups, providing their children with a quiet environment that would allow them to concentrate on their work. To accommodate the specific educational needs of the Gypsies, Karpati devised a project (never to be realised) to build a school that was to become an integral part of the life of the entire Gypsy community. Such a school was supposed to house, among other things, a nursery, a kitchen, a launderette, showers and toilets, a teacher's room, rooms for the children and even a delivery room for pregnant Gypsy women (Ibid., 192).

Karpati's call for "special" Gypsy education was partly realised through the creation of the so-called *Lacio Drom* (literally "good journey") classes in Italy, the "bridge schools" in Spain, and the "caravan schools" in France and England. The first *Lacio Drom* classes were established in 1963 by the Italian Ministry of Education in collaboration with the University of Padua and the *Opera Nomadi* association.[12] They constituted special classes that aimed to prepare Gypsy children to work in an ordinary school environment. During such classes, Gypsy children were taught basic literacy and numeracy skills and encouraged to develop "critical" skills (Karpati 1962). As with the *Lacio Drom* classes in Italy, bridge schools in Spain were conceived as a form of compensatory education (i.e., as preparatory to the incorporation of Romani children into mainstream schools). More specifically, the aim of bridge schools was "to facilitate the access of Gypsies to school through centres located near their homes, dedicated specifically to them and adaptable to their circumstances" (Garreta Bochaca 2006, 264). The caravan schools introduced in England by the National Gypsy Education Council[13] in 1967 highlighted the need for policies that did not penalise Roma, Travellers and Gypsies for their nomadic way of life. Gypsy Council volunteers taught children pre-school literacy skills and prepared them to join ordinary classes. The Council urged the British government to implement better provision for Roma, Traveller and Gypsy children and emphasised that "respect [should] be paid to the culture of the Travellers even in the classroom" (Acton 1997, 3).

Despite all efforts, early provision for the Roma failed to have a significant impact on the academic attainment of Romani children. Moreover, it has been demonstrated that "special" classes and remedial education in general end up reinforcing precisely the patterns of segregation between Roma groups and the wider society that they were meant to eradicate (COSPE 2006). From the 1980s onwards, voluntary and special provision has gradually been replaced with the enrolment of Romani children in mainstream schools in EU member states.

Educational Initiatives for Gypsy Children at EU Level

Over the past three decades, the problematic situation of Gypsy education has been openly addressed by European institutions. In particular, the European Commission and the Council of Europe have become increasingly involved in designing and implementing Gypsy school provision.[14]

Early EU resolutions aimed specifically at Roma, Travellers and Gypsies in Europe date back to the 1970s and the early 1980s. Of crucial relevance are the Committee of Ministers' Resolution "On the social situation of nomads in Europe", adopted on 22 May 1975, and Resolution 125 issued by the Council of Europe and the Ministers of Education in 1981 "On the role and responsibility of local and regional authorities in regard to the cultural and social problems of populations of nomadic origin". Both resolutions called on EU member states to grant Roma, Travellers and Gypsies the status of ethnic minorities and the same advantages enjoyed by other minorities, "in particular concerning respect and support for their own culture and language".

Three years later the European Parliament adopted two further resolutions (on 16 March 1984 and 24 May 1984) urging the European Commission to take proactive action in the field of Roma education. Following these resolutions, the European Commission published a report—entitled *School Provision for Gypsy and Traveller Children* (Liégeois 1987b)—on the situation of Roma education in Europe. The report offered a series of working proposals and recommendations, which were subsequently examined and discussed by Ministers of Education, teachers, associations concerned with Romani issues and organisations run by Roma. This led to Resolution 89/C 153/02 being passed by the Council of Europe and the Ministers of Education, a resolution that has been described as "a milestone for Gypsy communities" (Liégeois 1999, 138). Among its main achievements are the raising of public awareness of the difficult situation of Roma school provision and the official acknowledgment of Romani cultural and linguistic heritage. In it, the Council and the Ministries of Education, having recognised that "the illiteracy rate among [Romani] adults is frequently over 50 per cent and in some places 80 per cent or more" (Council of Europe 1989, 3), devise:

> A set of measures concerning school provision for Gypsy and Travel-ler children aimed, without prejudice to any steps already taken by Member States to cope with specific situations which they face in this area, at developing a global structural approach helping to overcome the major obstacles to the access of Gypsy and Traveller children to schooling. (Council of Europe 1989, 1)

Such measures included support for educational establishments, support for teachers, pupils and parents, training and employment of new teachers (who should preferably be of Romani origin) and increased provision of documentation and information to schools, teachers and parents.

In 1996, the European Commission published a new report on the imple-mentation of the measures envisaged in Resolution 89/C 153/02. It revealed that positive action had been taken in response, but also that the situation of Gypsy communities remained "difficult, and frequently dramatic" (Euro-pean Commission 1996, 75). This was confirmed by the persistent high rate of non-attendance of Romani pupils, the high level of illiteracy (90 per cent) of the adult Romani population, and frequent rejection and segregation of Romani children in the classroom (European Commission 1996, 75).

The report identified the need for a flexible and diversified range of proposals and educational activities for the Roma, and for the wide dis-semination of information and documentation. It suggested the following guidelines for future work:

- Promoting innovative educational activities;
- Encouraging the development of projects at the local level (micro-projects) and pilot projects aimed at enhancing intercultural education;
- Intensifying exchange both among and within individual EU member states concerning educational projects and initiatives;
- Establishing synergies and ensuring a transversal dimension to actions aimed at Romani communities.

The early 1990s were characterised by an effort to coordinate activities and EU-wide programmes, and by the establishment in 1995 of a "Specialist Group on Roma, Gypsies and Travellers". This was the first body of the Council of Europe with the aim of regularly monitoring the situation of the Roma in Europe and advising the Committee of Ministers on Roma issues. Subsequent initiatives at EU level included Recommendation 4/2000 on the education of Gypsy children in Europe, adopted by the Committee of Ministers (subsequently implemented in 45 Member States of the Council of Europe), and a resolution issued by the European Parliament in April 2005 on the situation of the Roma in the European Union.[15]

Persisting School Segregation of Roma, Gypsies and Travellers

Despite the growing commitment of European institutions in the field of Roma school provision, the situation regarding Roma education in Europe remains extremely problematic (EUMC 2006; ERRC 2007). Romani pupils are kept at the margins of the education system and often confined to "ghetto classes". Although the Grand Chamber of the European Court of Human Rights deemed this practice unlawful (ECHR 2007), there is evidence that segregation and systematic exclusion of Romani pupils at school are a wide-spread phenomenon (EUMC 2006). To a certain extent, such discriminatory educational practices resemble those enacted in a number of central and Eastern European countries, where Romani children are routinely placed in special schools for children with learning disabilities on the racist assumption that these are the only suitable institutions given their intellectual abilities (Liégeois 1987b; Piasere 1991; ERRC 1998; OSI 2004).

In central and Eastern Europe, the Roma suffer severe discrimination and social exclusion in four key areas: education, employment, housing and healthcare (ERRC 1998). The collapse of the Soviet bloc had a negative impact on the living conditions of the Roma in this area. Moreover, the critical condition of the Roma caught the attention of international organisations, including the United Nations, the Council of Europe, the European Parliament and the Organisation for Security and Cooperation in Europe (OSCE), and NGOs such as the Soros Foundation. With the introduction of the Copenhagen criteria in 1993, the improvement of the Roma's situation has become part of the standard criteria aspiring member-states have to meet before joining the European Union.[16] According to a report from the European Roma Rights Centre, despite increasing awareness of the dire situation of the Roma living in this area, "segregated education of Roma remains a prevalent feature of the educational systems in Bulgaria, Czech Republic, Hungary, Romania and Slovakia" (ERRC 2007, 8). In these countries, Romani pupils are confined to "special schools" and "special classes" devised for children with learning and developmental disabilities, or "ghetto schools". The report shows that, although this segregation pattern has been widely condemned at governmental level, there remains a lack of specific and coordinated policy measures aimed at overcoming the physical separation of Roma children in schools and providing them with adequate education.

Segregation practices are not confined to central and Eastern Europe, as revealed by the report *The Education of Gypsy Children in Europe* published by the European Commission in 2002. The document, also known as the *Opre Roma* Report, provided a comparative analysis of the situation of Roma education in Spain, France and Italy. It concluded that "the experience of European Gypsy/Roma pupils is one of a climate of exclusion and segregation", and argued that the persistent "lack of adequate infrastructures and practical teaching models leads to the socio-educational ghettoisation of these groups of Gypsy/Roma children" (*Opre Roma* Report 2002, 47).

The report also revealed the persistent inability of the school system to cope with the educational needs of Romani children, as demonstrated by the "high percentage of absenteeism and dropping out of students". According to the report, only 30–40 per cent of Romani children regularly attended primary school and few were likely to attend secondary school. The study reported illiteracy rates of Roma/Gypsies to be above 50 per cent, and in some cases as high as 90 or 100 per cent. In other words, more than 500,000 Romani children were thought to lack any basic literacy skills (*Opre Roma* Report 2002, 10–11).

The Case of the UK

Although the first school for Gypsies in England was established in 1926,[17] there was no national policy concerning Gypsy and Traveller education in the UK until the 1980s. In 1967, the Plowden Report *Children and Their Primary Schools* stated that Gypsy and Traveller children were "probably the most deprived children" in England and Wales due to persistent harassment and marginalisation.

In the late 1960s and throughout the 1970s, Gypsy and Traveller education was in the hands of voluntary organisations such as the National Gypsy Education Council (NGEC), the Advisory Council for the Education of Romany and other Travellers (ACERT) and the National Association of Teachers and Travellers (NATT). At this time, Gypsy and Traveller educational provision mainly consisted of segregated and remedial education, characterised by a discrepancy between the commitment of local education authorities to school provision for Gypsy and Traveller children and some LEAs' disregard of their responsibilities.[18] At the end of the 1980s, Gypsy and Traveller school provision was still dominated by considerable fragmentation (ACERT 1986). However, the mid-1990s saw a shift in educational policies from segregation to an increased awareness of Traveller issues within a broader European framework.

The current situation of Gypsy school provision in the UK shares a number of similarities with the situation of Romani communities in Europe, especially in relation to the drop-out rate of Gypsy children, bullying and racism (Derrington 2009; Bhopal 2011), and the number of children identified as being in need of special education. Roma, Gypsy and Traveller pupils in the UK have been identified as "the group most at risk in the education system" (Ofsted 1999, 11). A report by the Office for Standards in Education in 2003 revealed that the majority of Traveller pupils "achieve standards that are well below the national average" (Ofsted 2003, 5). With an average attendance rate of 75 per cent, the report continued, Gypsy and Traveller pupils display "the worst attendance profile of any minority ethnic group".

While primary school provision for Roma, Gypsies and Travellers reportedly "continues to improve", the study estimated that around 12,000 Traveller pupils of secondary age were not registered at school. As was already highlighted in a previous Ofsted report (Ofsted 1999, 12), although many authorities and educational institutions "recognise and celebrate ethnic diversity", "there is considerable hesitancy with regard to Gypsy Traveller backgrounds". As a result, the structure of the curriculum is "often divorced from the mainstream efforts of schools to promote race equality for all pupils" (Ofsted 2003, 6). The discrepancy between official views on equality and the inclusion of all pupils in the education system and discriminatory practices and inadequate school provision has detrimental effects on the attainment of Roma, Gypsy and Traveller children, who feel it necessary to hide their ethnic identity from educational authorities. The report concluded that "the vast majority of Traveller pupils linger on the periphery of the education system" as they remain "an 'unseen' minority ethnic group" (Ibid.).

Persistent Problems of Gypsy School Provision

As the reports and studies cited above demonstrate, Gypsy school provision has hitherto failed to increase the level of school attainment of Romani children. Despite the fact that in this field "everything, or nearly everything, has already been tried" (Liégeois 1994, 210), a number of problems seem to persist. Issues of access and non-attendance (whether due to economic reasons or a lack of adequate site provision) continue to be major concerns raised by educators. The segregation of Romani children into separate or substandard arrangements remains a widespread phenomenon (Council of Europe 2012, 116), together with their outright exclusion from formal schooling.[19] Indeed, exclusion starts even before schooling through the use of discriminatory categories, as in the case of Italian Sinti and Romani children who are labelled by the authorities as "nomads" or "foreigners" despite being Italian citizens.

Furthermore, the performance of Romani children at school is regarded as problematic. Teachers complain about their behaviour, which they describe as "difficult", "disruptive" or "uncooperative".[20] Few educators acknowledge that such behaviour is governed by implicit, culturally specific rules that may not be immediately evident to them.[21] Romani pupils may experience great isolation inside the classroom, where they are outwith the protective care of older siblings and other members of their ethnic group. Such isolation makes them particularly vulnerable to bullying and racist behaviour, as already highlighted by the Swann Report (DES 1985) and confirmed by later reports (Ofsted, 1996; Bhopal et al. 2000; Cemlyn et al. 2009; Myers, McGhee and Bhopal 2010).

The school performance of Romani children is assessed in terms of "handicap" and "intellectual deficit".[22] According to teachers, Romani children are unable to concentrate on a task for a sustained period, they have a poor range of vocabulary and lack logical thought (Tauber 2003). Such a negative appraisal of Romani children's cognitive abilities is based on results obtained through culturally insensitive educational and psychological testing. In some cases, the low educational attainment of Gypsy children has been interpreted as a manifestation of Gypsies' backwardness and primitivism (Okely 1997). This shows that educators are still influenced by the evolutionary paradigm according to which Gypsy culture is "frozen" at a stage of lower development, and confirms their belief that the school system should help Gypsies rise to the challenges of the modern world. Although nowadays the Roma are not defined openly as "primitive", they are not yet recognised as a people with an autonomous culture and a separate educational system, and their children are considered as "intellectually deprived" and "socio-culturally disadvantaged".[23]

All of the problematic aspects mentioned above have conspired to create the image of a group whose children are "unteachable" and "non-adapt-able" (Piasere 1986): they seem to constitute a classical instance of "ethnic school failure" (Ogbu 1987). For many, the solution to the behavioural and learning problems of Romani children is to remove them from mainstream provision and place them into specialised classes. However, while specialised education may be beneficial in providing initial access to the school system, it is crucial that these classes are viewed as a temporary measure and integrated into the school establishment. In fact, they are often regarded as an easy solution to "get rid" of problematic children who might slow down the learning of other children in the "normal" class (Gomes 1998). This situation has led some scholars of education to question whether a compensatory model of education may help to promote, rather than overcome, exclusion (Igarashi 2005; O'Nions 2007).

Having identified the persisting problems affecting the educational attainment of Romani pupils in mainstream education, it is important to emphasise that these problems should not be regarded as causes, but rather as consequences, of the scholastic failure of these children.[24] A number of structural factors are key to explaining the academic failure of many Romani students. Such factors pertain to the general situation and living conditions of Roma/Gypsies, including financial problems and high unemployment rates,[25] poverty and lack of access to basic health services (EUMC 2006). This situation has a significant negative impact on the ability of Romani pupils to attend school regularly and on their educational achievement.

In addition to structural factors, the academic performance of Romani pupils is influenced by a range of culture-specific factors, entailing an emphasis on communication and educational systems that are widely divergent from those of the non-Roma. These factors will be examined in more detail in Chapter 3.

CONCLUSIONS

What characterises Gypsy school provision from the outset is an element of compulsion. Historically, the forced schooling of Roma has been a means for pursuing their assimilation into mainstream society. State authorities saw it as a way to achieve "de-ethnicitisation" and control over their Romani population; missionaries perceived it as a way to convert and morally elevate an otherwise "degraded race"; and early educationalists as a way to "rescue" and "civilise" them. It is not surprising then that Roma, Gypsies and Travellers perceive compulsory schooling, which is considered an acquired right among the non-Roma, as an alien institution. The most extreme manifestation of forced schooling has been the policy of removing Romani children from their families, a practice that left a permanent scar in the collective historical memory of some Romani groups and continues to affect their view of school.

Today, Romani children are no longer routinely taken away from their parents, but are often exposed to racism and bullying and expected to assimilate into mainstream non-Romani culture. A climate of general mistrust of the mainstream education system persists, mainly because the school aims to educate the Gypsies according to non-Romani values, and not just provide them with basic instruction. In the past, Gypsies were educated "for the state", to become useful citizens. Nowadays, the Roma are educated to improve their condition, to achieve "social success" and "orientate themselves in modern society" (Tosuner, Pagano and Vermeren 2012, 113). But what is the position of the Roma on this?

School providers have thus far failed to include Romani community forces alongside the school and recognise them as educational agents. This oversight undoubtedly contributes to the failure of Gypsy school provision, which continues to be based on a view of the Roma as passive bearers of—rather than active participants in—the education process. This view requires drastic revision to take into account the Romani approach to literacy and education (see Chapter 3). Faced with a choice between going to school—and becoming assimilated into mainstream society—or maintaining their separate identity, most Roma have (predictably) chosen to reject school. What is often interpreted as rejection of schooling *per se* is in fact a result of the Roma's determination to preserve their separate identity

3 Education and Literacy Acquisition from a Romani Perspective

Once upon a time a grammarian wanted to spend some leisure time taking a boat ride on the river. So he rented a boat from a Gypsy whose business this was. During the ride the grammarian asked the Gypsy boatman, "Do you know anything about literature? Do you know how to write? Do you know how to read?".

And the boatman answered, "No, I'm always working, always trying to make ends meet, trying to feed my family, and never had time to learn to read. To me it's just a waste of time—I know my work, all there is to know about boats, and that's all I have to know".

And the grammarian said, "What a shame—you've wasted half your life with boats and know nothing about the more refined things in life".

So they went arguing back and forth about the need to know about reading and literature and the more refined things in life. All of a sudden a big whirlpool came up and things got scary. The boatman asked the grammarian, "Hey, do you know how to swim?".

"No".

"Oh, what a shame—you've spent half your life studying grammar and literature and writing, and you didn't learn how to swim? Well, if you don't learn how to swim now, it's going to be the *end* of your life!".

(Tong 1989, 21–22)

The relationship between the Roma and the school system is highly problematic. Tensions and conflict in this area are usually attributed to external factors, such as the difficulties experienced by the Roma in gaining access to school, or are blamed on their difficult relationship with the wider institutional sphere. There exists a widespread belief that Romani children are simply "not interested" in education, or, worse still, that they are simply "unable" to perform at the same intellectual level as the other children.[1] Another common view, which was examined in the previous chapter, is that which categorises the Roma as "culturally deprived" and lacking educational structures, and therefore in need of "rescuing" from the perils of illiteracy. Both views conspire to create the perception of the Roma as a case of "ethnic school failure" (Ogbu 1987).

However, the crucial question to ask in this regard is not, "Why do the Roma fail at school?" but rather, "Why have the Roma thus far not regarded school as an educational agent?". The main purpose of this chapter is to answer this question by providing a Romani perspective on the education system and explaining the Roma's view on literacy and its uses.

As will be shown, the Romani education system is informal and inextricably linked to the daily life of the community, while the non-Romani model is decontextualised and considered as preparatory to "real" life. In addition, the two educational systems rely on different communication methods: the Romani system is based on the oral mode, as opposed to the formal school system that relies almost exclusively on written communication. The chapter considers the role of the oral tradition within Romani society and looks at the oral features of the Romani language. It argues that failure to acknowledge the centrality of orality in Romani culture is a major reason for the lack of adequate education provision for Romani children.

Notwithstanding their difficult relationship with the school, the Roma appreciate that it can provide them with an invaluable tool: literacy. What the Roma mean by "literacy", however, hardly coincides with the non-Romani view. In this respect, the chapter shows that, while the dominant Western approach to literacy is characterised by a narrow focus on alphabetic writing, the Romani approach to literacy is highly diversified and comprises a range of alphabetic and non-alphabetic writing systems with important socio-economic functions. The chapter then moves on to analyse some early Romani writing systems (such as trail signs and graphic codes used by nomadic Western European Roma) and instances of instrumental uses of alphabetic writing among the Roma and the French Manuš, whose alphabetic practices are characterised by a mixture of oral and written modes of communication. Finally, the chapter recommends that the instrumental and socially situated nature of the Romani approach to literacy should be taken into account to ensure that literacy provision for Romani children is functional to their socio-economic environment.

TWO DIFFERENT APPROACHES TO EDUCATION

There are a number of significant differences between the Roma and non-Roma as far as the education of their children is concerned. Romani and non-Romani societies use different strategies to transmit knowledge, skills and shared values to future generations (a process known in the social sciences as "enculturation" or "socialisation"). The non-Roma utilise formal educational structures and institutions, while the Roma have no separate structures for enculturation. Among the latter, new skills are learned exclusively through imitation and everyday practice, and do not entail a long training period within formal institutions. Conversely, in a non-Romani educational context the school is regarded as an educational agent and has a crucial socialisation role. In this context, "instruction" (i.e., the transmission of ready knowledge) and "education" are not separate processes. As pointed out by Liégeois, schooling

> has taken on more and more of the family's educational role . . . We speak of the "educational system" when we mean the school system; we delegate total responsibility to the "Minister of Education" or "Department of Education". (Liégeois 1987b, 46)

Among the non-Roma, the education system has the task of providing not only specialised information and skills, but also "forming" the individual and shaping his/her values, beliefs and behavioural patterns in a certain fashion. From this perspective, formal education does not consist exclusively of acquiring literacy and numeracy skills, but is considered an instrumental tool for identity formation, strengthening the individual's cultural and historical memory and heightening his/her political and civil consciousness. This (Western) perspective on the school system seems to reflect the values of the majority society. But what happens when minority cultures with different views of education are forcibly included within such a system?

The education system of the Roma is largely characterised by the following features:

a) Romani education encourages independent behaviour and personal initiative.

Among the Roma, child socialisation is based on a "pedagogy of experience", which allows the individual considerable freedom. This is radically different from the approach used at school, where knowledge is usually conveyed through frontal lessons that encourage passivity and conformism.

Children are treated as "young adults" and not as "adults-in-the-making". From childhood, young Roma play an active role in their group and have to fulfil a number of tasks for which there is no formal, separate training. They enjoy more freedom than non-Romani children, but carry a greater amount of responsibility and individual accountability:

> In traditional Romani communities children are encouraged to be independent from an early age. This prepares them for the social and economic responsibilities of adolescence when they will be expected to marry, work full-time, and raise a family of their own. Independent behaviour is reinforced in a number of ways such as encouraging children to seek and prepare their own food, dress themselves, put themselves to sleep without supervision [. . .], and care for younger children. (Smith 1997, 245)

b) Romani education is shaped by a principle of "intergenerational continuity".

Romani education does not place barriers between generations. There are three main categories of educators in Romani society: (1) grandparents, who represent the link with the past and with the *mule* (the dead); (2) parents, that is, "the people to imitate, the people whose behaviour inspires curiosity and a spirit of adventure, persons of authority but rarely authoritarian" (Piasere 1986); and (3) older children (especially older brothers and sisters), who act as mediators between the parental generation and their age group. This system enables Romani children to become active participants in the education process, not just passive recipients of information.

c) Romani education does not take place in decontextualised structures.

Among the Roma, education is not imparted separately from the group and is not considered preparatory to real life. Enculturation practices are thoroughly "imbricated" in their socio-cultural structures. Education is a collective process and constitutes an organic system within which the family, that is, the educational unit, operates in harmony with the rest of the group.

> [Among the Roma] the child's education is collective. He[/She] lives communally, alongside three or four generations, and his[/her]socialisation takes place within this context which assures cohesion, coherence, continuity and security. Generations are neither separated nor opposed; children and adults work together, live together and suffer together. Children learn through immersion in the family, through their respect for adults and in being respected for themselves. (Liégeois 1987b, 46)

Conversely, formal school learning is based on a thorough decontextualisation of the learning process. This disengagement from the social context, as Jerome Bruner points out, "makes learning an act in itself and makes it possible to embed it in a context of language and symbolic activity" (Bruner 1966, 62). This brings us to another crucial point related to the decontextualised features of formal education: in a classroom environment, teaching is almost exclusively based on verbal formulation. Verbal communication dominates the learning process, and words constitute a "major invitation to form concepts rather than the action" (Ibid.). However, in Romani society knowledge is acquired through "observational learning" that does not require explicit verbal formulation but rather is based on observation and mimesis (Scribner and Cole 1973, 555). A further fundamental aspect linked to the dominant use of verbal communication in formal education is that the main vehicle of knowledge is the majority language, which for the Roma is likely to be a foreign language.

We can see that the differences between the two systems are remarkable. In this regard, Liégeois refers to "two different philosophies of education" that confront and largely oppose each other (Liégeois 1987b, 164). Describing the relationship between the Romani approach to education and formal school learning in terms of conflicting educational philosophies is useful to illustrate the extent to which the two educational systems diverge. However, adopting the notion of mutually exclusive "philosophies of education" risks reinforcing the belief that the dissimilarities between Romani culture and school culture are irreconcilable, which is not necessarily the case.[2] The Roma's informal and intergenerational approach to education is certainly different from the Western formal educational system. However, this difference has less to do with an ideological and philosophical opposition and more to do with culturally determined factors. In particular, what are usually described as "different learning styles" of Romani children are influenced by a predominantly oral use of language, whereas the language used at school is in most cases a written language. This reliance on oral communication is inextricably linked to the centrality of orality in Romani culture.

Romani Culture and the Romani Oral Tradition

Although Romani culture can hardly be defined as either a "pre-literate" or a "primary oral" culture, that is, a culture "with no knowledge whatsoever of writing or even the possibility of writing" (Ong 1982, 31), it does rely heavily on oral communication for the transmission of information and knowledge. The oral tradition of the Roma consists of both narrative (mostly folktales and *märchen*,[3] but also myths, parables, legends, riddles and proverbs) and lyric forms (songs, ballads and "slow songs"). Gypsy oral folklore has been published by Romani writers and scholars, as in the case of Károly Bari, Matéo Maximoff and Derek Tipler. More frequently, however, oral texts have been recorded, transcribed and published by non-Romani scholars.[4]

What are the main themes of the Romani oral tradition? The most common motifs are the celebration of the Roma's intelligence and cleverness, respect for the dead, the importance of hospitality, the dislike of a work-centred life, the contempt in which the Roma are held among the majority population and ways in which cultural survival is achieved. Diane Tong (1989) pointed out that the tradition of storytelling among the Roma incorporates key Romani values, beliefs and customs. Although some stories are unique to the Roma, researchers have established that the themes of Romani folklore are closely linked to the wider Indo-European folklore tradition (Groome 1879; Tong 1989; Wiernicki 1995). This can partly be seen as an outcome of cross-cultural contact, since "the culture of European Roma", as Krzysztof Wiernicki reminds us, "is heavily influenced by that of the peoples among whom they have lived for such a long time; and this also applies to their oral narratives and fairy tales" (Wiernicki 1995,

5). However, it is important to point out that, rather than passively repro-
ducing or even "stealing" elements of the existing Indo-European oral tradition (Sawyer 1962), the Roma had an active role in spreading folktales
across Europe (Groome 1899, lxiii; Tong 1989, 10).[5]

Oral narrative storytellers, since they cannot rely on written texts for
purposes of memorisation, have to contextualise their narratives through
the embedding of the story into a known framework. They also rely on
certain stylistic features to make their stories memorable: repetition, formulaic expressions, rhyme, alliteration and the use of rhetorical devices
such as hyperbole (Ong 1982, 33–36). In addition to these characteristics,
which apply to oral narration in general, Romologists have identified features typical of Romani narration. Romani oral narratives encourage identification between audience and narrator through a conflation of past and
present verb tenses (Williams 1986) and by using devices such as temporal
deixis and the switch of narrative points of view (Dick-Zatta 1985b). The
most common form of oral narrative among the Roma is the fictional tale,
usually called *paramiči* or *paramisi*. There are several types of *paramiči*,
including heroic or epic tales, wonder tales, magic tales and droll stories.

The specific functions of the Romani oral tradition seem to vary according to the group concerned. Jelena Čvorović maintained that among Serbian Gypsies "there are several types of stories: some serve as entertainment
only, such as 'scary' stories about the dead and various jokes; others are
'educational' stories, to which the Gypsies refer as their 'school'. Some stories are a mix of these types" (Čvorović 2009). Rena Cotten argued that
the various story-types detected among the American Rom have different
forms and functions (Cotten 1954, 261), and identified three main (non-
fictional) tale-types:

- The *svata*, which Cotten described as "the textbooks of Gypsy culture" (Ibid., 262), have an educational purpose: to instruct the young
  "in the ways of the Gypsies" and to familiarise the adults "with countries and places they do not know from personal experience"; (Ibid.)
- the *hira*, which are "tales about known, living or remembered persons", and are the equivalent of "biographies, newspapers, social
  register and rogues' gallery of the society"; (Ibid., 264)
- the *kris*, that is, stories of court trials that took place among the
  Vlach Roma, whose function is to provide "clarification of basic legal
  points". (Ibid., 265)

Jane Dick-Zatta, who studied the oral tradition of the Slovenian Roma
in Italy, argued that they have no established corpus of fairy tales, myths
and non-fictional narratives (Dick-Zatta 1986, 2), and demonstrated how
the Roma's oral narratives have essentially a pedagogic function. Among
them, narration is an important social activity. Oral narratives are perceived by the audience as the "truth"; the narration of real events. The

truthful nature of oral narratives among the Roma, however, does not fulfil the same objective criteria as the notion of truth among literate societies (Ibid.). Real events are formulated in symbolic terms and often "recreated anew" to bestow teachings and admonishments of general validity. In this case, what is regarded as the truth is not the correspondence of truth and reality, but is founded on a relationship of trust between the audience and the storyteller, who often deploys formulaic expressions such as "May God punish me" or "May I die if I am not telling the truth" to ensure the audience that his/hers are "true Romani words" (*čače romane lava*).[6] In the context of Romani oral narratives, the identity of the storyteller and his/her relationship with the audience is therefore paramount: the storyteller is often a member of the same family group, usually an elder or at any rate an adult. It is by listening to the narrator's life experiences that young members of the audience learn how to live and behave like Roma in relation to the external world. It is thus essential that such narratives are handed down from the older generation to the next.

To sum up, Romani oral narratives seem to have multiple objectives and functions. Nevertheless, it is possible to argue that oral narration among the Roma has the overall aim of transmitting important social knowledge regarding the group, including information about the Roma/non-Roma relationship. Such information is essential to the cultural survival of the community and provides an essential means of cultural identification. This mode of identification does not merely involve the performer and the oral text, but extends to the audience and has the power to shape it into a communal soul (Ong 1982, 46). Among the Roma, oral narratives are therefore a direct expression of the experience of the group: they are not simple words but a guide to social action.

Oral Features of the Romani Language

Given that the Romani language is used primarily in oral settings, it presents a number of characteristics typical of oral languages. Since oral cultures, as Walter Ong pointed out, cannot rely on writing to "structure knowledge at a distance from lived experience", they have to "conceptualise and verbalise all their knowledge with more or less close reference to the human lifeworld, assimilating the alien, objective world to the more immediate, familiar interaction of human beings" (Ong 1982, 42–43). A major implication of this phenomenon is that in non-literate societies language remains anchored to everyday experience, and this seems to be true of Romani (the Romani language, also known as *Romani chib*). Among non-literate Roma, Romani acts primarily as a basic means of communication and interaction with other group members, rather than a tool for conceptual analysis. To use Luria's expression, Romani is used as a vehicle of "situational", rather than "conceptual" or "categorical", thinking (Luria 1976, 52–55).

The oral status of Romani has not been significantly affected by the increasing levels of scholarisation detected among the Roma (Matras 2005a). This is partly because Romani is not normally deployed as the main language of instruction and literacy acquisition. The creation of a standard written variety of Romani is relatively recent, and its use for educational and official purposes limited to a minority of Romani literate individuals (mainly writers and intellectuals). For the time being, as Yaron Matras remarked, "[. . .] all Roma who have access to education are educated in the state language, and so their command of literacy in the state language always precedes any attempts, be they institutionalised or private, to acquire literacy in Romani" (Matras 1999, 482).

Another aspect of Romani as an oral language is its crucial social function in relation to the wider Roma/non-Roma relationship. Historically, the recognition of Romani as a separate language has been opposed consistently by the non-Roma, who made it an object of persecution,[7] together with other defining components of Romani identity.[8] Its use in the public sphere therefore carries great symbolic significance and acts as a powerful tool for self-identification. As Matras pointed out, "the one feature that stands out as a common denominator of the Rom is, by definition, their use of the Romani language" (Matras 2004, 54). This is confirmed by the fact that the word *Romanes*, which is often used as a noun meaning Romani as a language, is in fact an adverb translatable as "like a Rom" or "in a Romani way".

Romani languages are learnt almost exclusively through direct contact rather than through formal instruction. This basic fact, together with the diasporic dispersion and social isolation of Romani groups, has provided a protective shield for the preservation of the Roma's oral traditions. In this context, Romani seems to act as a filter that enables the passage of sensitive information that has to be kept within the group boundaries. As Kiddle highlights, the Gypsies, as "the inheritors of an oral culture", "have always been aware of the potential advantages this gives them in being able to keep outsiders at bay and they remain so" (Kiddle 1999, 126). On the one hand, the use of Romani determines ethnic membership, on the other it helps to avoid unwanted interaction with members of the majority group:

> For Roma/Gypsies there is always a very close link between social position (membership of a given group or section of society) and linguistic behaviour. [. . .] Modulated according to the speaker's needs, language is a marker both of the degree of social proximity one may wish to have and, by the same token, of the social distance one wishes or needs to maintain. (Liégeois 2007, 47)

Dick-Zatta (1990) has shown that among the Slovenian Roma the oral code of communication serves as a "cognitive amplifier" in the context of Roma/non-Roma relations. The function of Romani is primarily that of centring attention on the Roma/non-Roma dichotomy. Such a dichotomy is central to the Roma's view of the world and to their notion of humanity, which they conceive in terms of "a continuum stretching between the 'nearest', one's own parents and children, passing through many intermediate steps, *slachta* (blood Rom groups), *družina* (a family group), *aver Roma* (other Rom groups), etc., to the 'farthest', who are the Ga[d]že" (Dick-Zatta 1990, 55).[9] Every aspect of Romani life (daily activities and customs, types of social behaviour, ways of interacting with the natural world) carries a symbolic meaning that can be interpreted in relation to this fundamental distinction. For example, eating a certain type of food may be regarded as being closer to the Roma's true way of life, or, conversely, may be seen as "Gadže-like" and thus confined to the other extreme of the continuum (Williams 1986). The role of this symbolic classification is to reinforce the Roma/Gadže dichotomy. While for the Gadže the Roma constitute an "Other" among "Others", for the Roma and Sinti the Gadže are the "Other" *par excellence*. Accordingly, individuals in these groups define themselves first "in terms of not being Ga[d]že" (Dick-Zatta 1986, 5). The same symbolic articulation based on categories of "closeness" and "distance" acts as basis for how the Roma and Sinti perceive their dispersal among the Gadže, which has a direct impact on their peripatetic practices.[10]

The need to mark out clearly the symbolic distinction between Roma and non-Roma is particularly important in the school context. In a classroom situation, Roma and Sinti find themselves vulnerable because they are forcibly placed in close proximity to the non-Roma (and other Roma and Sinti groups). For them, this is a potentially dangerous situation because the direct sharing of a social space with the Gadže clashes with the strategy of geographical and symbolic dispersion mentioned above. It is in this context that the symbolic role of Romani as an identity marker becomes crucial. As has been observed, Romani is often used by Roma and Sinti pupils to exchange information while at the same time excluding the Gadže (Gomes 1998; Tauber 2003). In doing this, these pupils manage to reinstate the all-important ethnic divide that was temporarily blurred by the geography of classroom organisation.[11]

The Roma's determination to preserve their language and oral tradition has serious implications for their involvement in schooling, and greatly contributes to their negative attitude towards alphabetic literacy. In a sense, the limited diffusion of schooled literacy among the Roma represents a guarantee that the oral status of their culture will be maintained. From this perspective, illiteracy constitutes an advantage, rather than a "handicap".[12] First, non-literacy inhibits a number of dynamics that would lead to drastic changes in their oral culture. These include cognitive changes triggered by literacy acquisition and literacy use, and significant changes in their social structure.[13] As shown by Goody and Watt, the widespread use of literacy has a drastic effect on group solidarity, and while in non-literate societies "every social situation can-not but bring the individual into contact with the group's patterns of thought, feeling and action", in literate societies "the mere fact that read-ing and writing are normally solitary activities means that insofar as the dominant cultural tradition is a literate one, it is very easy to avoid" (Goody and Watt 1968, 59–60).

At a more fundamental level, avoidance of schooled literacy can be interpreted as a form of resistance against acculturation (Hancock 2000a; Levinson 2007, 8, 11). As mentioned earlier, for the Roma/Gypsies the school is not a neutral place, but part of the Gadže's world. As Tauber remarks:

> School is not only a place where one learns how to read and write: school is a cultural place, an institution where a whole society is edu-cated. School is the result of centuries of development and manifes-tations of a specific way of thought—a thought the non-Gypsies call "culture", a thought the Sinti call *Gadžengro šero*: "the Gadže way of thinking". (Tauber 2003, 21)

Although the Roma refuse to recognise the educational function of the school, they do recognise its crucial importance as a place to learn read-ing and writing skills.[14] Judith Okely stated clearly that English Travel-lers "express a desire for literacy and numeracy" (Okely 1983, 162), and that "there is indeed a demand for schooling among some Travellers and especially if it does not entail major compromises with their mobile self-employed way of life" (Ibid., 161). Gomes (1998) and Tauber (2003) make a similar point in relation to the Sinti in Italy. Moreover, there is evidence that the need for literacy among Roma and Gypsies is increasing (Liégeois and Gheorge 1995; Kiddle 1999; Derrington and Kendall 2004). This is partly because "illiteracy no longer provides protection from the aggression of other cultures as channelled through the school" (Liégeois and Gheor-ghe 1995, 30), and because of the requirement for literacy in the changing job market. Literacy skills are now in more demand among the non-Roma and are a necessary requirement to access the job market: possessing basic literacy is essential in obtaining a driving license, carrying out a trade, accessing public services and dealing with local bureaucracies. For this rea-son many Roma have begun to regard literacy skills as strategically and economically important, and they would be willing to enter the dominant school system to obtain them.

When assessing the complex attitude of Romani groups towards literacy, it is essential to emphasise that their notion of what counts as literacy dif-fers from the dominant Western model. Generally, the Roma have an inter-est in gaining basic literacy skills that are applicable to practical, everyday uses and contribute to their economic independence (Okely 1983; Smith 1997; Levinson 2007). Martin Levinson has listed some of these desired skills as:

Understanding of local economies and their populations, manual dex-
terity, mechanical ingenuity, highly developed memory, salesmanship
and bargaining skills, home and care skills, knowledge of herbs, skills
with horses and other animals and expertise about metals. (Levinson
2007, 10)[15]

Regrettably, such skills hardly coincide with those promoted by non-Romani educational institutions, as the school system supports a notion of formal literacy tailored to a non-Romani model. This form of literacy, which
is based on a narrow interpretation of literacy as standardised schooled
literacy, stands in dramatic contrast to the informal and pluralistic view of
literacy that seems to characterise that of Romani groups.

THE WESTERN MODEL OF LITERACY

According to the conventional Western view of literacy, to be fully literate
an individual is expected to master reading and writing at a basic level.
These skills are supposed to have a direct effect on cognitive processes and
abilities as literacy is seen as a neutral, uniform technology having cumula-
tive effects on cognition. A prominent example of this view is the work of
the anthropologist Jack Goody on the cognitive and social implications of
literacy and writing. According to Goody, Western literacy is endowed with
intrinsic properties that play a crucial part in the development of "logic",
"criticism" and "individual thought" (Goody and Watt 1968; Goody 1977).
He proposes a "literacy factor" as the distinguishing criterion in classifying
human societies.

Goody's approach, and indeed the general Western approach, is based
on what is aptly described by Harvey Graff as a "literacy myth" (Graff
1991, 3). Brian Street has convincingly challenged this "myth" (which he
calls the "autonomous" model) by pointing out that anthropological evidence "suggests that there is scientific and non-scientific thought in all societies and within all individuals" (Street 1984, 25). The cognitive opposition
between Western and "traditional" societies is flawed because "observers
have simply failed to remark the scientific nature of much of the thinking
of so-called 'primitive' peoples and have perhaps overstated the 'scientific'
nature of thinking of their own societies" (Street 1984, 26).[16]

Non-Romani definitions of literacy are almost exclusively preoccupied
with writing, and alphabetic literacy is mistakenly taken to be "literacy"
tout court. However, the claim that alphabetic writing is the only source of
"logical" and "scientific" thought is not supported by sufficient empirical
findings (Graff 1991, 4). Such a claim also fails to question the relationship
between literacy and writing, and overlooks important functions played by
literacy practices in the social context.

Far from being a monolithic, self-evident phenomenon, literacy is a varied and complex reality. This fact is captured well by Graff, who states that:

> There are many kinds of "literacies". One need distinguish not only between basic or elementary kinds of literacy and higher levels of education, but also among alphabetic, visual and artistic, spatial and graphic, mathematical, symbolic, technological and mechanical literacy. An understanding of any one type requires care in qualifying terms and specifying what precisely is meant by reference to "literacy". These many "literacies" are all conceptually distinct, but nonetheless interrelated. (Graff 1991, 11)

By restricting the scope of literacy to alphabetic literacy one risks reinforcing the dichotomy between literate/non-literate societies, which is as misleading and biased as the old-fashioned primitive/modern polarity (Lévi-Strauss 1962). Contrary to common belief, human societies are unlikely to be defined as purely "oral" or "literate", but instead present a combination of oral and literate modes of communication. In reality, both oral and literate societies are characterised by "mixed"—partly oral and partly written—communication.[17] Raimondo Cardona (1990) argues that the possibility of finding a society completely unaware of the existence of writing is rather remote. He emphasises that the lack of an alphabetical writing system does not automatically imply the absence of all forms of writing, since writing is a much broader phenomenon encompassing "the production and the use of graphic systems for communicative purposes" (Cardona 1990, 207). In line with this broader perspective, it is important to recognise that all societies have developed their own specific writing typology: the Roma forming no exception.

A further crucial dimension usually overlooked by the Western approach is the pivotal role alphabetic literacy plays in social and political contexts, especially its role in promoting and perpetuating state hegemony to the detriment of minority groups.[18] Writing is a code, a system of signs that can only be deciphered by using another semiotic system, the spoken language. However, far from being merely a secondary semiotic system (in other words, a mere transposition of spoken language), writing is a multi-faceted phenomenon, "whose meaning, including any consequences it may have for the individual and society, depends crucially on the social practices surrounding it and on the ideological system in which it is embedded" (Ingold 1994, 533). Alphabetic literacy constitutes not only a material technique for acquiring a range of skills, but also a medium of representation conveying a wide range of symbolic connotations.

Furthermore, literacy is deeply embedded in the specific context within which it develops and operates, as emphasised by recent approaches known as New Literacy Studies (NLS). Unlike the traditional view of literacy as a set of decontextualised, neutral skills, the NLS approach regards reading and writing as practices that are rooted in different socio-cultural situations.[19] It calls for a shift from studying literacy as a uniform, universal phenomenon to the investigation of multiple and culturally specific literacies. By focusing on the situated nature of literacy, it pays particular attention to its functions and uses, that is, how individuals engage with literacy practices in practical terms and for what purposes (Collins and Blot 2003).

In addition to the socially situated nature of literacy, NLS emphasise its hegemonic use. The key tenet of the concept of hegemony, as formulated by Antonio Gramsci, is that political (and socio-economic) dominance can be attained through a particular form of consent. Hegemony imposes the supremacy of a dominant group not through direct, physical force but through an internalised form of social control, the indirect imposition of the values and views of those who are in power (Gramsci 1997). Scholars of NLS argue that literacy is inextricably connected to hegemonic processes through which a political system achieves and maintains its consensual basis without the use of physical force. "Literacy is not a likely technique for domination or coercion; [. . .] however, it has proved a much more viable option [. . .] for establishing and maintaining social and cultural hegemony" (Graff 1991, 12). Writing practices are embedded in the contested domains of ideology and hegemony, both of which can be sites of oppression and resistance (Street 1993).

The role of literacy as an empowering tool for marginalised and minority groups has been developed by authors such as Paulo Freire and Donaldo Macedo (1987). For them, "literacy cannot be reduced to the treatment of letters and words as purely mechanical domain", but should be seen as a "set of cultural practices that promotes democratic and emancipatory change" (Freire and Macedo 1987, xii). Critical literacy can be defined as

> [the] analytic habits of thinking, reading, writing, speaking or discussing which go beneath surface impressions, traditional myths, mere opinions and routine clichés; understanding the social contexts and consequences of any subject matter; discovering the deep meaning of any event, text, technique, process, object, statement, image or situation. (Shor 1993, 32)

This understanding of literacy as a tool of empowerment is of crucial importance when considering, on the one hand, high illiteracy rates among the Roma and, on the other, the use of writing for counter-hegemonic purposes by an increasing number of Romani writers and intellectuals, which will be discussed in more detail in Chapter 5 and Chapter 7.

THE ROMA'S DIVERSE APPROACH TO WRITING

Despite the fact that the Roma were aware of the existence of alphabetic writing from an early stage, they have deliberately kept themselves at the margins of the communication system of the dominant social group and, as I argued earlier in this chapter, they have managed to retain a mainly oral system of communication. This system is closely linked to the specific features of the Roma's socio-economic approach.

The Romani economy does not require writing. It is based on mutual aid and cooperation, rather than being centred on capitalist accumulation (and registration) of wealth and economic surplus.[20] Therefore, literacy is not required for the rationalisation of economic exchanges. Furthermore, literacy is not functional in the dispensing of justice, which is a collective process that takes place within the group without the need for separate, decontextualised legal structures.[21] Nor does the Romani social system include the presence of a separate clergy, traditionally the main repository and transmitter of literacy skills.[22] Finally, as seen above, the Roma rely mostly on oral (rather than written) modes to pass down their stories and narratives.

To conclude, communication based on alphabetic literacy is not central to the Romani social system. It would be wrong, however, simply to equate the marginal role of alphabetic literacy among the Roma with a complete "lack of writing" and with an attitude of utter rejection. Alongside oral modes of communication, the Roma have developed over the centuries a diverse range of writing practices for internal use to convey information exclusively to other group members. Of great significance in this context are non-alphabetic graphic systems (Piasere 1995; Williams 1997).

Uses of Non-Alphabetic Graphic Codes: The Patrin

A prominent example of a non-alphabetic writing system used by the Roma is that of the trail signs or *patrin* (also known as *patteran*), which literally means "leaf". The *patrin* signs were adopted by nomadic Romani groups to assist orientation while travelling, and were vital when the Roma used to travel on foot or on carts pulled by horses. These signs have a long history and have been recorded by several authors.

The first to mention the *patrin* was Thomas Dekker in *Lanthorn and Candle-Light* (1930).[23] In it, Dekker describes the *Moone-men*, also referred to as "gypsies" [*sic*] or "Egyptians", as a wild and dangerous people, "barbarous in condition" and "beastly in behaviour" (Dekker 1930, 344), a people whose wandering habits resemble the ever-changing face of the moon. According to Dekker, Gypsies have the appearances of beggars, a propensity for violence and are "more scattered than Jews, and more hated" (Ibid.).

Dekker deeply resented the Gypsies' nomadic way of life. He compared them to lice and detested their "secretive" practices, which he associated with playing tricks. In particular, he had suspicions that they used trail signs for secretive communication among themselves. He noticed that they had developed the habit of placing small "boughs" at particular points on the road:

One shire alone and no more is sure still at one time to have these Egyptian lice swarming within it, for, like flocks of wild-geese, they will evermore fly one after another. Let them be scattered worse than the quarters of a traitor are, after he's hanged, drawn, and quartered, yet, they have a trick, like water cut with a sword, to come together instantly and easily again. And this is their policy, which way soever the foremost ranks lead, they stick up small boughs in several places, to every village where they pass which serve as ensigns to waft on the rest. (Dekker 1930, 345)

"Gypsy trail-signs" are also described in *The Zincali* by George Borrow (1841). Borrow was an English author who worked for the British and Foreign Bible Society and travelled extensively throughout Europe. He devoted his writings to the English and European Gypsies (Borrow 1851, 1858, 1908), including the Spanish Gypsies (Borrow 1841).

Borrow presents three kinds of *patrin* (or *patteran*, as he calls them): (1) two or three handfuls of grass "lying at a small distance from each other" at crossroads; (2) a cross "drawn at the entrance of a road, the long part or stem of it pointing down that particular road"; and (3) a cleft stick "stuck at the side of the road, close by the hedge, with a little arm in the cleft pointing down the road that the band have taken, in the manner of a signpost". In the book *Romano Lavo-Lil*, a Gypsy character gives the following definition of the *patrin*:

Patrin is the name of the signs by which the Gypsies who go before show the road they have taken to those who follow behind. We flings handfuls of grass down at the head of the road we takes, or we makes with the finger a cross-mark on the ground, we sticks up branches of trees by the side the hedge. But the true patrin is handfuls of leaves flung down; for patrin or patten in old Roman language means the leaf of a tree. (Borrow 1908, 99)

Ursula, one of the Gypsy characters in Borrow's *Romany Rye*, describes the *patrin* as follows:

"Do you know what patteran means?".

"Of course, Ursula; the gypsy trail, the handful of grass which the gypsies strew in the roads as they travel, to give information to any of their companions who may be behind, as to the route they have taken. The gypsy patteran has always had a strange interest for me, Ursula".

"Like enough, brother; but what does patteran mean?".

"Why, the gypsy trail, formed as I told you before".

"And you know nothing more about patteran, brother?".

"Nothing at all, Ursula; do you?".

"What's the name for the leaf of a tree, brother?".

"I don't know", said I; "it's odd enough that I have asked that question of a dozen Romany chals and chies, and they always told me that they did not know".

"No more they did, brother; there's only one person in England that knows, and that's myself—the name for a leaf is patteran. Now there are two that knows it—the other is yourself". (Borrow 1858, 146)

Another nineteenth-century author who recorded the use of the *patrin* among the Roma is the American scholar Charles Godfrey Leland. In his book *The English Gypsies and Their Language* (Leland 1873, 24), Leland compares two versions of a trail sign used by the German Sinti (the oldest *patteran*, according to the author) and the English Gypsies (Figure 3.1).

Like Borrow, Leland refers to these road signs as instances of the "Gipsy [*sic*] *patteran*" (Leland 1873, 24), and argues that the term derives either from the Greek term πατουνα (sole of the foot, track), or from the Hindustani word *panth* (road).

It is questionable whether the *patrin* signs retain the same function today as in the nineteenth century. Due to the growing use of cars and trailer caravans in the twentieth century, the scope for trail-signs seems to have diminished among itinerant Roma and Gypsies (see Fraser 1967, 387).

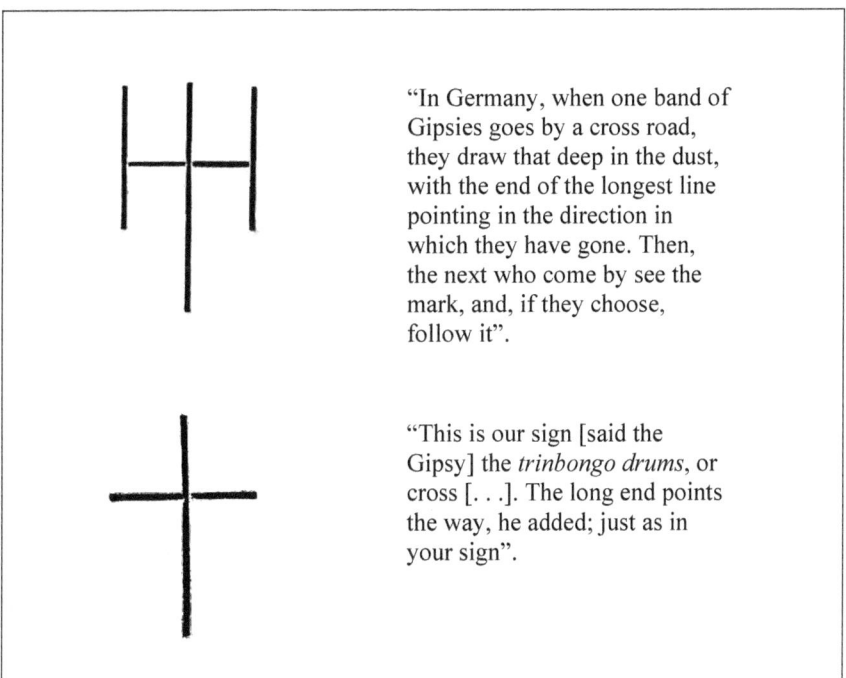

"In Germany, when one band of Gipsies goes by a cross road, they draw that deep in the dust, with the end of the longest line pointing in the direction in which they have gone. Then, the next who come by see the mark, and, if they choose, follow it".

"This is our sign [said the Gipsy] the *trinbongo drums*, or cross [. . .]. The long end points the way, he added; just as in your sign".

Figure 3.1   Trail signs (Leland 1873, 24).

However, recent occurrences of trail sign use have been detected among the Slovenian-Croatian Roma. The Croatian Rom Giuseppe Levakovich, also known as *Tzigari*, revealed in his autobiography:

> When we want to show somebody the way, we either scatter along the road some leafy boughs about fifty centimetres long, pointing in the right direction, or we scatter tufts of grass at crossroads. When we arrive at a square, if we see a bough embedded into the ground or tied to a stone with a red ribbon, this means that it is not a good place to stop. The use of pebbles should be avoided, since they get moved very easily, and grass is the best material to use, because it is usually scattered longitudinally. (Levakovich and Ausenda 1975, 129; my translation)

Furthermore, there is a sophisticated system of trail signs that the Slovenian Roma still use which they call *"tragi"* (the Romani term for "sign"). In his study *Māre Roma*, Leonardo Piasere (1984) distinguishes three categories of itinerant signs used by the Slovenian Roma: signs of "tranquillity", "emergency" and "danger".

Tragi signs fulfil a number of communicative functions, for example indicating a direction taken by group members ("direction" signs) or informing about the safety of a specific itinerary ("transit" signs, "halt" signs, etc.). The medium used for *patrin* consists of natural objects such as

Table 3.1   "Tragi" Signs

SITUATION	SIGN
Tranquillity	Three tufts of grass, with a stone above the first tuft/a ribbon tied to the branch of a tree
Emergency, imminent danger	Grass scattered in the middle of the road
Potential danger	Long reed leaves tied in a knot in the middle of the road

Source: Piasere (1985, 162–163).

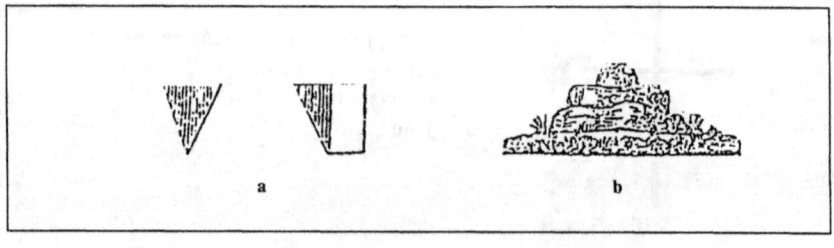

Figure 3.2   Trail signs: a) Harp-shaped drawings; b) A pile of three stones (Piasere 1995, 89).

twigs, leaves, grass, stones, hay and a variety of waste material arranged in a particular fashion (Figure 3.2). *Patrin* signs are "open secrets" (Bell 2007), visible to everyone, although likely to pass unnoticed on the roads of Europe as only the Roma can read and interpret them correctly.

The *patrin*, "nomadic signs" *par excellence*, need to be contextualised within the relationship of nomadic Romani groups and their natural environment. The Roma's "semiotic appropriation" of the environment using the *patrin* differs dramatically from the utilitarian and exploitative approach to nature of the non-Roma (Williams 1997). Nature supplies the Roma with a "semantic space" onto which they can symbolically "inscribe" the ephemeral messages conveyed via their non-alphabetic graphic practices. This semantic relationship with nature enables the Roma to survive among the non-Roma by providing them with a separate communication system and thereby a means of distinguishing themselves from the non-Roma.

Uses of Non-Alphabetic Graphic Codes: Chine Signs

In addition to trail signs, Romani groups in the Balkans and central and Eastern Europe use other non-alphabetic graphic codes previously described by Romologists. In the article *Wanderzeichen der Zigeuner*, Heinrich von Wlislocki presented a list of signs (*Wanderzeichen*) allegedly used by Gypsies in Hungary, Transylvania, Romania, Serbia, Poland and Turkey, and translated the specific messages associated with each of them (Wlislocki 1994, 144).

Wlislocki's list depicts a graphic system closely linked to the Roma's peripatetic way of life that combines "spatial mobility and non-subsistence commercialism" (Rao 1987, 3).[24] Groups that utilise peripatetic strategies include pastoral nomads, commercial nomads and service nomads. The spatial mobility that characterises these groups allows them to be effective in exploiting a broad range of scattered resources and grants them flexibility in terms of economic survival strategies.

The peripatetic activities of the Roma/Gypsies are aimed largely at the provision of services to sedentary communities, and Romani women have been key in performing peripatetic services. As Judith Okely explains in relation to the English Gypsies, women are traditionally expected to work outside the boundaries of their group:

> Gypsy men may expose their women to certain risks and do not monopolise the external economic activities themselves because women are in some contexts more successful at Calling than men would be. [The Gypsy woman] by eliciting the pity of the Gorgio, [. . .] can extract a greater economic return. (Okely 1983, 204)

The female itinerant practices that Okely refers to as "calling" are also known as "*chine*" (Rao 1976), and include selling a variety of items (small

Table 3.2   Chine Signs

GRAPHIC SIGN		MEANING
1. A cross	✕	There is nothing to be taken here
2. A double cross	✖	Here the Gypsies have been treated inhumanly
3. A circle	O	People here are very generous
4. A double circle	◉	Very good people
5. Two vertical strokes with two longitudinal strokes above	☰	This is the house of a magistrate/official
6. Two crosses with a stroke under each one	X X	Here Gypsies have been accused of theft
7. Several vertical lines	‖‖	Here we "have found": i.e., we have stolen something
8. A triangle	△	Something can be gained from tarot reading
9. A cross inside a circle	⊗	Do some damage here!
10. Two waving lines	≋	The lady of the house would like to have children
11. Two vertical lines joined by a waving line	|∼|	The lady of the house does not want more children
12. A circle crossed by two waving lines	✿	An old woman has died
13. Two circles crossed by two waving lines	∞∞	An old man has died
14. A triangle crossed by a waving line	⩗	The master of the house has died
15. A triangle crossed by two waving lines	⩗	The lady of the house has died
16. Two crosses joined by a waving line	x∼∼x	The wife has been unfaithful to her husband
17. Two waving lines joined by a cross	✖	The husband has been unfaithful to his wife
18. A vertical line with a longitudinal line above and a cross underneath	⊤⨯	A wedding is currently being planned

Adapted from Wlislocki (1891/1994); Payne (1935).

utensils, wares), begging and fortune telling. Romani women often draw *chine* graphic signs with charcoal on the walls or the gates of houses after their visits, which serve two main purposes. First, the signs provide women with clues and information that are essential for successful economic transactions. For example, signs such as △ and ○ mean that in a particular place "something can be gained from tarot reading" and that "people here are very generous", whereas the sign ✕ indicates exactly the opposite. Other *chine* signs perform an important function concerning women's safety in a possible dangerous situation. For instance, the sign ⓒ (meaning "people here are very good") provides reassurance about the safety of a place, as opposed to a sign such as ✖✖, which warns women of the risk of approaching a particular house.

There are clear similarities between *patrin* and *chine* signs. Both codes have a particular significance within the specific socio-economic milieu from which they emerged. Furthermore, both graphic systems are largely "nameless" practices. When Leland asks an English Gypsy (as reported in *The English Gypsies and Their Language*), "So you all call it *patteran*?" the reply is "No; very few of us know that name. We do it without calling it anything" (Leland 1873, 24).

The information conveyed by *patrin* and *chine* signs is characterised by a high degree of "cultural invisibility".[25] This has to be understood in the context of an oral Romani culture in which knowledge is passed down through imitative learning and hands-on experience, rather than through formal instruction. The invisible nature of *patrin* and *chine* signs is in line with the Roma's reluctance to reveal important aspects of their culture, especially in the presence of non-Roma. As observed by Anne Sutherland:

> The Rom are extremely secretive and suspicious of non-Gypsies and on the whole do not want anything known about them by the outside world. Some secrets have practical reasons behind them, such as hiding extra income from welfare workers, concealing illegal activities from the police, and so on, but many times secretiveness is simply a protective barrier for their group against a more powerful outside society. (Sutherland 1975, 29)[26]

Anonymity and invisibility were key ethnic strategies that enabled Romani groups to resist cultural assimilation and prevent discrimination. For a persecuted minority the act of "naming", of making themselves open to scrutiny, amounts to becoming vulnerable because, to use Williams' words, "what the Gage are able to observe, sooner or later they understand. It becomes part of their discourse. They come to own it" (Williams 1997, 44; my translation).

The cultural invisibility of Romani graphic codes has led to misunderstandings among non-Gypsy authors who tend to portray the *patrin* as indicators of the mysterious—if not treacherous—character of the Gypsies.[27] The following passage from Adriano Colocci's *Gli Zingari* (The Gypsies, 1889) is a good example:

The life of the Gypsy on the road *has a mysterious side.* [. . .] We have met a group of Hungarian Gypsies on the Apennines around Fossato who were confidently roaming those mountains and were more knowledgeable about the surroundings than the local inhabitants themselves. In Kadi-Keu (Asia) we met a group of Neapolitan Gypsies who were heading toward Iskimid as if they were simply heading from Naples to Caserta. Building on existing research, we have come to the conclusion that the international "Court of Miracles" has *its own special topography, known only to thieves, fugitives, smugglers and Gypsies.* (Colocci 1889, 181; my translation and emphasis)[28]

The implicit reference to the *patrin* in the quote draws on the connection between their use and Gypsy nomadic practices. However, Colocci fails to explain, let alone understand, how this communication system works. All we learn is that the Gypsies have a mystifying ability to travel extensively in unknown territory, and we are led to believe that this ability is a form of treachery. Furthermore, Gypsies are identified together with a range of deviants (thieves, fugitives and smugglers) that allegedly share this code.[29] The image of the Gypsies as a cunning and dangerous people was a widespread trope throughout the nineteenth and twentieth centuries, and was greatly responsible for the criminalisation of the Gypsy way of life. This negative perception extended to other itinerant people (seasonal workers, commercial nomads, travelling showmen and circus people) and was largely the result of a sedentarist bias that "pathologised" nomadism and associated it with idleness and lawlessness (Lucassen 1993).

Non-Romani narrative constructions of the *patrin*, such as Colocci's, promote the secretive nature of Romani graphic codes and their possible criminal uses. Such a belief is best countered by analysing the socio-economic function these codes serve. As explained previously, Romani non-alphabetic graphic systems are used to support a wide range of activities specific to the Romani economy and are closely related to the Roma's peripatetic lifestyle. They constitute "restricted", "reserved" signs, or "signs with a limited diffusion" for "internal use" among the Roma/Gypsies. Their ethnic positioning remains clearly on the Gypsy side of the Gypsy/non-Gypsy divide.

Instrumental Uses of Alphabetic Writing: The Case of the Slovenian-Croatian Roma and the French Manuš

In relation to non-Roma, Romani groups nowadays use writing for a variety of purposes. Since they depend on the provision of services to the non-Roma for their survival, it is imperative that they can communicate effectively with their non-Roma clientele. In addition, since the communication system of the dominant group is based on alphabetic literacy, the

Roma have developed some communicative competence in the use of alphabetic codes. However, this use of alphabetic writing has largely remained "external" and "instrumental".

The instrumental use of alphabetic writing among the Roma—unlike the more "exotic" use of non-alphabetic graphic codes—has so far attracted

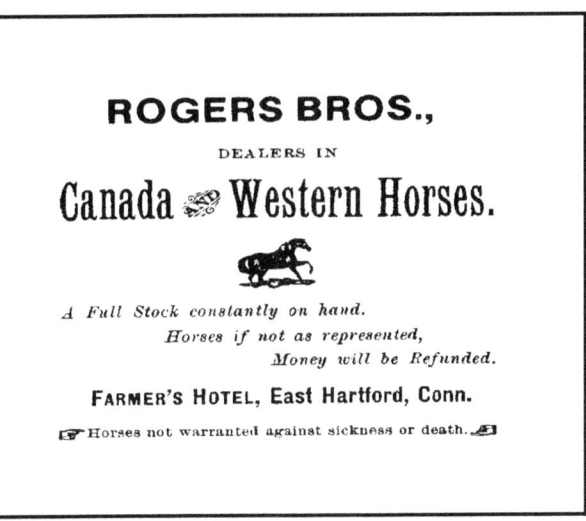

Figure 3.3   Advertisement (Salo and Salo 1982, 300).

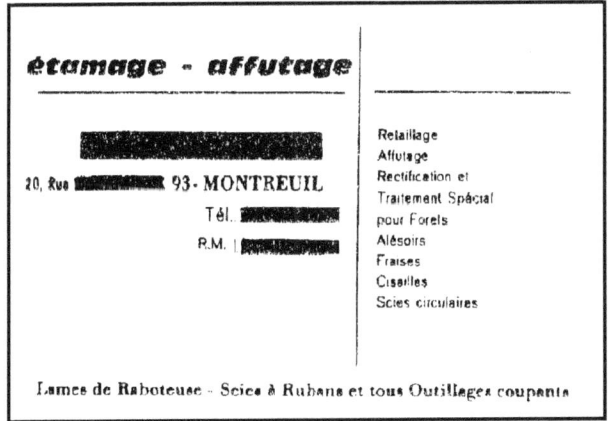

Figure 3.4   Business card (Williams 1998, 85; available online at: http://halshs.archives-ouvertes.fr/docs/00/08/93/ 65/PDF/Williams_1997_MDP.pdf).

only limited interest from non-Romani scholars and authors. As a result, very little is known about Roma's everyday literacy practices or—to use Barton and Hamilton's (1998) expression—about their "local" literacies. Yet these practices are of considerable importance when analysing the Roma's approach to literacy, and a number of researchers have documented instances of instrumental literacy among Romani groups. These include Brunello (1996), who reports the use of writing by Roma from Serbia and Kosovo in begging practices in north-east Italian cities, and Salo and Salo (1982), who refer to the utilisation of literacy for a range of commercial purposes, from advertising to self-promotion through business cards, among the Romanichal Gypsies in America (Figure 3.3).

The use of writing among Slovenian-Croatian Roma living in northeast Italy represents an interesting case of instrumental literacy. Within this group, alphabetic writing is a marginal code employed by a small group of individuals in daily interactions with non-Roma. Writing is usually restricted to the female members of the group and confined to activities such as filling out forms, reading legal and administrative documents and understanding regulations and official notifications (Toninato 1999). There is increasing evidence of an "internal", more "personal", use of alphabetic writing by Romani women authors (analysed in more detail in Chapter 5). Nonetheless, the dominant approach to literacy remains an instrumental one, as confirmed by the low literacy levels in this group.

Furthermore, alphabetic writing among Slovenian-Croatian Roma is largely limited to a number of clearly defined, repetitive bureaucratic or commercial activities. These activities neither presuppose nor entail the agency of a specific writing subject. They can be seen as instances of a purely instrumental use of writing that indicates a kind of *degré zero de l'écriture*, to borrow Roland Barthes' terminology (Barthes 1953). Like most Romani groups, the Slovenian-Croatian Roma do not regard writing as a prestigious activity but as a practice confined to a literate minority kept at the margins of society (mainly women). This external use of writing acts as a "social strategy" for reducing the risks of cultural assimilation and inhibiting the full completion of the social implications of literacy (Toninato 1997).

Instrumental uses of the written code do not easily fit on either side of the written/oral divide and are best defined as a hybrid "oral" approach to writing and literacy. Illustrative examples include the writing practices of the French Manuš described by Patrick Williams (1998). According to Williams, the literacy practices of the Manuš transcend the oral/written dichotomy (and the corresponding "Roma *vs.* non-Roma" opposition), and their written texts—such as letters and postcards sent to family members who live far away or are temporarily absent from home—act as a "surrogate" for human contact. When Williams acted as a "scribe" for a Manuš man who wanted to write a letter to a cousin, he observed that the letter was in fact a patchwork of formulaic expressions that did not convey any news, but was simply meant as a sign of the cousin's affection. The author of such letters is not a clearly identifiable subject, but an anonymous entity transmitting, or rather performing, a repetitive and stereotypical communicative act.[30] Because the written text is repetitive and formulaic, it can "act" as a reification of the physical presence of other group members. Moreover, the use of writing in Williams' example is subordinate to the spoken word and aims to preserve its integrity. The focus is neither on writing itself nor on the information conveyed by the written text, but on what writing signifies. Writing acts only as an instrument, a physical carrier of an intra-family link. Williams aptly describes letter writing among the Manuš as an "oral use of writing".

The alphabetic practices analysed above illustrate both the diverse use of literacy by the Roma in their daily activities and in interactions with the non-Roma, and the principles behind this use. To sum up, Romani literacy practices are contextualised, close to the real-life world and actively contribute to the economic independence of their users. They are also characterised by a certain degree of hybridity, in that they incorporate oral elements into written texts. These practices deserve some space alongside formal literacy activities within the school curriculum as the implications of this would be twofold. At a general level, acknowledging the fact that literacy includes oral, written, alphabetic and non-alphabetic forms would be an essential step towards the creation of a plural notion of literacy (UNESCO 2004). At the pedagogical level, it would enable Romani pupils to make use of their local knowledge and experience (Olson and Torrance 2001, 14) and learn literacy skills that are actually relevant to their world, thereby helping to bridge the persisting gap between Romani and non-Romani education contexts.

TOWARDS A NON-BINARY CONCEPTUALISATION OF ROMANI LITERACY

In addition to non-alphabetic graphic systems in internal communication among the Roma, we nowadays find written alphabetic practices that form an increasingly significant aspect of Romani literacy. Pivotal instances of these practices include the expanding field of written Romani literature (analysed in Chapters 4 through 6), the rise of Romani writing for political uses (see Chapter 7) and the use of hybrid (Roma/non-Roma) literacy practices at school (see Chapter 8). This diversified use of alphabetic writing performs two core functions. For Romani authors, the act of writing has a primarily counter-hegemonic function (Street 1993). I propose to term this the "*pars destruens*" of Romani writing, that is, its crucial role in uncovering the inconsistencies of literary clichés and challenging misleading depictions of Romani identity. In addition,

Romani writing has a function emphasised by academics and intellectuals that can be termed *"pars construens"*: the use of writing to provide Roma/Gypsies/Travellers with a common voice, while at the same time opening up new spaces of renegotiation of Romani identity vis-à-vis the dominant group.

As already remarked, the multifaceted use of literacy among the Roma is inadequately captured by the traditional literate/non-literate dichotomy. In this respect, it seems preferable to adopt Piasere's representational model of writing as a communication system that includes both Roma and non-Roma addressers and addressees.[31] Four possible communicative situations can be distinguished according to this model (Figure 3.5).

The model associates four relationships ("Roma→Roma", "Roma→non-Roma", "non-Roma→Roma" and "non-Roma→non-Roma") with four ideal types of communication. The "Roma→Roma" situation is characterised

1) Roma→Roma

2) Roma→non-Roma

3) non-Roma→Roma

4) non-Roma→non-Roma

Figure 3.5 Roma/non-Roma communicative situations (adapted from Piasere 1995, 84).

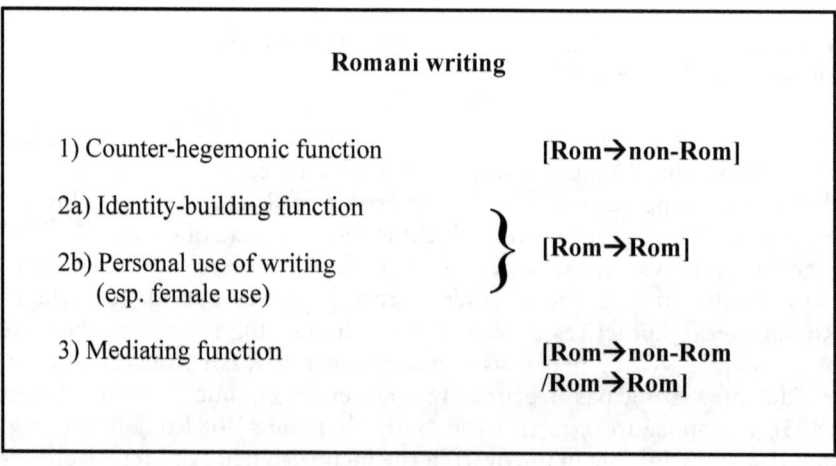

Romani writing

1) Counter-hegemonic function   [Rom→non-Rom]

2a) Identity-building function

2b) Personal use of writing   } [Rom→Rom]
    (esp. female use)

3) Mediating function   [Rom→non-Rom /Rom→Rom]

Figure 3.6 Romani writing: main functions and uses.

exclusively by oral modes of communication, whereas writing (narrowly identified with alphabetic writing) is confined to "non-Roma→non-Roma" and "non-Roma→Roma" communicative situations. In the relationship "Roma→non-Roma" we find a restricted instrumental use of writing. However, the model requires further qualification (see Figure 3.6).

As this study aims to show, the use of writing (in both its alphabetic and non-alphabetic form) is also found within Romani groups in both situations: "Roma→non-Roma" (i.e., external use) and "Roma→Roma" (i.e., internal use). Codes such as the *patrin*, and graphic codes associated with economic practices performed mainly by Romani women, are "restricted", that is, they typically occur within a "Roma→Roma" communicative situation (internal use). On the other hand, instrumental uses of writing, such as those documented among the Manuš and the Slovenian-Croatian Roma, typically occur in a "Roma→non-Roma" situation.

In applying this representational model to Romani literary production, we see that the counter-hegemonic function of Romani literature (its *pars destruens*) mainly occurs in "Roma→non-Roma" communicative situations. However, Romani written literature also contributes to identity-building processes that take place in "Roma→Roma" communicative situations, which until recently were considered as exclusively characterised by the oral code. Finally, it is important to emphasise that the Roma use writing for mediation purposes in both "Roma→non-Roma" and "Roma→Roma" communicative situations.

CONCLUSIONS

The chapter has tackled the issue of the "academic failure" of Romani pupils at school by adopting a Romani view on literacy and education. In particular, the chapter has analysed the features of the Roma's education system in a cross-cultural perspective. The comparative analysis of Romani and non-Romani education systems has revealed a number of significant differences. The dominant school system encourages decontextualisation and hyperspecialisation, which are typical of literate societies where communication is centred on writing. Furthermore, this system has so far disregarded the Roma's education system and traditionally been used as an institutional tool to assimilate Romani minorities into mainstream culture. This generates conflict whereby Romani parents do not regard the school as a place where their children should be educated (i.e., assimilated), and Romani children are exposed to conflicting demands and expectations. Ideally, the school system should be able to mediate between these two conflicting systems to find common ground between them. But where is this common ground to be found?

At present, the relationship between Roma/Gypsies and schooling continues to be characterised by cultural misunderstanding and lack of communication. However, what seems in many respects an irreconcilable opposition could be transformed into "differences that can be understood and accommodated" (Liégeois 1994, 312) by recognising, and not dismissing, the cultural capital that Romani pupils have acquired within their own environment. Second, literacy education should be closely connected with this unique cultural capital. In other words, the school system should openly address what Margaret Mead has defined as "the drama of discontinuity" (Mead 1943, 638), that is, the gap between different education environments: the school on the one hand and the "community" on the other. As will be shown in Chapter 8, the mediating role of literacy in this context is crucial.

Another reason for the low academic attainment of Romani pupils is the compulsory, inflexible nature of schooling. Instead of focusing on the compulsory aspect of education, the emphasis should be on the "desirability of learning" (Mead 1943, 634) and what the Roma/Gypsies want and need to learn. As shown in this chapter, Roma/Gypsies have a long-term interest in literacy and writing: it is precisely this interest, then, that should provide the basis for building an entirely different relationship between Roma and schooling. But the next important question to pose is: What kind of literacy skills are actually used and needed by Roma/Gypsies?

As identified in this chapter, there is considerable ethnographic evidence that the Roma master a wide range of literacy practices, both alphabetic and non-alphabetic. The plural and complex nature of these practices contributes to undermining the centuries-old stereotype of Romani culture as exclusively "oral" or "illiterate". On a more general level, the Roma's diversified approach to writing prompts us to reconsider dominant critical notions of literacy as a unified, monolithic phenomenon: a Literacy with a big "L" and a single "y". Literacy practices have to be seen instead as always "situated" in a specific socio-historical context.

Finally, the study of Romani literacy practices has revealed that the Roma's interest is not in a specialised notion of schooled literacy, but manifested instead in a highly diversified and mainly instrumental use of literacy. What the Gypsies expect from the school system is not to educate their children but to provide them with a range of skills applicable to real life situations, and that may enable them to achieve freedom and economic independence. For this reason, literacy programmes aimed at Roma should not be restricted to academic literacy, but should aim to develop a wider range of literacy skills that are dynamically interconnected with the life of the pupils. In other words, it is necessary "to move everyday life into the school" (Scribner and Cole 1973, 558) by making letters and words relevant to the Roma's world.

Part II
The Rise of Romani Literature

4 The Rise of Romani Writing
An Overview

The recent emergence of Romani literature prompts a number of questions. First, what are the crucial factors that have promoted its rise and rapid growth? Is it possible to talk about *a* Romani literature, or would it be more accurate to talk about the existence of several Romani *literatures*? What are the defining features of Romani literature(s), how do they differ and what do they share? And finally, what are the main challenges faced by Romani writers? This chapter will address some of these key questions.

A main precondition for the emergence of Romani literature is a steady rise in literacy levels among the Roma, including fluency in digital literacy and IT. Another enabling factor in the development of Romani writing is the recent standardisation of Romani and its use for purposes of inter-ethnic communication. In addition to these material factors, there is also an important cultural phenomenon at work, which is a change in the Roma's attitude towards literacy: an unprecedented phenomenon, despite being confined to a literate elite. This change reflects a positive view of education among the Roma and marks a shift in their perception of literacy as a tool to preserve and revitalise Romani cultural heritage. It is often accompanied by a certain level of political mobilisation and/ or a commitment to gaining cultural and political legitimation for the Romani people.

Romani literature today is characterised by a highly varied corpus, encompassing a wide variety of genres, ranging from transcriptions of oral narrative and autobiographical accounts and memoirs to novels, short stories, drama, plays and poetry collections. It includes the works of professional authors and those of occasional and "ephemeral" writers. Within it, there are instances of full authorship and co-authorship between Romani authors and non-Romani writers and scholars (the latter characterising especially early examples of Romani literature).

Having developed within and across a great number of national and ethnic boundaries, Romani literature is linguistically hybrid. Following Toninato (2006, 238–239), it is possible to distinguish between four categories of Romani texts:

- Poetic texts written and published exclusively in non-Romani languages: see for example the poetic collections published in Italy by Paula Schöpf (1997), Luigi Cirelli (1994) and Mansueto Levacovich (1991), or those published by Romani authors in England (e.g., Morley 2000);
- multilingual literary collections by Romani authors published in both major and minority languages: see for instance the collection *The Roads of the Roma*, published by the University of Hertfordshire Press in 1998, the anthology *Romane krle/Voci zingare* (Gypsy Voices) published in 1992, Rajko Djurić's *Bi kheresqo bi limoresqo/ Sans maison sans tombe* (1990) and Luminiţa Mihai Cioabă's collections (Cioabă 1994, 1997);
- multilingual literary collections by both Romani and non-Romani authors: see the anthologies published in Italy by Santino Spinelli from 1994 onwards;
- texts written and published exclusively in Romani languages.

The analysis of the multilingual features of Romani literature can be further extended to investigate its prospective readership. It seems reasonable to infer that texts written exclusively in major languages are mainly aimed at a non-Romani readership (as has often been remarked by the authors themselves), whereas texts written solely in Romani are aimed at other Roma. It is worth noting, however, that once they are in a written form and made public, texts in general are subject to all manner of possible readings and interpretations. In this respect, the identification of two types of readership (Romani/non-Romani) on the basis of language choices can be useful for heuristic purposes, but should not overshadow the fact that Romani literary works are ultimately "open works" (to use Umberto Eco's words) whose uses and subsequent transformations remain largely unpredictable. In all, one could say that many Romani authors regard their ideal readership as one which is formed by both Roma and non-Roma individuals willing to lay the basis for a more constructive confrontation with their people.

I chose in this book to deal in particular with multilingual texts in which the Romani version of the poem is accompanied by a translation into one or more major languages such as Italian, English, French, Spanish and German. I consider such texts particularly significant because they address multiple readerships and thus hold the greatest potential for mediating between the dominant and minority culture. Within the multilingual texts analysed here, the use of Romani is crucial. The Romani language is regarded by many authors and intellectuals as perhaps the only factor enabling the Roma to overcome inter-group divisions and find a common voice in the public sphere. As we will see, the rise of a Romani written literature has considerably strengthened the unifying role of Romani.

ROMANI LITERATURE AND THE ROMANI LANGUAGE

Romani is the largest minority language in the EU today (Bakker 2001). It is spoken by five million Roma in Europe and by some eight to twelve million Roma scattered worldwide (Bakker et al. 2000, 41). Historically, the use of Romani has been discouraged and at times actively suppressed (as seen in Chapter 2) in an attempt to assimilate the Roma. For a long time, Romani was not considered a proper language, but a jargon or argot supposedly used to cover up the criminal activities of its speakers. The demotion of the Romani language to a jargon is closely linked to the categorisation of the Roma as a deviant social group. In several European literary works the language spoken by Gypsy characters is represented as a "secret" speech often entirely made up and exclusively aimed at entertaining and amusing the audience.[1] It was only at the end of the eighteenth century that scholars discovered the Sanskrit origins of Romani, which then became an object of study.

Due to the diasporic features of the Romani speaking community, Romani is a highly fragmented language (Soravia 1977, 1994; Courthiade 1990, 1993; Hancock 1995). It bears remarkable affinities to languages spoken in contemporary India: up to three quarters of the Romani vocabulary is of Indian origin (Hancock 1995, 26). In addition, Romani has been influenced over time by a number of European and non-European languages spoken in countries situated along the complex path of the Roma's migrations (including Iranian languages, Greek, Romanian, German and Italian).

Romani is characterised by a high degree of dialectal variation (Matras 2002). In an attempt to map out Romani dialects as accurately as possible, scholars have divided them into groupings and sub-groupings on a regional basis. The first, which dates back to the arrival of the Roma in Europe, is the Balkan-Carpathian-Baltic group; a second group is circumscribed to the Balkans; and a third group (Vlax Romani), the largest of all, extends from Russia, Sweden and France to the Americas (Hancock 1995; Matras 2002). The identification and categorisation of Romani dialects is a problematic undertaking, and classification solely based on geographical criteria is unsatisfactory. Therefore, additional factors, such as current historical circumstances, nomadic practices and sedentarisation patterns, must also be taken into account. The dynamic interplay of all these variables explains processes of linguistic transformations and phenomena of structural and lexical borrowing detected within dialectal varieties of Romani. The influence of majority contact languages on the grammatical and lexical structure of Romani, for example, may vary greatly depending on the specific features of the Roma's presence (in terms of duration and frequency of interaction with the local population), and on external factors such as the specific policies adopted towards them. In the case of the so-called "para-Romani" languages, the influence of other languages has been so great that it determined the replacement of the original grammatical structure of Romani with that of the local language. As a result, para-Romani languages, despite being closely related to Romani—from which they derive a great number of lexemes—can no longer be considered part of it.

Although Romani is not an official language of the EU it is included among European minority languages based on the European Charter for Regional or Minority Languages.[2] In view of the principles established by the Charter, Romani qualifies (together with Yiddish) as a non-territorial language to which special language provision should apply.[3] Unfortunately, this is not yet the case, and in some European countries its existence has not even been acknowledged. This lack of official recognition is often accompanied by the refusal to acknowledge the status of the Roma as a distinct ethnic group. Therefore, the rise and diffusion of Romani writing is of great significance. On the one hand, the creation of Romani written literature contributes to increasing public awareness of the cultural and political rights of the Romani people. On the other hand, it enables Romani authors and intellectuals to perform a symbolic reappropriation of their language, a language whose destiny has so far mainly been in the hands of non-Roma. The promotion of written Romani is thus an act of political significance.[4] Furthermore, the written use of Romani may lead to a renewed appreciation of its aesthetic qualities and its discovery as a poetic tool in its own right.

ROMANI LITERATURES: AN OVERVIEW

The wide geographical and linguistic variety of Romani literature renders any efforts to systematise an autonomous Romani literary field impossible. To mirror this fragmentation, the expression "Romani literatures" should be used instead of "Romani literature", as the latter suggests a uniformity that simply does not exist. The following overview, far from being a comprehensive account, constitutes an attempt to map out the main "literary centres" of Romani literature. These centres roughly correspond to two geographical areas: (1) Eastern Europe and the Balkans and (2) Western and Northern Europe.

Historically, a significant body of Romani written literature has originally emerged from Eastern Europe and the Balkans, mainly due to the particular nature of Communist policies adopted towards Romani minorities in this area. Although governmental approaches to the Roma varied considerably across the European Communist states, there were also some significant intra-Communist similarities.[5] The Roma were generally perceived as members of a social, rather than an ethnic, group who needed to become "useful" citizens. In some instances, the Roma were recognised as a separate ethnic group and their language acknowledged.[6] This however did not prevent Communist regimes from repeatedly trying to assimilate Romani groups. As Zoltan Barany writes: "For the Communist states the Romani minorities represented a nuisance that impeded their construction of a new society" (Barany 1994, 326–327). The Roma's nomadic practices in particular were regarded as a major obstacle to their socio-economic integration, as this prevented them from entering the dominant labour market system. Romani groups remained at the bottom of society, poverty stricken and marginalised, with their low levels of literacy seen as problematic for their political participation. The dominant approach adopted by Communist states to solve the "Gypsy question" was to subject them to forced sedentarisation and compulsory schooling in the majority language.

The policies of the Eastern European Communist regimes succeeded in raising the living standards and educational levels of their Romani population, enabling a literate elite to emerge and thus laying the basis for the development of Romani literature in the area. However, these improvements came at a high social cost: the Roma were expected to renounce their identity and their traditional way of life came under threat. In the former Czechoslovakia, where the Roma's oral tradition was threatened by strong assimilationist policies, the emergence of Romani written literature in the late 1960s has been described as "a direct reaction of the Roma to the Communist attempts at their state-controlled assimilation" (Hübschmannová 2009, 98). What is more, in the post-Communist period, despite hopes for more tolerant Roma policies, the Roma remain marginalised and despised by the majority population. This is why the Roma in central and Eastern Europe have been more readily engaged in protests against the poor living conditions of the Romani population—whereas in Western Europe they have opted for a strategy of social "invisibility". Education, art and literature in particular have been perceived by Romani public intellectuals in central and Eastern Europe as tools of cultural resistance.

Romani Literatures in Eastern Europe—Papuśa

One of the first authors of poetry in Romani was Bronislava Wajs (known as Papuśa, that is, "doll"), a female poet belonging to the Polska Roma's group. Born in Poland in 1910, she learnt to read and write without attending school and endured the painful experience of the military occupation of her country by Nazi troops. She participated actively in the war, fighting as a partisan, and afterwards devoted herself to literary activity. Papuśa's ballads, originally intended for oral performance and inspired by a nostalgic recollection of her nomadic way of life, have reached us thanks to a Gadžo poet, Jerzy Ficowski, who since 1949 has transcribed Papuśa's poems. In 1956, Ficowski published Papuśa's bilingual (Romani/Polish) collection of poetry under the title *Songs of Papusza*.

Unfortunately, just three years after the publication of her work, Papuśa was forced to give up writing due to the growing hostility her fellow Roma subjected her to. Expelled from her group in 1956, Papuśa spent the rest of her life in solitude, eventually abandoning poetry, and died in 1987. In spite of her tragic life, Papuśa left a lasting poetic legacy and is unanimously regarded by Romani authors as "the mother of Romani literature".

Like Papuśa, a considerable number of Romani poets are originally from Eastern Europe,[7] especially the former Soviet Union, Hungary, Romania, Slovakia, the Czech Republic and the former Yugoslavia.[8]

Romani Authors from the Former Soviet Union

Romani literature in the former Soviet Union has a long and established tradition, with evidence of organised intellectual activities dating back to a few years after the October revolution. The 1920s and 1930s saw the publication of Romani fiction, poetry and plays. The All-Russian Union of Gypsies was created in 1925 and in the same year the periodical *Névo Drom* (New Road) was launched. The journal *Romani Zorya* (Romani Dawn) was created in 1927 and first published in 1929. A number of Romani schools were founded and the theatre *Romen*, the first professional Gypsy theatre in Russia, was established in Moscow in 1931.[9] Its first production, performed on 21 December 1931, was the play *Žizn na kolesach* (Life on Wheels) written by Romani author Alexander V. Germano. Born to a Czech father and a Moravian Romni, Germano (1893–1954) was one of the first known Romani writers. He was an educator, a writer of poetry, fiction and theatre, and in the late 1930s translated some of Alexander Pushkin's works into Romani. He was a member of the All-Russian Gypsy Union and one of the founders of Moscow's Romani writers' group *Romengiro Lav* (Romani Word), which featured among its members leading Romani authors such as Nina Dudarova, Ivan Rom-Lebedev, Nikolai Pankov and Olga Pankova.

All publications in Romani were officially suspended between 1938 and 1970, but after this a new generation of Romani writers and intellectuals began to emerge, which included Nikolai Satkievich, Ilko Mazuro, Karlo Rudevic and Alexander Belugins. These authors combined the commitment to Romani human rights, civil rights and education with efforts to strengthen their cultural and literary traditions. The late Alexander Belugins (pen name Leksa Manuš), born in Riga, Latvia, was a prominent Romani scholar, writer and translator. His poems, translated into several languages, have appeared in numerous international journals such as *Lacio Drom* and *Roma*. Manuš was an accomplished linguist who worked at the Institute of Scientific Information of the Russian Academy of Sciences in Moscow. He was fluent in several Romani dialects and several European languages, and translated into Romani the Indian epic *Ramayana*. Like other Romani poets, Manuš found in the Indian origins of his people a source of pride, and actively promoted the idea of a Romani identity based on a common language and culture.

One of the leading contemporary authors from the former Soviet Union is Valdemar Kalinin. He was born in Vitebsk, Belarus, in 1946 and currently lives in England while working as an educator, poet and translator.[10] His literary work positions itself within the tradition established in the 1920s by authors such as Pankov, Germano, Olga Pankova and Rom-Lebedev. He is author of the collection of poetry *Romany Dreams* (2005), published in a trilingual version: Belorussian, English and Romani (written in both Cyrillic and Latin alphabets). Kalinin has earned a number of prestigious prizes and literary awards, including the Poetry Prize at the International Literary Competition *Amico Rom* in 2001 and the Roma Literary Award of the Open Society Institute in 2003.

Romani Authors from the Former Yugoslavia

Roma have been present in the region known today as the former Yugoslavia since the late thirteenth century (Crowe 1996, 195), meaning the Romani literary landscape in this region is particularly rich and varied. Scholars tend to distinguish between two main literary traditions in the area: the literary production of authors such as Rajko Djurić, whose work is markedly influenced by the written non-Romani tradition, and that of poets from Kosovo and Macedonia (especially poets from Šuto Orizari), whose creations are closer to the oral and folk tradition and thus situated "in-between" the oral and written traditions (Courthiade 1985).

In Tito's post-war Yugoslavia, the Roma enjoyed some degree of autonomy and were able to establish a number of political and cultural organisations. In particular, Roma in Macedonia[11] were engaged in cultural and political activism as there was a rise in the number of literate Roma and the use of Romani in the public sphere was encouraged. In 1980 Śaip Yusuf, author of the first description of Romani grammar, published with Krume Kepeski a bilingual (Romani-Macedonian) grammar: *Romani gramatika/Romska gramatika*. The association *Pralipe* (a term also spelled *Phralipe*, that is, brotherhood) was founded in Skopje in 1948. It played a crucial role in the formation of a Romani literary movement and later supported the creation of a theatre company, *Pralipe*, established in 1970 in Skopje by Rahim Burhan. The company, which became the foremost Romani theatre company in Europe, was disbanded by the Yugoslav Communist Party and relocated to Germany in 1990.

The emergence of a written Romani literature in Yugoslavia[12] was instrumental in fostering the Roma's ethnic awakening. Romani intellectuals and activists from the former Yugoslavia became prominent members of the international Romani intelligentsia. Among them are Rajko Djurić and Slobodan Berberski,[13] who is considered by some as the real "pioneer of Romani poetry in Serbia" (Djurić 1993, 178).

Due to the events of the war in the early 1990s, a large number of Romani writers and intellectuals were forced to emigrate to Austria and Germany. Among them were the above-mentioned Rajko Djurić, together with Jovan Nikolić and Alija Krasnići. Born in Malo Orašje (Belgrade) in 1947, Rajko Djurić belongs to the Gurbet group[14] but was educated among the Serbs and is one of the most influential Romani writers on the international literary scene. His interests range from poetry to philosophy, sociology and journalism. Djurić's poetry incorporates themes and motifs drawn from Romani folklore, but is ultimately the result of the fruitful encounter between Romani and non-Romani literary traditions. This bestows his poetry with universal resonance and appeal.

Among Djurić's collections are *Bi kheresqo bi limoresqo* (Without House or Grave, 1990), *O rom rodel than tela-o kham* (The Rom is Looking for a Place Under the Sun, 1980), *Purano svato-o dur them* (Ancient Words of a Distant World, 1980), *A taj U* (A and U, 1982) and *Les disciples d'Héphaistos* (The Disciples of Ephesus, 1994). Djurić combines his literary work with political activism. He was president of the International Romani Union (IRU) between the fourth World Romani Congress (WRC) in 1990 and the fifth WRC in 2000, and publicly campaigned for the promotion of the Romani language and the development of what he deemed "new" Romani literature (Djurić 1993). Due to his opposition to Miloševic, Djurić was forced to leave Belgrade in 1991 and moved to Berlin.

A poet, songwriter and performing artist, Jovan Nikolić was born near Belgrade in 1955. In 1982 he published his first book of poetry, *Dosti khatinendar/Gost niotkuda* (The Guest from Nowhere), which was followed by several other volumes of poetry. In 1999 Nikolić migrated to Berlin and currently lives in Cologne. A founding member of the IRWA (International Romani Writers' Association), Nikolić is an internationally renowned author and his poems, translated into ten languages, have been included in several international anthologies. He has been awarded important literary prizes for his work and has received grants from the Heinrich Böll Foundation, the Berlin Academy of the Arts, the German PEN Centre and others. His most recent publications include the volume *Zimmer mit Rad* (Room With Wheel, 2004), published only in German, *Kosovo mon amour* (2004, co-authored with Ruždija Russo Sejdović), *Weisser Rabe, Schwarzes Lamm* (White Raven, Black Lamb, 2006) and *Seelenfänger, lautlos lärmend* (Soul Catcher, Silently Noisy, 2011).

Romani writer and activist Ali (Alija) Krasnići was born in a town near Obilić (Kosovo) in 1952 and belongs to the Gurbet Roma group. He started studying law at the University of Obilić, but later decided to devote his efforts to literature and became one of the best-known Romani writers in the former Yugoslavia. However, the outbreak of war in Kosovo forced him and his family out of the country. Krasnići is author of the first book of tales written in Romani to be published in the former Yugoslavia, *Čergarendje jaga* (The Fires of the Tent-Dwelling Gypsies), published in 1981 by the Gandhi Foundation. He is an extremely versatile writer who has published more than forty books, including children's books, and his works encompass a variety of genres including prose, poetry and drama. He is also author of a Romani dictionary and a translator.

Romani Literature in the Former Czechoslovakia

The formation of a Romani written literature in the former Czecho-slovakia is a recent development, as it only began to emerge between the end of the 1960s and the beginning of the 1970s. The Communist government constantly pursued an ethnocentric policy aimed at the complete assimilation of the Roma within mainstream society. A sub-stantial increase in the level of scholarisation among the Roma during the period following World War II—despite having a negative effect on the intra-generational transmission of oral narratives—was one of the main factors that led to the rise of a literary written production. The Slovak Roma founded the *Union of Gypsy-Romanies (Zvaz Cikanov-romov)* in 1968 after the dramatic events of the Prague Spring, and their example was followed by the Roma of the Czech Republic in 1969. The Union's periodical, *Romano lil*, together with the numerous publications founded throughout the 1960s, contributed effectively to strengthening the links within the Romani population and promoting their ethnic and cultural awareness.

Two established Romani authors from Slovakia are Elena (Ilona) Lacková and Dezider Banga. Lacková was born in Velký Šariš, Czecho-slovakia, in 1921. The daughter of a Polish mother and a Romani musi-cian father, she enjoyed reading from childhood but her first literary works were lost during the hard times of World War II. She has writ-ten several novels, tales and plays about the Romani Holocaust, and particularly well known is *Horiací cigánský tábor* (The Burning Gypsy Camp), written in 1949 and published in 1956, which focuses on the wartime persecution of the Roma. This play, performed by amateur Gypsy actors, was a resounding success and led to her appointment as a Communist Party official. Her autobiography was recorded in Romani by Milena Hübschmannová and later published in Czech and translated into English as *A False Dawn*, becoming the first autobiography of a Romani woman to be published in the UK. In 2001, Lacková received the Chatam Sofer Medal from the Slovak Museum of Jewish Culture for her Holocaust writings.

Born to a smith's family in 1939 near Lucenec in the Slovak Republic, Dezider Banga studied philosophy at the University of Bratislava. He is an academic and editor writing in both Slovak and Romani who between 1964 and 1992 published several collections of poems and short stories. Additionally, he published books of fairy tales (*Čierny vlas*, 1970) and is the editor of the children's bilingual magazine *Luludi*. He is also the author of a Romani spelling book.

Other prominent Romani writers from this region include Tera Fabiánová, Margita Reiznerová, Ilona Ferková, Andrej Giňa, Olga Giňová, Vlado Oláh, Emil Ščuka, Olga Vnadová, Jan Horváth and Vlado Oláh.

Hungary[15]

Since the late 1950s (that is, after the Hungarian Revolution in October 1956) a number of initiatives have been introduced at governmental level to counter anti-Roma discrimination and support Romani culture and education in Hungary.[16] The first officially recognised Romani organisation (*Cigányszövetség*, meaning Gypsy Council) was created in 1958 but was closed down in 1960 (Crowe 1991, 120). The following year it was decreed that Hungarian Roma do not constitute a national minority. In 1985 the National Gypsy Council was established, followed in 1986 by the Hungarian Romani Cultural Association. The latter, chaired by Romani writer Menyhért Lakatos, funded several cultural projects and artistic productions. In 1989 the Romani organisation *Phralipe* was created, led by author and activist Béla Osztojkán. These initiatives, aimed at "integrating" Roma/Gypsies into Hungarian society, have produced mixed results. The Romani population in Hungary remains marginalised and discriminated against. However, the Roma's educational attainment is higher than in other parts of Europe and this has certainly favoured the rise of a Romani written literature in this region. There are a number of well-established Romani writers in Hungary, for example Károly Bari, József Holdosi, Attila Balogh, Menyhért Lakatos and the already-mentioned Béla Osztojkán.[17]

Károly Bari is a poet, dramatist, painter and author of several books of poetry, including *Holtak arca fölé* (Above the Face of Death, 1970), *Elfelejtett tüzek* (Forgotten Fires, 1973), *A varázsló sétálni indul* (1985) and *Winter Diary* (1997). Besides his poetic work, Bari is a folklorist whose work is of great anthropological interest as he has published numerous anthologies of Romani folk tales and songs. Of particular importance are his collections of songs about the Holocaust. Bari is also a keen linguist who has worked as a translator, while his critical comments and reflections upon the nature of literary creation have been published and translated into English (Bari 1997b).

József Holdosi began publishing poems in 1970. In 1978 he published the successful novel *Kányák* (The Kites), which was translated into German (1984) and Polish (1989), and this was followed by the novel *Glóriás*, which appeared in 1982.[18]

Attila Balogh (born in 1956) is a Romani poet writing in Hungarian. He worked as an activist and was a founding member of the organisation *Phralipe*. He is also a founding editor of the literary magazine *Cigányfúró* (Gypsy Drill) and a member of the Hungarian Journalists' Association and of the Hungarian PEN Club. Balogh has published several books of poetry and prose, including *Lendítem lábamat* (1980), *Versek* (Poems, 1991) and *József Attila a Peep-showban* (Attila Jozsef at the Peepshow, 1998). Balogh has received several prizes for his intellectual achievements and his commitment to the Romani cause.

Romania

The rise of a written Romani literature in Romania is a recent phenomenon: the first publications to appear in the country date from the 1920s and 1930s (Djurić 2002, 82). Some of the most well known Romani authors from Romania include Gheorghe Păun Ialomiţeanu, Vasile Ionescu and Luminiţa Mihai Cioabă. Born in Romania in 1957, Luminiţa Mihai Cioabă is a talented poet and prose writer based in Sibiu. She has published several collections of poems edited in various languages (Romani, English, Romanian and German), such as *The Roots of the Earth* and *The Rain Merchant*,[19] two plays, a collection of short stories (*The Lost Country*, 2002) and collections of fairy tales and ballads. Her works feature a sophisticated use of poetic language, aimed at evoking themes and imagery considered by the author as the symbolic "roots" of Romani identity. Cioabă's seemingly effortless style has been described by Romanian author Mircea Ivănescu as follows:

> Her verses, which at first gave the impression that they had been scattered alongside the free racing of the pen, just marking and rewriting instant sensations the same way they are recorded in a teenager's diary—reveal a profound coherence, an intensity and a force that belong to genuine lyrics. (Cioabă 1994, 13)

Cioabă has received literary awards in Romania and Italy and won the Poetry Prize at the International Literary Competition *Amico Rom* in 1995. She is one of the founding members of the IRWA and currently manages the *Roma Social-Cultural Foundation* ("Ion Cioabă"), which seeks to empower Romani ethnicity, promote Romani cultural heritage and publish "books, textbooks, pamphlets, calendars and recordings in Romani, that will be translated into Romanian, German and English for the purpose of dissemination, and made available to governmental and non-governmental institutions and foundations".[20]

Bulgaria

In post-war Bulgaria, the Roma managed to establish a national Romani organisation, a theatre and a newspaper.[21] However, from 1947 onwards the Communist regime pursued a policy of assimilation of the Gypsy population. The Gypsy theatre in Sofia was closed down in 1951, in 1958 nomadism was outlawed and in the early 1960s the government began a twenty-year campaign to force Roma with Turkish names to accept Bulgarian names. At the same time, the government prohibited the manifestation of Roma's ethnic and cultural specificity. After 1989, however, the Roma were able to create their own associations and publish their periodicals, and became active in the public sphere.[22]

Romani literature in Bulgaria began to emerge after the 1950s. Usin Kerim (1929–1983) was the foremost Romani writer in Bulgaria and author of several collections of poetry including *Pesni ot katuna* (1955), *Stikhotvoreniia* (1968), *Sŭrtseto mi* (1978), *Khalište: Stikhotvoreniia* (1987) and *Kato prašen skitnik se zavruštam* (1989). Other prominent Romani authors in this country include Sali Ibrahim, Assen Merkov, Mihail Petrov and Hristo Hristov.

Romani Literatures in Western Europe

The past two decades have witnessed a rapid expansion of Romani literatures westwards, and a second centre of Romani literature is now forming in central and Western Europe. This phenomenon is partly due to the migration of Romani writers after the fall of Communism and the tragic events of the war in the former Yugoslavia. This does not mean, however, that the rise of Romani literatures in Western Europe is purely the result of such migration. In fact, Romani literatures in Western Europe have their own well-established tradition and peculiar features, such as the use of one or more majority languages, which enabled Romani authors such as Matéo Maximoff, Mariella Mehr and Ceija Stojka to become known beyond the boundaries of their ethnic group.

France

Matéo Maximoff was the first Romani novelist and one of the most prolific Romani authors of all time. Born in 1917 in Barcelona from father Rom Kalderaš and mother Manuš,[23] he was taught to read and write by his father. Maximoff wrote most of his books in French and a few—mostly unpublished—stories and narratives in the Kalderaš dialect. In the final part of his book *Dites-le avec des pleurs* (Say That With Tears, 1990), Maximoff discusses his decision to write in French rather than Romani. He is committed to reach the widest possible audience, while also emphasising the mediating role of the Romani writer, whose main task he considers to be that of using his/her mastery of the written medium to serve as an interpreter and a historian in the name of his/her people (Maximoff 1990, 204).

Maximoff's writing career began after his experience of World War II, during which he was imprisoned in a concentration camp in Lannemezan until 1943. Maximoff made his literary debut with the novel *Les Ursitory*, published by Flammarion in 1946. The publication of this book, set in Romania and telling the story of a family feud, was followed by that of tales, short stories and several novels. In 1957 Maximoff published *Savina*, a novel set among the Kaldéraš Roma in Russia at the time of the Tsars. *Vinguerka* (1984) and *Ce Monde qui n'est pas le mien* (1992) were also inspired by the life of Kaldéraš Roma in Russia at the beginning of the nineteenth century, a time when Romani slavery was not yet abolished. Finally, *Routes sans roulottes* (Roads without Caravans, 1993) relates the author's family history over more than a century, from 1810 to 1944, when he returned with his family to Paris towards the end of World War II.

A central concern in Maximoff's work is to document the sufferings and persecution of the Roma through the ages. His novel *Le prix de la liberté* (1955) deals with the theme of Romani slavery, inspired by the revolt of Romani slaves in what is today Romania.[24] The book *Condamné à survivre* (Condemned to Survive, 1984) illustrates the tragic fate of the Roma from the time of the October Revolution in Russia to Nazi Germany. He also devotes particular attention to narrating the life of the Roma interned in concentration camps. For example, in *Dites-le avec des pleurs* he narrates the history of his family before, during and after World War II and, against the attempts at erasing their lives from history, he documents the sufferings of his people under the Nazi regime.

In his works, Maximoff combines realistic elements with Romani folklore and magic, which is why his literary style has been compared to that of magic realism (Hancock, Dowd and Djurić 1998, 154). The theme of Romani magic is the main focus of his books *La septième fille* (The Seventh Daughter, 1969) and *La poupée de Maméliga* (The Doll of Maméliga, 1986), a book of horror stories with the subtitle *Le Livre de la peur* (The Book of Fear).

Maximoff's work situates itself within the long-established Romani storytelling tradition, and arises from the encounter between the autobiographical and the collective. It is also characterised by personal recollections interspersed with ethnographic elements. An acute observer of his culture, Maximoff published a number of articles on the Romani tradition for the *Journal of the Gypsy Lore Society* and the French journal *Études Tsiganes*. He effectively acted as a participant-observer who endeavoured to preserve Romani memory, rescuing it from falling into oblivion. After joining the Pentecostal movement in 1961, Maximoff became an Evangelical pastor, combining his intellectual commitment with religious activity. He translated the New Testament into Romani before his death at the age of 82.

Other prominent Romani authors writing in French include Sandra Jayat,[25] Jean-Marie Kerwich,[26] Alexandre Romanès,[27] Sterna Weltz-Zigler, Lick Dubois[28] and Vania De Gila-Kochanowski (Jan Kochanowski), an eminent linguist. Born in Poland in 1920 but brought up in Latvia, Kochanowski was deported during World War II and later joined the Resistance. After the war, he settled in France and continued his studies: he graduated in linguistics from the Sorbonne in 1960 and in 1984 completed a second doctoral dissertation in ethno-sociology at the University of Toulouse. In addition to his academic work—which will be discussed in Chapter 7—he published the novel *Romano Atmo "L'âme tsigane"* (1992), which describes the life of the Gypsies around the time of the

Latvian Revolution of 1905–1906, and the collection of short stories *Les Romané Chavé par eux-mêmes: Le roi des serpents et autres contes tsiganes balto-slaves* (1996).

Romani Authors from Spain and South America

José Heredia Maya (1947–2010) was a poet, playwright, academic and activist born in Albunelas (Spain). He studied Spanish literature, specialising in Federico García Lorca, and taught Spanish Philology at the University of Granada. In 1972 he published his first collection of poems, *Penar ocono*, followed by *Charol* (1983) and *Experiencia y juicio* (1999). He is also author of the well-known theatrical production *Camelamos naquerar* (We Want to Speak), staged for the first time in 1976, three months after the death of Franco. It is a hybrid work, including dance, music, poems, flamenco *coplas* and legal texts from the fifteenth, sixteenth, eighteenth and twentieth centuries, a powerful representation of the persecutions suffered by the *Gitanos* throughout the centuries with a strong political overtone. Other theatrical productions by Heredia Maya include *Macama Jonda* (1983), *Sueño terral* (1990) and *Un gitano de ley* (1997), based on the life story of Ceferino Giménez Malla (also known as El Pelé, Patron Saint of Roma and Sinti), a Spanish Gypsy executed in 1936 by Republican soldiers during the Civil War for having defended a priest, and later beatified by the Catholic Church. Besides Heredia Maya, other prominent Romani writers from Spain include Nicolas Jimenez Gonzalez—a sociologist and activist author of poetry and short stories— Agustín Vega Cortés and Joaquín Albaicín,[29] one of the founding members of the IRWA.

Romani authors writing in Spanish include the Argentinean political activist Jorge F. Bernal, whose poems have appeared in Spinelli's collections (see Spinelli 1995), and Jorge Emilio Nedich, author of a number of novels including *Gitanos para su bien o su mal* (1994), *Ursari* (1997), *La extraña Soledad de los Gitanos* (The Strange Solitude of the Gitanos, 2001), *El Pepe Firmenich* (2005) and *El aliento negro de los Romaníes* (The Black Breath of the Romanies, 2005).

Romani Authors in England, Australia, America and Canada

Romani authors based in England include Ray Smith, author of the collection *One Hand Clapping* (1995), Ely Frankham, Josie Townley, Lucy Ann Adams, Tom Odley, Kathleen Cunningham, Hester Hedges, Charles Smith, David Morley and Louise Doughty. Morley, a poet, critic and academic, is Professor of Creative Writing at the University of Warwick and has won several awards for his literary endeavours and his work as an educator. He has written several collections of poetry, including *Clearing a Name* (1998), *Mandelstam Variations* (1991), *Scientific Papers*

(2002), *The Invisible Kings* (2007) and *Enchantment* (2010). Doughty, an English writer of Romani ancestry, is the author of the internationally acclaimed *Fires in the Dark* (2003), a historical novel about the Nazi persecution in the former Czechoslovakia, and *Stone Cradle* (2006).

Among Australia's leading Romani authors are Jimmy Storey (born in England), author of the poetry collection *Over There* (1983), Marie Olaussen, Lee Fuhler and Norman Talbot, whose poetry has been translated into Italian.

As for Romani poetry in America, the work of Nadia Hava-Robbins is highly original. After emigrating from the former Czechoslovakia, Hava-Robbins began writing poetry to "explore [her] people's origin". A performing artist and storyteller, she successfully combines poetry, music and dance, and is a member of the International Society of Poets. Her poems have been published as part of the National Library of Poetry anthologies.

American author Cecilia Woloch, of part-Romani descent, published *Tsigan*, a book-length poetic exploration of the author's quest for her Romani roots. In the course of her personal journey of self-discovery, she becomes increasingly aware of being part of a wider history and experiences the way in which the Roma are perceived in Europe.

The Canadian-born Romani academic and writer Ronald Lee has written extensively on Romani history and the Romani language, including the compilation of a Romani dictionary. His autobiographical novel *Goddam Gypsy* (reprinted in 2009 as *The Living Fire/E Zhivindi Yag*) explores the world of Roma living in Canada in the 1970s, highlighting tensions and cultural conflicts between Canadian ethnic minorities and the majority population and dealing with the complex relationship between Roma from Canada and America and European Roma.

Romani Authors from Germany, Austria and Switzerland

During the 1980s and 1990s a growing number of Romani authors from Germany, Austria and Switzerland began to publish their work in an effort to counter persistent discriminatory attitudes and violence towards their people. In Germany and Austria the events of the Holocaust have indelibly marked a generation of Romani authors,[30] which includes Philomena Franz, Otto Rosenberg,[31] Walter Winter[32] and Alfred Lessing.[33]

Philomena Franz was born in Germany in 1922 to a Sinti family of musicians. She was sent to Auschwitz in 1943 and later transferred to the concentration camps of Ravensbruck and Oranienburg. She managed to survive, but lost her family. After the war ended she started writing and her book *Zwischen Liebe und Hass* (Between Love and Hate), originally published in 1985 and reprinted in 2001, is an account of her imprisonment in the concentration camps. The first part of the book is devoted to describing the author's happy childhood, which contrasts dramatically with the atrocities of Auschwitz. Franz also writes poetry and has published a collection of fairy tales, *Zigeunermärchen* (2001). In 1995 she was conferred the *Bundesverdienstkreuz* (Order of Merit of the Federal Republic of Germany) and in 2001 awarded the *Preis Frauen Europas* for her contribution to European integration and intercultural understanding.

The leading Romani authors in Austria include Ilija Jovanović, Miso Nikolic, Karl and Mongo Stojka and Ceija Stojka. Born to a family of Lovara Roma in Austria in 1933, Ceija Stojka is an author, painter and singer. As a child, she and her family were deported to Auschwitz-Birkenau and then Bergen-Belsen. She managed to survive the atrocities of the concentration camps together with her mother and four of her five brothers, but she lost her father and her seven-year-old brother Ossi. As in Philomena Franz's case, Stojka's writing dwells on the dramatic contrast between her memories of the happy family life she led before the deportation and the pain and suffering she endured as a Roma prisoner. She published three autobiographical accounts of the Holocaust, including *Wir leben in Verborgenen: Erinnerungen einer Rom-Zigeunerin* (We Live in Hiding: Memories of a Roma-Gypsy woman) in 1988, which focuses on the period 1939 to 1945. In 1992 she published another autobiographical account, *Reisende auf dieser Welt* (Travellers on This World), in which she described her life in Austria after the war, while *Träume ich, dass ich lebe? Befreit aus Bergen-Belsen* (Am I Dreaming that I Am Living? Freed from Bergen-Belsen), published in 2005, focuses on her detention in the Bergen-Belsen concentration camp. The book *Meine Wahl zu schreiben—ich kann es nicht* (My Choice to Write—I Have None), published in 2003, is a bilingual collection of poems in German and Romani.

Jovanović is a Serbian Rom who has lived in Vienna since 1971. His first collection of poems, *Bündel/Budžo*, was published in a bilingual Romani/ German version in 2000. His most recent book is *News from the Other World*, a bilingual collection of poems in Romani/English, published in 2010. He has acted as chairman of *Romano Centro*, founded in Vienna in 1991 and one of Austria's foremost Romani associations. He has been awarded the Theodor-Kömer prize (1999) and the *Bundes-Ehrenzeichen* (2008) for his contribution to intercultural dialogue.

The leading Romani author in Switzerland is Mariella Mehr. She was born in Zürich in 1947 and belongs to the *Jenisch* (also Yenish) group.[34] Like many other *Jenische*, she experienced the trauma of being forcibly separated from her family as a child and, later, of having her own child taken into care. This procedure was part of a brutal assimilation policy that targeted specifically Romani children. It formed part of the programme *Hilfswerk für die Kinder der Landstrasse* (Relief Work for Children of the Country Road), set up to allegedly "protect" Romani children and to ultimately "normalise" the deviant behaviour of nomadic Gypsies. The programme was carried out by welfare organisations such as the *Pro Juventute*[35] between 1926 and 1973—when it was closed down after the publication of a number of articles in the Swiss weekly *Der Schweiserischer Beobachter* which shed light on the racist and abusive acts perpetrated by such organisations—and by the founder and director of the programme, Dr Alfred Siegfried.

The traumas and abuses suffered at the hands of the enforcers of the *Kinder der Landstrasse* campaign have had an indelible effect on Mehr's life and work. Her first book *steinzeit* (Stone Age), published in 1981, is an autobiographical novel dealing with her childhood memories of physical and mental abuse. Her other work includes the novels *Zeus oder der Zwillingston* (1994), *Daskind* (1995), *Brandzauber* (1998) and *Angeklagt* (2002); the poetry collections *In diesen traum schlendert ein roter findling* (1983), *Nachrichten aus dem Exil* (1998), *Widerwelten* (1998) and *Das Sternbild des Wolfes* (2003); and the plays *Silvia Z.* (1986), *Kinder der Landstrasse* (1987) and *Anni B.* (1989). She has won several literary awards and in 1998 received an honorary doctorate from the University of Basel. Because of its multilingual circulation[36] and thematic focus, Mehr's work is not limited to autobiographic, ethnically specific events, but carries a much wider, universal significance. Mehr currently lives and works in Italy, linking her literary activities with a political commitment to her people.

Romani Literature in Italy

Romani literature published in Italy is structurally and linguistically diverse. Early examples consist of transcriptions of oral narratives and memoirs, with a case in point being the collaborative autobiographical account of the Istrian Rom Giuseppe Levakovich, published in 1975 under the title *Tzigari* (Levakovich and Ausenda 1975).[37] A more recent example of narratives originating from the collaboration between Roma and non-Roma is the book *I Kañjarija: Storia vissuta dei Rom Dasikhanè in Italia* (The Kañjarija: History of the Roma Dasikhanè in Italy), edited by Massimo Converso[38] in collaboration with the associations *Opera Nomadi*, UNIRSI and with the collaboration of the *Biblioteche Romane*.[39] Finally, the journal *Lacio Drom* published several transcriptions of oral narratives, including tales, non-fiction and fictional stories and autobiographical narratives and testimonies.

Over the past few decades there has been evidence of a growing literary production among Italian Romani authors, especially among the Roma from the Abruzzi (e.g., Santino Spinelli and Luigi Cirelli), the Sinti (e.g., Paula Schöpf, Vittorio Mayer Pasquale, Olimpio Cari, Gnugo de Bar, Floriano Debar and Pućo) and the Slovenian-Croatian Roma. Furthermore, several Romani poets from the former Yugoslavia have published their collections in Italy, mostly in a bilingual version (Romani/Italian). Among them are Rasim Sejdić (1943–1981) and Šemšo Advić (who now lives in Sweden). Sejdić, a gifted poet and narrator from Bosnia, had been writing poems from the age of fourteen.

His family belonged to the Bosnian Xoraxané group, and while his first poems were in Serbo-Croatian subsequent collections were published in Romani with an Italian translation (see, for instance, the collection *Rasim, poeta zingaro*, 1987). Sejdić's stories, transcribed and collected by Giulio Soravia, consist mostly of tales, stories of the dead, ghosts and vampires and fanciful tales (mostly published with an Italian translation in the journal *Lacio Drom*). Meanwhile Advić, a poet born in Banja Luka, published his first collection of poetry in 1985. His following book, *Ratvaról iló romanó/Sanguina il cuore dei Rom* (The Heart of the Roma is Bleeding), appeared in 1993. Advić's poetry epitomises the classic themes of Gypsy literature, but also deals with specific historical events such as the tragedy of war in the former Yugoslavia, which sowed death and destruction among the Roma of that area. His poetry attempts to combine the pursuit of linguistic refinement with richness of content, and constitutes a notable example of emerging Romani literature.

The literary production of Italian Roma and Sinti includes the works of Santino Spinelli, a Rom from the Abruzzi. He is author of two bilingual (Romani/Italian) collections of poems, *Gili Romani* and *Romanipè/Ziganità*, inspired by traditional themes of Romani literature. Spinelli's poetry is characterised by an acute awareness of the gap between the Roma and non-Roma, and by the latter's inability to understand the Roma's reality. The author is able to convey powerful and suggestive images through a skilful use of rhymes and assonances. His work is designed to recreate the traditional *gili romani*, the "Romani song", an endeavour aided by the author's experience as a musician and a gifted composer.

For a considerable number of Romani authors, poetic activity is a way to express their sense of ethnic identity. Luigi Cirelli and Mansueto Levacovich, together with the main exponents of the literature of Sinti authors, can all be ascribed to this trend. Cirelli published his book *Senza meta* (Without Destination) in 1994 as part of the poetry collection *Poeti e scrittori Rom* (edited by Angelo Arlati). His poems, written exclusively in Italian, are a celebration of his ethnic roots, and one of their central themes is love in all its nuances, ranging from sensual love to spiritual devotion. Within them, the figure of the mother holds a central role. The main focus of Cirelli's work, however, is the difficult relationship between the Roma and non-Roma. According to the author, the root of the problem lies in the narrow-mindedness and hypocritical attitude of the non-Roma towards his people. He complains bitterly about the Roma's lost freedom and the attitude of indifference of the surrounding society. In this context, poetic language seems the only form of communication capable of bridging a seemingly impenetrable ethnic divide.

In 1991 Levacovich, an Istrian Rom whose father, Giuseppe Leva-kovich, narrated his autobiography to the anthropologist Giulio Ausenda, published the anthology *Popolo mio dei Rom* (My Romani People), written exclusively in Italian. Levacovich's works constitute the first evidence of a written production among the Slovenian-Croatian Roma living in northern Italy. His literature is dominated by a pessimistic *Weltanschauung* and characterised by a harsh denunciation of the complete lack of dialogue between the Roma and non-Roma, who are separated by a formidable barrier of hatred and prejudice. The poet ultimately invokes death as the only solution to the never-ending persecution suffered by the Roma. Levacovich associates his work as a poet with a strong commitment to promoting Romani human and civil rights. Another politically engaged author is Demir Mustafa (born in Skopje in 1960 and currently living in Florence), whose poems and short stories were published in 2002 with the title *Poesie e racconti* by CISU, an Italian academic publisher based in Rome.

Conclusions

This chapter has provided an overview of Romani literature, which, as we have seen, is polycentric and polylingual and largely reflects the diasporic dispersion of the Romani people (Toninato 2006). Two main Romani literary "centres" have been identified: Eastern Europe and the Balkans, and Western and northern Europe. Romani written literature first developed in Eastern Europe in the early twentieth century and has subsequently expanded westward.

Romani literature has to face a number of serious challenges that will ultimately determine its future. Literacy levels among Roma and Sinti groups remain relatively low, and their dire living conditions mean that mere day-to-day survival takes precedence over literacy acquisition. This situation has so far prevented the creation of a sizeable body of written texts in Romani and the formation of a wide Romani readership. The lack of a widely shared written language is a major hindrance to the rise of Romani literature. Essentially, Romani remains an oral language that has only recently been codified. As a result, those Roma and Sinti who can read and write have become literate in a non-Romani language and often prefer to express themselves in writing in these languages. Meanwhile, the diffusion of Romani texts is highly problematic, as a Romani literary field struggles to establish its autonomy.[40] As we will see, for most Romani authors the quest for literary autonomy is intertwined with an active commitment in the political sphere. It is highly likely that, as the context of the Roma/non-Roma relationship continues to be characterised by inter-ethnic tension and the constant attempt, on the part of the dominant group, to control and assimilate the Roma, this will continue to be the case.

Other challenges to the establishment of Romani written literatures are directly associated with widespread cultural attitudes on the part of both Roma and non-Roma. First, Romani writing suffers from a generalised critical neglect due to its "non-canonical" features, which will be discussed in Chapter 6. Second, the establishment and diffusion of Romani written literature is hindered by the fact that most Romani groups continue to adopt a strategy of "restricted literacy" and regard writing as the exclusive domain of the dominant group. However, despite the great challenges faced by Romani literature, there are encouraging signs for its future. As writing has become increasingly acceptable in the eyes of the Romani community, the number of Romani authors is constantly growing. There is also evidence of a coordinated attempt to establish a pan-European network of Romani writers. At an international meeting of Romani authors held in Cologne from 17–19 November 2001, the following declaration (known as the "Cologne Declaration") was issued:

> We, Roma authors from eight European countries, who met in Cologne at the invitation of Deutsche Welle, have decided to found an international association of Roma authors. [. . .] The object of the association is to protect the interest of Roma authors and to bring their literary work, irrespective of the language in which it is written, to public attention.

The following year the IRWA was founded at Karjaa, Finland. Among the founding members were Romani authors Veijo Baltzar[41] (president), Mariella Mehr (vice-president), Jovan Nicolić (vice-president), Charles Smith, Margita Reiznerova, Valdemar Kalinin, Joaquin Albaicín, Rahim Burhan and Luminiţa Mihai Cioabă. As maintained in the mission statement of the association, the IRWA's main objectives are to promote Romani literature and "to strengthen the language and culture of Romani people".[42]

The association has devised a number of important projects, most notably the creation of a Romani Library. This pan-European project, which began in May 2003 and was completed in March 2006, was coordinated by the Department of Linguistics at Karl-Franzens University (Graz). The project had two main aims. First, it sought to "contribute to nurturing and reinforcing the cultural identity of Romani as a language of contemporary literature and in particular to encourage the younger generation to read and [. . .] write creatively". Second, the project was an attempt to fight anti-Roma prejudice. From this point of view, increasing the availability of works written by Roma can effectively contribute to "enliven intercultural dialogue and to promote the recognition of Roma literature as an integral part of European and World literature and culture".[43] The project entailed the selection and diffusion of literary works—mainly contemporary—by Romani authors in a multilingual edition (thirty volumes in six European languages). A number of publishers supported the project, including the University of Hertfordshire Press (United Kingdom), Drava Verlag (Austria) and L'Harmattan (France).

5   Roma Writing Themselves

The chapter provides an overview of the key themes and tropes in Romani written literature.[1] The focus is not on a specific literary tradition, but rather on a number of themes and images that are central to the Romani identity as a whole. The authors whose work has been included in this study belong to different Romani groups and use a variety of languages, but they all live under comparable socio-political circumstances. What all these authors have in common—and what ultimately justifies their inclusion in this study—is their ethical approach to writing and their desire to communicate aspects and issues in Romani history and culture that have been neglected or misleadingly interpreted by the majority group. These problematic issues are often thematised in their work and become a source of literary inspiration. They include nomadism, the Romani Holocaust, racial discrimination, violence and social marginalisation.

A specific section has been devoted to the work of Romani women writers. Despite focusing on a limited number of authors, some remarks and interpretations put forward here may be extended to refer to female writers of other Romani groups. This is not to say that the problems faced by women—or the ways in which they choose to address these problems—are necessarily the same in all Romani groups. There are, however, some important similarities shared by Romani women authors, most notably the need to communicate, to find their own voice to express a point of view alternative to dominant experiences and to develop self-awareness about the use writing, its possibilities and implications.

THE REWRITING OF ROMANI NOMADISM

Nomadism is among the key components of what is generally known as the "Gypsy way of life", and is a highly controversial phenomenon due to it being the object of ideological manipulation and polarised interpretations. In the past, nomadic Roma were accused of being idle and treated as socially dangerous subjects. Nowadays, generalised hostility towards nomadism continues to permeate the political, legal and media spheres and has frequently led to the criminalisation of the Roma's peripatetic practices.[2] Paradoxically, anti-nomadic views and policies coexist alongside a romantic idealisation of nomadic Gypsies in European art and literature. What is important to emphasise is that both the widespread stigmatisation of nomadism and its artistic romanticisation are ultimately based on equally ethnocentric strategies, whereby Romani nomadism is taken out of context and reinterpreted according to dominant ideologies. It is not surprising, then, that Romani authors consider it necessary to reveal to the non-Romani reader the reality that lies beyond misleading interpretations of nomadism.

Before analysing specific texts dealing with this central theme, it is necessary to point out that Romani nomadism cannot be reduced to either an elective "lifestyle" or a state of alleged freedom from bourgeois conventions. It must be seen instead as a social practice closely linked to the specific characteristics of the Roma's socio-economic system. In this context, nomadism fulfils several functions. As emphasised by Liégeois (1994, 77), nomadism "makes social organisation possible, allows adaptability and flexibility, enables the exercise of economic activities". Contrary to stereotypical views, Romani groups are not necessarily nomadic. There is of course no such thing as a "genetic propensity" that might explain why some groups have embraced a nomadic way of life and some have not.[3] Romani groups in Europe, as Piasere (2004, 12) has shown, are characterised by varying degrees of nomadism. The latter should not be viewed as being in opposition to sedentarism, but as part of a continuum of various possible combinations. Generally, Romani groups in northern Europe display a greater tendency to engage in nomadic practices, while groups in southern Europe tend to be more sedentary (Ibid., 10). In addition to being a geographically diversified phenomenon, the Roma's nomadic practices have evolved over the years in response to changing social, political and environmental circumstances. Perhaps the most notable change is the transition from a rural to an urban economy based on manufacturing. Nowadays, it is thought that only 20 per cent of the Roma are nomadic (Liégeois 2007, 32; Piasere 2004, 14). This does not prevent Romani groups that are sedentary at one given time from deciding to resume their peripatetic strategies later. Such a decision may involve reasons that are not strictly economic, but depend on the "dispersed" structure of Roma society (Piasere 1991).

In addition to constituting a complex socio-economic strategy, nomadism represents a powerful symbol of Romani identity. The experience of travelling is a pivotal aspect of *Romanipe*, the Roma's specific way of looking at the world and perceiving their place in it (Liégeois 1986; McVeigh 1997; Levinson and Sparkes 2004). Nomadism is regarded by the Roma as an act of proud reassertion of their diversity from the settled society. This is why, even when they are no longer nomadic, many Roma continue to treasure their nomadic past. Among the Roma, self-perceptions of nomadism are often in opposition to external representations, especially the fictionalisation of Romani nomadism. Romani poets explicitly engage with hetero-ascribed images of nomadism in "autoethnographic" texts[4] where authors invest them with a new meaning.

Several Romani authors highlight the problematic side of their nomadic way of life in an effort to move away from romantic stereotypes. The image that perhaps best encapsulates the ambivalent nature of nomadism is that of the road. Poets such as Iliaz Šaban write about a "long road" that leads nowhere and about a "journey of sorrow":

> We took a road into night
> unaware of where it might lead.
> We left behind a great land
> and started our journey of sorrow.
>
> We strayed over many a byway
> carrying our heavy loads.
> We buried our dead along the way;
> in the forest our fathers grew old.
>
> In the midst of the darkest place
> we sat ourselves down to rest.
> We paused to revive our spirits
> and as we sat there, we slept.
>
> No bread we ate nor water drank;
> not a crust passed our lips.
> When morning came we got up again
> and continued along the road.[5]

Some poets describe nomadism as "a life of wandering/forwards, backwards" along roads forgotten by time.[6] Others see themselves as "tramping along the road", "barefoot, ravenous", with no place to shelter. They perceive themselves as doomed to die on the road. In the following poem by Rajko Djurić, the Roma are depicted as a people "without house or grave":

> O-o-o
> goes my endless lament
> o-o-o
> to my father-o
> my graveless father
> my homeless people
> toys of the wind
> dregs of the world
> Where then
> Where then from here?

o-o-o/to my mother-o
gentle mother
where is there a stone
on which to raise me up
that I might call your name?
The sky is our cover
and wherever I fly
the ground is barren
without a heart.[7]

In the poems above the very concept of travelling is devoid of its original
meaning and reduced to an endless, circular wandering, a kind of vicious
circle triggered by the hostile attitude of the host group. The destiny of our
people, say Romani poets, is to pursue a hopeless search for tolerance and
human understanding.

Poor Rom, where is your future.
The gagio is strangling you, you have no place to live.
Poor Rom, you are wasting your breath,
who is ever going to listen to you?
Hearts of stone,
they do not know how to warm themselves around the fire.
Look ahead without fear,
we have a God
He will show us the way,
He will hold our hand
and He will say to us: "Walk on . . . walk on"[8]

Let us go to a place
where the hearts are filled with love
where the bread may be shared with us.
Let us go to a place or maybe nowhere
a place where mutual love still lives on
where we may find embraces and kisses.
Let us go
nobody knows where
Maybe to a secret place
where people search and find themselves in the others.[9]

In the poems above, the Roma's itinerancy is depicted as a kind of forced
exile from settled society. Such literary self-representations are in strik-
ing contrast with the images of artificial gaiety characterising non-Gypsy
textual renditions of Romani nomadism. If nomadism appears to have
been so frequently misunderstood by the non-Gypsies, there are further
aspects of the Roma's identity and way of life that have been distorted and

misrepresented. Romani poets appear to point out to the reader that what is frequently portrayed as an allegedly carefree existence is in fact dominated by violence, oppression and social exclusion.

THE CURSE OF EXCLUSION

Racial (and ethnic) categories can be manipulated to create division and legitimise segregation among different ethnic groups. Over the course of centuries the Roma have been stigmatised as dangerous subjects and the colour of their skin has been the object of superstitious beliefs. As seen in Chapter 1, during the Middle Ages the blackness of the Gypsies was considered a clear indication of their supposed evil nature. It was also interpreted as a sign of inferiority, paving the way for their exploitation by the dominant group: in what is now Romania they were reduced to slavery over a period of five hundred years (Hancock 1987). Later, the Roma's ethnic diversity was reformulated in racial terms. Under the Nazis, Gypsies were classified again as "dangerous" and even as "racially degenerate" and "inferior", and therefore singled out for extermination (Kenrick and Puxon 1995; Lewy 2000). At present, systematic discrimination on ethnic and racial grounds is still deployed to exclude the Roma from mainstream society.

What is the impact of racism on the Roma's self-representations? There is no simple answer to this question as there can be several responses to racism from minority groups and individuals, ranging from self-victimisation to political protest and violence. Ian Hancock, who compared the experience of the Roma with that of African-Americans, underlines the negative socio-economic and psychological consequences of anti-Roma racism and anticipates that, unless this problem is addressed by European institutions as a matter of urgency, the Roma could resort to violence and rioting as a form of self-defence (Hancock 2000). Discrimination and enduring racist abuse had a definite detrimental impact on the Roma population across Europe. In some cases, the hetero-ascription of racial traits to the Roma has seeped into their self-representations. Anthropologist Alaina Lemon provides us with a pertinent example of this phenomenon in quoting the words of a "Kelderari welder" living in Russia, who told her: "We are *negry* [. . .]. We are treated like a second class here, like your blacks in America" (Lemon 2000, 75). However, in some cases anti-Gypsism has led to an increased awareness among the Roma of the need for political self-determination, as demonstrated by the rise of an international Romani intelligentsia actively engaged in fighting against racism. Another response to anti-Roma racism and violence is found in Romani literature.

A great number of Roma identify violence as the main thread running through their group's history and a constant component of their everyday lives: it is thus small wonder that violence should constitute one of the salient *topoi* of Romani literature. In the poem "I Was Born in Black Suffering" by Iliaz Šaban, the meaning of the colour black is reformulated from the point of view of the Roma:

> Oh yes, that's me all right
> tramping along the road
> barefoot, ravenous—
> and on bad days
> the wind blows
> rain pours
> and there's nowhere for me to shelter . . .
>
> *Why did you bring me into the world, mother dear?*
> you bore me to a life of black suffering
> maybe you gave birth to me on a dark road like this
> my lips tremble, rain soaks me through
> and there's not even you, dear mother, to see me.[10]

While for the non-Roma the Roma's blackness represents first a biological trait, almost a reified object, in Šaban's poem blackness loses its biological connotation and becomes a symbol of suffering. Šaban's textual reappropriation of blackness can be compared to Aimé Césaire's rereading of black subjectivity. In presenting the notion of *Négritude*,[11] Césaire wrote: "I accept [*négritude*], no longer cephalic index, or plasma, or soma, but measured by the compass of suffering" (Césaire 1994, 23). As in Césaire's literary endeavour, Šaban's text is characterised by an act of self-recognition ("Oh yes, that's me all right/tramping along the road"), and identifies blackness with suffering and social exclusion. To the Romani poet, exclusion and social marginalisation are primarily the result of discriminatory practices adopted by the dominant society. By shifting the semantic domain of blackness from a biological to a social dimension, the poet contributes to a process of redefinition of Romani identity from within.

In Šaban's poetry, social exclusion provides the main key to interpret the Roma's life and *Weltanschauung*. Taken to its extremes, this negative condition can lead to a loss of cultural identity and, ultimately, to real or symbolic self-annihilation. "I am not a man", writes Romanian poet D.T. Artezian; "The day I was born, I was a little child / my mother gave me a name / When I started growing up / I cursed the day I was born".[12] The poet Ruzdija Seidović defines the Rom as "weed",[13] but such self-demeaning statements should not be dismissed as acts of self-victimisation: they need to be contextualised within the Roma/non-Roma power relationship. Moreover, these statements are employed by the poets as part of a textual strategy aimed at provoking the reader and drawing his/her attention to the extreme violence that pervades so many aspects of Romani life.

The following poem by Santino Spinelli effectively illustrates the devastating impact of anti-Roma violence on the domestic sphere. The text conveys a message of strong condemnation of the hatred of the non-Roma for his people:

> A knock on the door in the deepest night
> the ferocious teeth of trained dogs
> an automatic gun pointed at a sleepy face
> shattered dream nightmarish hallucinations
> black uniforms piercing stares
> disgust and hate slanderous accusations
> violent hurricane innocent eyes . . .
> the door closed a dream disappeared
> tears on the ground . . . torn hearts.[14]

The poem's structure is organised around the juxtaposition of a number of key images: the knock on the door, the ferocious teeth of trained dogs, the automatic gun and the black uniforms. The dramatic nature of these images is reinforced by the use of metonymy and the poem's abrupt opening. In it, the Roma are victims of a faceless, heartless authority. The police officers who attack a peaceful Romani family have no human features because there is nothing human about their violence.

To recreate the quick succession of the events of the raid, the author makes use of a nominal style. Verbal forms occur in the past participle and invariably convey a negative meaning. This creates an impression of a disproportionate use of force and an imbalance between the passive attitude of the victims of the raid and the brutal behaviour of the police. Violence is portrayed in a cyclic form—a violent act marks the beginning of the poem and another one closes it—and is likened to a natural phenomenon (the hurricane) to emphasise its unrestrained, destructive force. This disproportionate outburst of violence has dreadful effects: the hearts of the victims are not merely "broken", but "torn" and "dismembered".

Violence is experienced by the Roma not only in a physical form, but also in terms of ethnic and racial discrimination:

> It stings the eye
> like a needle
> like a spear
> like a knife.
> A little black man
> did not want to be alone any longer,
> burdened with books
> he went and lived among white people
> he wanted to study with them
> he wanted to live with them

they did not like him.
They asked each other
a scornful look on their faces:
What is that black doing here? It stings the eye
like a needle
like a spear
like a knife.[15]

An insurmountable black/white dichotomy lies at the heart of Jovanović's poem. The little black man's attempt to live among white people is thwarted by his physical appearance. Social exclusion reinforces the boundary separating the Roma from the non-Roma to the point that it becomes impossible to bridge. The message of this poem is painfully clear: no matter how hard a Romani individual may try to overcome social and cultural barriers, his/her efforts are invariably doomed to fail.

The Roma/Gadže opposition is also the dominant theme in the poetry of Mansueto Levacovich. His poem *Senza speranza* (Without hope) portrays the Roma/Gadže relationship as antithetical. The Gadže, with very few exceptions, appear to refuse any contact with the Roma. The poet likens this act of exclusion to a curse cast upon the Roma by the Gadže:

> *Gagio*, and you *gagi*:
> you who follow our way
> preaching love and peace
> without knowing what they mean.
> We Rom are humiliated and persecuted,
> beaten up, squashed, tired and hungry.
> We beg you to stop.
> Our sufferings are many, so many . . .
> No Gypsy, no Gypsies.
> We are your destiny.
> Our ancestors persecuted your ancestors,
> we persecute you.[16]

The curse, thought to weigh upon the Gypsies in medieval times, is reinterpreted here from a different point of view. This curse, the poem seems to indicate, is not due to the supposed "evil nature" of the Gypsies. It is rather a direct result of the condition of social exclusion imposed on the Roma by the Gadže.

A sense of helplessness and disillusion haunts Levacovich's poetry. His verses amount to a poetic *cri de coeur*, a denunciation of the injustice and human rights infringements perpetrated against the Romani people:

> *Gagio*, and you, *gagi*:
> you who celebrate compassion

as one of the most precious
qualities of the human soul,
you who say that no society
is conceivable,
and no bond
is possible among humans
without it:
it includes
justice and charity.
Oh mother, we are so poor,
and all we ask for is such a tiny crumb.
The *gagio* and the *gagi*
deny us even this right
which belongs to us.
My poor children,
I am frightened about your future.
The *gagio* and the *gagi*'s faces
are veiled;
their hearts are full of hatred.
We will not receive any comfort
from these people.
Oh my children: your future
is filled with tears and suffering.[17]

What lies at the root of the terrible curse afflicting the Roma? And why has it been depicted in such fatalistic terms? According to the poet, the Gadže cannot but hate the Roma and have no intention of ending their persecution. They remain unmoved by the appeals of the Roma and are incapable of pity: their hatred has made them "blind and indifferent". The Roma and non-Roma have two completely diverging views of the world. On their part, the non-Roma despise the Roma's way of life, which they dismiss as a form of resistance to mainstream social norms. Meanwhile, the Roma accuse the Gadže of fomenting a persecutory attitude towards them. Ultimately, the Roma/Gadže relationship is reduced to a fierce power struggle within which the Gadže occupy a dominant position. The Gadžo is the "absolute ruler of this world" says the poet, but his position of power entails another curse. Within the Christian perspective embraced by the poet, by persecuting and murdering the Roma the Gadže condemn themselves to damnation.

The ultimate message conveyed by Levacovich's text is that ethnic and racial hatred is a vicious circle that harms both oppressed and oppressors. For an increasing number of Romani authors, poetry is a way to break this vicious circle. Through writing, they hope to lay the basis for a constructive encounter with the members of the majority group. To achieve this, however, they first need to re-establish the historical truth of violence and persecution against their people.

KEEPING ALIVE THE MEMORY OF THE ROMANI HOLOCAUST

The publication of written testimonies and memories of the Romani Holocaust is a relatively new and neglected aspect of Romani literature.[18] It has often been assumed that commemoration of the *Porrajmos*[19] among the Roma is rare because they have allegedly "lost" memory of those tragic events (Fonseca 1996). In Romani culture, "remembrance" and "commemoration" are in fact distinct processes (Stewart 2004). However, the assumption that the Roma generally avoid talking about the Holocaust because they no longer remember it or even "ignore" its significance is fundamentally flawed. "Let me assure you", wrote Nadia Hava-Robbins, "that there is scarcely a Rom, as there is scarcely a Jew, [who] is not aware of the Holocaust".[20]

There are no grounds to doubt the existence of oral narratives about the Holocaust among the Roma. Some of these narratives have been published in books and academic journals (Pahor 1980; Stojka 1992; Kenrick and Puxon 1995; Sonneman 2002; Bársony and Daróczi 2008) or made available through the creation of dedicated documentation centres.[21] There are a number of reasons why the Roma's Holocaust memories have started to appear only recently in the public domain. Essentially, these narratives were not published earlier because they were not meant to be recorded and have thus been intentionally kept within the protective boundaries of the group.

It is a well-known fact that memory is a culturally determined phenomenon. Moreover, memory and forgetting are mutually inclusive processes (Halbwachs 1992; Connerton 1989). In the case of the Roma, it is absence and *silence*—rather than remembrance—that play an important role in the construction of the Romani past and in structuring their relationship with the non-Roma (Williams 2003). The Roma have been able to preserve their identity and culture because they have successfully adapted to a range of ever-changing social, economic and historical circumstances. As already mentioned, the ongoing process of shaping and reshaping that is at the core of Romani identity—a process that in fact applies to any form of identity—is based on a complex strategy of partial avoidance of the dominant group (Piasere 1991). This ethnic strategy entails, among other things, a limited involvement of the Roma in the Gadže's social and communication system. The mechanism of forgetting can be understood as an instance of this strategy, which explains why some Roma decide to hide their ethnic roots. Most Romani poets, however, have a completely different approach to the matter. Like other witnesses of the Holocaust, they feel a moral obligation to speak out about the genocide:

My eyes wanted to cry
My voice wanted to scream

My fists wanted to fight
My heart wanted to flight
My soul wanted to hide
but My conscience would not let me
it makes Me speak
it makes Me write.[22]

For these poets, writing represents a form of testimony that enables them to respond to those who still deny the historical truth of the genocide. As in the case of other Holocaust survivors who decided to write about their experience, the act of remembering is extremely painful, but it is the only way to redeem the memory of those who perished.

The ethical imperative of bearing witness often entails a certain level of self-effacement on the part of the authors, since for them what comes first is not their individual suffering but that of the group as a whole. Bearing witness is what prompted Austrian Romani poet Ceija Stojka to write. In an interview with Karen Rosenberg, Stojka confessed that she did not begin writing with the intent of being published (Rosenberg and Stojka 1995, 18). She wrote down her memories so that her children would not forget this painful chapter of Romani history. Most of all, she sees her writing as an act of resistance against indifference and current attempts at downplaying the extent of the Romani Holocaust.

> For a short time [after the events of the Holocaust] the anxiety subsided: from 1945 to maybe 1975 it was peaceful. We were here, we were accepted, we were Austrian citizens. And then came the eighties—they were awful: you heard, "Auschwitz never existed". And I thought, "How can they say 'There was no Auschwitz'—I have it right on my arm". (Rosenberg and Stojka 1995, 19)

For Stojka, writing has two main objectives: to do justice to the victims and reinstate, against Holocaust deniers, the truth of the *Porrajmos* (remembering for the past). Second, Holocaust writing responds to the need to educate future generations so that they may learn from the past and be warned about the risk that it may happen again (remembering for the future).

Stojka's texts reveal a sense of urgency to reclaim the events of the Holocaust. This is clear in the ensuing poem:

I
Ceija
say
Auschwitz lives
and breathes
still today in me
I still feel today

the suffering
Every single blade of grass every flower there
is the soul of a dead one
I have seen
everything is there again
everything is near again[23]

This sense of urgency is expressed in an essential, almost a-poetical language. The author makes no attempt to narrate or describe the events of the Holocaust. Her text corresponds to a performative act of bearing witness, as demonstrated by the use of the first person "I", which is immediately followed by the author's name, "Ceija", at the start of the poem. Of great significance is the use of verbal forms in the past tense ("I have seen") alongside verbs in the present tense ("I still sense"), as if to establish continuity between past and present. The existence of the Holocaust cannot be denied because it is indelibly inscribed in the author's memory and on her body (as Stojka writes, "Auschwitz lives/and breathes/even today in me/I still sense to this day/the suffering"). The author/survivor's existence thus constitutes the main guarantee that her testimony is truthful. Moreover, the fact that she gave her testimony a written form ensures that the memory of the event lives on.

Another powerful Holocaust testimony is the following poem by Rasim Seidjć:

Their feet crushed the Romani violin
only Romani ash remains
fire and smoke
rise up towards the sky.
They took the Roma away
the children separated from their mothers
the women from their men
they took the Roma away
Jasenovac is full of Roma
tied to cement pillars
hand and foot bound by heavy chains
kneeling in the mud.
Only their bones
remain in Jasenovac
a denunciation of inhumanity
there will be other dawns to light up the sky
and the sun is still warming the Roma.[24]

In this poem Romani art (here represented by the violin) metonymically symbolises the Romani people. The opening lines are dominated by images of destruction and annihilation: the violin is trampled on, the Romani people are reduced to ashes and the unity of the family and the mother/child dyad are shattered. The poet recreates the terrible violence that swept away his people by contrasting symbols of lightness (the violin) and love (both filial and marital) with those of heaviness and abjection (cement pillars, heavy chains, kneeling in the mud). In contrast to the gruesome images of the initial lines, the closing lines of the poem present us with images of life and light (the dawn, the sun), as if to declare that even the most devastating act of ethnic cleansing has ultimately failed to achieve the expected result ("there will be other dawns to light up the sky/and the sun is still warming the Roma").

The tangible traces of the genocide (their bones) cannot be erased and remain a stark reminder of man's inhumanity to man. But what happens when that act of inhumanity continues to be silenced and denied? Together with the images of the broken violin, a recurrent image within textual renditions of the Romani Holocaust is that of the "forgotten Holocaust", which seems to re-enact the centuries-old negation of a separate Romani identity:

> Silence, desolation, dark night
> the sky is gloomy, heavy with silence!
> the mournful dirge fills the air!
> From these stones, grey stones,
> from every debris, from the shattered frames,
> a desperation made of blood and tears rises.
> My spirit gets caught up in the wire fences
> And my soul clings to the bars,
> prisoner in the enemy's house!
> Who am I? Nobody! Who are you? Nobody!
> Sinti, who are you? Nobody! Only shadows,
> fog! Fog that idle customs hold back
> as prisoner of the greatest infamy
> in the history of mankind![25]

Here silence has two main connotations: on the one hand, it indicates absence of life, the silence of the victims, reduced to mere shadows and forcibly deprived of a voice. Conversely, there is the silence of the living, the shameful attempt to conceal the historical reality of the Holocaust. Against the silence of the living, the poet has the duty to speak out and prevent the denial of the murder of so many Roma and Sinti. Rhetorical questions and answers are intertwined, and are clearly marked in the text through the use of exclamation marks. Other textual strategies adopted by Roma Holocaust poets include the use of surrealistic language and imagery, as exemplified by the poem "Auschwitz" by Santino Spinelli:

Sunken face,
veiled eyes,
cold lips;
silence.
Torn heart
breathless
speechless
no crying.[26]

It is often claimed that the unspeakable atrocities of the Holocaust should not be given a conventional narrative form (Young 1988). In this text the sequential order of events is substituted by a mere accumulation of images. The poem opens with the image of a lifeless, disfigured human face. The impression of death is conveyed through the absence of flesh from the face, light from the eyes and warmth and sound from the lips. The climax of this symbolic process of removal is reached in the central image of the torn heart, underscored by the anaphoric repetition of the words *bi* (without) and *nikt* (none). A similar textual device is deployed in the following poem:

Black ice-cold hands turning towards the sky,
the mud covers the crushed head,
a muffled cry rises,
nobody listens to it.
A helpless people
led to the massacre,
nobody has seen
nobody has said anything.
Corpses resurrected
from the swamp,
horrible faces shown to the sun
a finger pointed
at those who kept silent.[27]

The images presented in this text—the corpse trapped in the mud, the muffled cry, the faces twisted with pain—may evoke in some readers scenes from Dante's *Inferno*. They contribute to the creation of a hellish landscape that recurs in other literary representations of the Holocaust (Levi 1958, 1986). The extermination camp is a place of utter despair, devoid of human warmth and populated by helpless victims. Every element of this landscape—the howls of despair, the imprisoned bodies, the disfigured corpses—should generate in the reader an overwhelming sense of anguish. The title of the poem alludes to a curse (*kusibbè*). This could be interpreted as a curse on the Roma, and evokes the biblical curse that in medieval times was thought to afflict the Gypsies and condemn them to a life of wandering. In the context of the poem, however, the curse—represented by the pointed finger—has been reversed against the non-Gypsies, who kept silent about the massacre of a harmless people.

RE-PRESENTING THE FEMALE SELF: THE CASES OF PAULA SCHÖPF, MARIELLA MEHR AND SANDRA JAYAT

It seems appropriate to begin this section on female authors by outlining the standing of women in Romani society, as this offers a useful background against which to situate their writings. Romani women must conform to a system of rigorous rules and restrictions, with particular limitations imposed on interactions with both their fellow group members and the non-Roma. In the first instance, women are subordinate to their husbands. They have no autonomous decision-making power and are not allowed to challenge male authority under any circumstances. In addition, they are often subjected to pollution taboos and cannot freely mingle with members of the opposite sex.[28]

With a handful of exceptions, Romani women have fewer opportunities to become fully literate. Early childbearing, social restrictions and demands placed on Romani women within the family have a direct impact on their educational attainment, which tends to be lower than that of their male counterparts. Nonetheless, recent studies revealed that those women who manage to achieve a good level of education have developed a unique relationship with literacy and writing (Toninato 1999). For them, writing offers a valuable tool for self-expression. This section focuses on three Romani female authors whose writings provide a rare insight into little-known (yet crucial) aspects of Romani identity: Paula Schöpf, Mariella Mehr and Sandra Jayat.[29]

Devoting a separate section of this chapter to Romani female writing may seem redundant since the themes and issues tackled by Romani female and male authors are largely the same. The perspective from which women writers perceive these issues, however, is radically different. What seems to characterise the "female poetic voice" in Romani poetry is a sort of "multiple consciousness", that is, an awareness of women's marginalisation and exclusion from the dominant group *as well as* from their own ethnic group. The poems of Paula Schöpf (also known as *Kiriassa*, that is, Cherry) offer a clear example of this multiple consciousness.

Paula Schöpf

Paula Schöpf was born in Bolzano in 1953, belongs to the Sinti group and lives in northern Italy and Germany.[30] Her first poetry collection, entitled *La mendicante dei sogni* (Beggar of Dreams, written in Italian) was published in 1997. Several of her poems have been included in the aforementioned anthologies edited by Spinelli. In her writing she sets out a pessimistic *Weltanschauung* centred on the belief that an unbridgeable rift divides the settled population from the Sinti. The latter are forced to live at the margins of society, like a group of outcasts, and Schöpf refers to a "nation of beggars". This is the same condition of social invisibility described by other Romani poets such as Spinelli (in "Song of the invisible people"), Banga (in "Tramps"), Šaban (in "I was born in black suffering") and Djurić (in "Without House or Grave").[31] The condition of social exclusion endured by so many Roma and Sinti manifests itself primarily in terms of an absence of communication with the non-Roma: the Roma/Gadže relationship is dominated by silence, indifference and hatred. On the other hand, the poet's efforts are aimed at opening up a dialogue with the non-Roma. Addressing a generic non-Romani reader she writes: "My friend, I would like to talk to you . . . /there are so many things I could tell you/ . . . if only you understood my voice". However, her attempts are condemned to failure because of a basic lack of understanding between the two cultures: " . . . you/can you understand me?".[32] For this reason, Schöpf defines her poems as "verses without voice" (*versi senza voce*), that is, poems doomed to remain unheard and unread. The Gadže's failure to understand the voice of the Romani poet is ultimately due to their unwillingness to establish a constructive interaction with the Other.

Performing a crucial change of perspective, the poet laments the same lack of communication within her group: "in the dark I write flows of words/which nobody will ever read/which nobody will ever understand/ . . . nobody takes notice/Everything is sealed/In my darkness".[33] Her isolation is absolute and hopeless: "Alone/My soul enters the silence/The chain of my thoughts is heavy/Alone/I want to be alone/Like the wind in the desert/Alone/Like the mountain in its deafening silence/I will fill myself with solitude".[34] Silence and sadness dominate women's lives:

> I will seek neither love nor life
> I will only seek solitude
> I will not look for regrets or memories
> In this sadness I will drown my life
> I will withdraw into the shell of silence
> Perhaps silence of sorrow
> Perhaps silence of cowardice
> The silence will take away my life.[35]

Like other female writers,[36] Schöpf highlights the situation of alienation experienced by Romani women. She writes about her "strange" solitude, about her own personal sorrows that culminate in an impulse of self-annihilation:

> I am carrying a demon on my shoulders
> A demon who decides upon my life
> As he likes
> Whether daytime or night
> Sunny or rainy
> And all I drink is sand and salt
> The demon on my shoulders
> Takes me to the desert
> Where my bones crumble under the sun
> The ashes are spread over my soul
> and dry out all my blood
> I am carrying a demon on my shoulders
> Who takes me away from the blue sky
> And leads me into the darkness where there is nothingness
> Where I no longer exist.[37]

The isolation experienced by Romani women seems to make them more inclined to empathise with those among the Gadže who live in similar circumstances, such as the poor and the disenfranchised: in short, the wretched of society.[38] The writer's *conscience malheureuse* of the female condition, sharpened by writing, is what ultimately enables her to unveil the sorrow that lies at the very heart of the human condition. In Schöpf's poetry, collective and individual claims are thus inextricably linked: the author focuses on the denunciation of the abuses suffered by the Roma and Sinti as a people and on women's individual struggle for autonomy and self-expression.

Mariella Mehr

The ability to sympathise and speak out for "voiceless" subjects also characterises the works of *Jenisch* author Mariella Mehr. She views the primary aim of her writing as giving a voice to helpless victims unable to fight against violence and indifference.[39] Like other Romani authors, Mehr devotes her work to the theme of violence. In her novels[40] and poetry she denounces and condemns violent and racist practices carried out against her people, such as the infamous "Children of the Road" programme mentioned in Chapter 4. In particular, she has brought attention to the situation of Romani women and children in the context of racially motivated violence. Although both *Jenisch* men and women were victims of assimilationist practices, Mehr emphasises that violence against female Roma was particularly severe and dehumanising, as women were targeted for compulsory sterilisation.

For Mehr, writing constitutes not only a vehicle of literary expression but also a fundamental act of survival that enabled her to find a way out of the vicious circle whereby victims of abuse become in turn perpetrators of violence. Mehr's autobiographic novel *steinzeit* (Stone Age, 1981) is particularly representative of this "cathartic" function of writing. The title refers to the implications of loneliness and the lack of love and human kindness she experienced as a child. She tries to convey the devastating consequences of hatred and violence through prose charged with expressionist intensity. Mehr's literary language is intentionally disjointed and ungrammatical, as if to mirror the dismantling of the protagonist's ego, whose identity is split into three personae ("silviasilviosilvana"). She presents herself in the following way:

> In my Jenisch mother tongue, I am a Jenisch; according to the language of racial hygiene and in anthropological science [I am]: homeless, asocial or carrying the legacy of an asocial and homeless stock, that is, a vagrant, one of those sub-humans, pernicious, morally deficient, incapable of social integration, a day's thief, notoriously idle, weird, worthless, work-shy, sexually deviant, socially dangerous, a psychopath who belongs to that scum that Hitler outlawed and neutralised. My sisters, my brothers and I were even deprived of our name, the name of our people, Jenisch.[41]

This self-destructive process starts when little Silvia asks her doctor who her real parents are and is told that her mother is a prostitute and an alcoholic and her father a misfit. Because of this lie, Silvia is unable to identify with a positive role model and is effectively cut off from her real family and her ethnic roots, which makes her even more isolated and vulnerable to abuse. Silvia grows into an adult (Silvana) who is an alcoholic, addicted to drugs, unable to integrate socially, depressed, anguished, rebellious and out of control. The sequence of violent episodes scarring her life is presented through the fractured perspective of "silviasilviosilvana". From this perspective, events are juxtaposed without any logical relation, the only underlying connection being the violence perpetrated against the protagonist at different stages of her life. This narrative strategy enables the author to distance herself from such traumatic events and give voice to the silenced perspective of the traumatised, while at the same time undermining existing literary and linguistic norms.

Sandra Jayat

The search for individual freedom is the main theme at the root of Sandra Jayat's poetry. Born in Italy in 1938 to a Sinti family, she later moved to Paris where she began a highly successful career as a painter and poet.

Clearly, her work as an artist has influenced her writing. Jayat's art is centred on her perception of colour, which she uses as a symbol to represent her state of mind. Her writings celebrate key cultural aspects of Romani culture, such as the central role of music, and are characterised by the search for musical effects through rhyming, repetition and the use of onomatopoeic expressions. Other important themes in her work are travelling and the love of nature. These key components are all found in her semi-autobiographic book *La longue route d'une Zingarina* (1978), in which she describes the flight of a fifteen-year-old Gypsy girl who refuses to accept her arranged marriage and travels on foot from Italy to France in search of a different life. The price she has to pay for her freedom is a life on the margins of both societies. Although the author does not refrain from exposing the difficulties encountered by her protagonist, her main emphasis is on the possibilities for female self-realisation.

One of Jayat's collections of poetry, "I Was Not Born To Follow", is at the same time a strong statement of ethnic pride and an affirmation of her personal worldview:

> They have imprisoned pure water
> In multiple plastic
> [...]
> They have put in plastic
> Paper flowers artificial flowers
> While man breaking out
> Waits for the law of nature
> Perhaps in the middle of a cry
> A dream dies like a bird
> A tree falls on time
> And grass bursts out of stone
> So put on your masks in the noise
> You! Who prevent others from living
> Restore to your thoughts
> The feeling of the wild rose
> I was not born to follow[42]

Jayat's poem "The Blue Eagle" is not just a lament for one's alienation and lack of freedom, but also a celebration of human resilience and of a woman's insuppressible will to live, underscored by the threefold repetition: "I exist [...]", "I exist [...]", "I exist [...]":

> I have washed so much sorrow in the river
> That the clear water cannot flow
> I have taken so many steps for friendship
> That the trees begin to bow

I have pulled so hard on tomorrow's arm
That the earth burns to exhaust me

I exist my friend
I exist in the storm
I exist outside the cage
Of my friend's scorn

I have hunted the eye of solitude so far
That my eyes strip the vision bare
I have gnawed freedom's fingers so often
That I have taken pen to escape
I have struggled for us to ignore our sex
Till I dance to the rhythm of defiance[43]

Jayat's work portrays Romani women as independent characters with a strong sense of justice. They refuse to accept a subordinate role in society and take full control of their lives, regardless of the consequences. This is far removed from the stereotypical view of Romani women as victims of their own culture. It also differs from the self-representations of other Romani female authors, such as Ceija Stojka and Philomena Franz, whose personal struggle is inextricably bound to (and, to a certain extent, obscured by) the dictates of collective experience. It is arguable that for Jayat the use of writing is ultimately the result of a double act of defiance: defiance against the conventions of the majority society that silences and marginalises the Roma's voices, and against those of her own ethnic group. In fact, Romani women writers often reveal and criticise aspects of their culture that are usually kept hidden from the majority, thus violating the strategy of invisibility widely adopted by their fellow Roma in an attempt to reduce the risk of cultural assimilation.

The texts of Romani female authors analysed above reveal to the reader that women in Romani society are often denied the right to have aspirations and hopes of self-realisation. Women's hopes and claims are probably doomed to remain unfulfilled, but the very fact that they have been formulated is highly significant. In a world dominated by the overarching Roma/non-Roma opposition, Romani female authors contribute to casting some light on a reality that has so far been silenced. They demonstrate that the unrelenting conflict with the non-Roma is not the only problematic issue affecting the life of the Romani people: these poems reveal that an even deeper conflict lies at the heart of Romani society, a conflict that, despite being silenced through the forceful imposition of male authority, remains unresolved.

What is the contribution of female writing to the resolution of this conflict? What kind of alternatives does female writing provide to male-dominated patterns of Romani identity? Women's strategy is not to merely openly challenge male authority, for this would surely lead to their expulsion from the group. Rather, they aim at circumventing social conventions and behavioural constraints through literacy and writing.[44] This negotiating process manifests itself in different ways and has different implications depending on the group in question. For some women, writing is a way to negotiate between their inner self and the strict control that the group imposes on their ideas and behaviour (as in the case of Slovenian-Croatian Romni Nada Braidic, who will be discussed in Chapter 8), ultimately leading to a positive encounter with the non-Roma. For authors such as Luminița Mihai Cioabă, writing has become a rewarding profession, a successful strategy for carving out her own autonomous space within the group.[45] In the specific case of Paula Schöpf, writing has exacerbated the conflict between personal and collective identity, but has also granted her a deeper awareness of the suffering that characterises the human condition. This restructuring of the individual consciousness through writing is particularly relevant to the study of Romani literature as a whole.

CONCLUSIONS

The analysis of the main thematic *foci* of Romani literature has highlighted some of its crucial features, which can be summarised as follows:

- Romani literature is firmly anchored in social reality and deals with issues of contemporary relevance, such as enduring anti-Roma violence and racism and the continuous attempt to control and limit Romani nomadic practices.
- Romani literature is chiefly concerned with the consequences of the conflictual relationship between the Roma and non-Roma, which is characterised by a high level of inter-ethnic conflict. Within this relationship the Roma, in that they are a voiceless and marginalised minority, occupy a subordinate position. To a certain extent, writing helps shift the balance of power within this relationship by providing Romani authors with a voice in the public sphere and enabling them to challenge misleading images and anti-Gypsy stereotypes. This use of writing, which can be defined as counter-hegemonic, paved the way for a more political use of writing among the Roma (see Chapter 7).
- As the case of Romani Holocaust writers has revealed, many Romani authors regard the act of writing as a duty and a moral obligation.
- Generally speaking, Romani literature promotes reflexivity and self-awareness, both at an individual and a group level. In the particular case of Romani women authors, alphabetic writing has provided them with a vehicle to express their alternative cosmologies and, to a certain

extent, to overcome and renegotiate limitations and restrictions on their freedom.

Finally, Romani authors are engaged in trying to reinstate elements of Romani history and culture that have been forgotten or misrepresented. By re-presenting these elements, Romani authors rewrite them and, in a way, "reinvent" them as part of an alternative conceptualisation of Romani identity.

6 Theorising Romani Literature
Literary Categories and Textual Strategies

By virtue of its long history and cultural heritage, Romani literature potentially has a strong claim to inclusion in the canon of European literature. Yet the Romani presence within the European literary scene has been neglected and marginalised. There have been few sustained attempts at theorising Romani literature, which is usually perceived as not "canonical" enough to deserve critical attention.

Among the key factors that continue to hinder the recognition of Romani literature outside Roma communities are material and structural factors internal to the Romani writing system and extrinsic factors directly related to the features of the literary canon. Structural factors include the scattered and limited diffusion of Romani texts, whose publication is mostly due to isolated, sporadic initiatives by associations promoting knowledge of Romani culture among the non-Roma.[1] In addition to such structural limitations, however, other, less evident motivations lie behind the critical neglect of Romani literature.

One of the main reasons why Romani writing has essentially been invisible to the eyes of the non-Roma is that nobody expected it to be there at all. The use of writing for literary purposes, in fact, clashes with deeply ingrained stereotypes of Gypsies as primitive and uneducated. Even when the existence of Romani texts has been acknowledged, they have not been regarded as an object of study for the literary critic, but as belonging to the domain of the folklorist or anthropologist. More generally, the "literary ostracism" affecting Romani literature is interlinked with the Western graphocentric perspective of non-literate societies as intrinsically deficient in literary capacity, or exclusively confined to the domain of the oral (oral literature being perceived as "less prestigious" than written literature).[2] Furthermore, the classification of Romani literature as non-canonical is due to the internal structure of the literary canon itself. As John Guillory argued, there seems to be a "structural homology" (Guillory 1987, 483) between the configuration of the dominant canon on the literary level and social dynamics that have the effect of excluding minority groups from hegemonic discursive practices. In other words, the structural features of the literary canon reflect the unequal distribution of power within society and promote the cultural hegemony of the majority group while marginal-ising minority writing.

Whatever its root causes, the critical neglect of Romani writing has resulted in a lack of suitable theoretical tools for analysing this literature. The aim of this chapter, rather than devising new tools to achieve a com-prehensive critical reading of Romani literature, is to explore what existing concepts and theoretical tools may best contribute to its study. The chap-ter begins by looking at three cognate literary approaches: the "ethnic", the "migrant" and the "minor". The basis for comparing Romani writ-ing and literatures by ethnic, migrant and minor authors is that they have all emerged in comparable social and cultural circumstances. They are all products of what Mary Louise Pratt calls "contact zones", that is, zones characterised by inherently asymmetrical power structures, where different cultures "meet, clash and grapple with each other, often in highly asym-metrical relations of domination and subordination" (Pratt 1992, 4). They all deal, to various extents, with issues of hegemony, empowerment and resistance to cultural assimilation, and they all entail processes of media-tion and negotiation of cultural meaning.

After assessing the applicability of these theoretical approaches to study Romani literature as a macro-category, the chapter explores the usefulness, at the textual level, of notions of linguistic deterritorialisation, hybrid-ity and intertextuality. The concept of hybridity, due to its emphasis on processes of crossing-over and creative borrowing in situations of cultural contact, is particularly well suited to describe the structural and textual features of Romani literature.

ROMANI LITERATURE AND THE ETHNIC PARADIGM

Romani literature can be productively compared to so-called "ethnic litera-tures", a label used extensively in the North American context to include writing by Black American, Native American, Asian American, Chicano/a and Italian American minorities.[3] Ethnic literature is literature "written by, about or for persons who perceive themselves, or were perceived by others, as members of ethnic groups" (Sollors 1986, 243). Connected to the notion of ethnic literature is the idea of "ethnicity", a term coined in the early twentieth century that initially had a pejorative connotation, denoting an ontological notion of otherness. In the latter half of the twentieth century it came to define cultural difference conceived in a non-hierarchical, construc-tivist fashion (Barth 1969; Glazer and Moynihan 1971; Sollors 1986, 1989; Hall 1996). Following the "constructivist turn" in the conceptualisation of ethnicity, a sort of consensus has formed that the writer's ethnic identity should not be regarded in essentialist terms, as a form of group affiliation determined by birth and common ancestry, but as a socially constructed narrative of belonging, a kind of "collective fiction" (Sollors 1989, xi).

With reference to the particular case of Italian American literature, Anthony Tamburri (1991) has identified the main functions fulfilled by ethnic literature. "One of the goals of ethnic literature", writes Tamburri, is:

> To dislodge and debunk negative stereotypes [about the ethnic group]. In turn, through the natural dynamics of intertextual recall and inference, the reader engages in a process of analytical inquiry and comparison of the ethnic group(s) in question with other ethnic groups as well as with the dominant culture. In fact, it is precisely through a comparative process that one comes to understand how difference and diversity from one group to another may not be as great as it initially seems; indeed, that such difference and diversity can not only co-exist but may overlap with that which is considered characteristic of the dominant group. (Tamburri (1991, 13)

In their writings, ethnic authors often express their ethnic difference through an attitude of resistance to the literary conventions and typologies at the heart of the Western canon. Even when these authors seem to conform to dominant literary modes, they retain a culturally specific focus by giving prominence to local histories and traditions.

At first glance there seems to be some basis for subsuming Romani literature under the "ethnic" category. First, both Romani and ethnic literature refer to a situation of sustained oppression and social discrimination to which minority groups are subjected. Both literatures emerged from a hostile environment where ethnic groups are involved in a struggle for political and cultural legitimation. They both have to deal with what Maria Lauret (2001, 7) defines as the historical "burden of representation", which is largely accountable for their political edge and subversive potential.

In a context in which minority ethnic voices are marginalised and excluded from hegemonic discursive practices, literature may provide alternative avenues of self-expression. This explains why writers from oppressed ethnic minorities view literature as a sort of "elective homeland", that is, as the symbolic repository of what is at risk of being erased in the process of forced integration into mainstream society. In such cases writing equates to a performative act of affirmation of the writer's self against the dominant group's attempts at minimising and homogenising the ethnic difference in its midst. This is why much of these writers' efforts are devoted to the process of "naming" or defining themselves, rather than simply accepting the image imposed on them by the dominant group. This self-defining act provides a complex representation of the minority group, highlighting the dynamism and internal variation inherent in the ethnic culture.

Of central concern to authors of ethnic literatures is the question of "voice" and, more specifically, the suppression of the ethnic minority's voice in the public sphere. The absence of a recognised voice is precisely what motivates a large number of Romani poets in their literary efforts. A poet who is also a Gypsy, wrote the Hungarian Romani poet Károly Bari, has a moral obligation to speak for his/her own people. He/she has the duty to preserve the cultural memory of his/her group's language and traditions, especially when their existence is threatened by the dominant group. Among the Roma, Károly Bari argues:

> The "writer with a mission" remains a potent ideal; poets are still seen as leaders of people, with programmes to save an entire nation [. . .] this is the only way [the Romani poet's] works can have any impact, the only way he himself can be regarded as the real thing. [A poet] is duty bound to acknowledge the essence of his communal heritage, especially if it acts not as an impediment, a barrier, but as a source of inspiration, an aid to the imagination. (Bari 1997a)

Another important aspect shared by both Romani literature and so-called ethnic literatures is the important role they attribute to oral history and traditions. On the one hand, the preservation of the group's oral heritage has a conservative function—that of contributing to the cultural survival of the ethnic group—while serving an important pedagogical function in informing readers about little known cultural traits of the ethnic group. On the other hand, by providing an insider's view on their own culture, ethnic writers may help to challenge the conventional way in which the dominant group tends to conceptualise minority cultures, forcing the reader to reassess and revise previously familiar identity categories. This view "from the periphery", as envisaged by Tamburri, may in turn trigger a reassessment of the way the "centre" (i.e., the dominant group) conceptualises itself in relation to minority cultures.

There seems to be sufficient ground to classify the literature of the Romani people alongside other non-canonical ethnic literatures. Nevertheless, categorising Romani literature as "ethnic" raises a number of problems. "Ethnicity" and "ethnic identity" are notoriously difficult concepts to define. The label "ethnic" is often applied to minority literatures as if ethnic identity were somehow self-evident and almost "transparent". Thus, ethnic literature is still approached as a mimetic rendition of the writer's ethnic identity, and his/her literary efforts are perceived as little more than autobiographical realism. However, the ethnic writer does not simply "mirror" reality—whatever this may be—but provides a textual reinterpretation of this reality in the hope of transforming it. Ethnic literatures cannot be dismissed as "social realism" as they do not amount to an "authentic, unmediated representation of ethnicity" (Palumbo-Liu 1995, 12). It is also important to note that not all authors commonly defined as "ethnic" deal necessarily with "ethnic themes". As John Reilly points out, "authors can and do elect to write literature in which they do not embed statements about ethnicity at all, so there is nothing inevitable about the ethnic burden carried by the structures of literature" (Reilly 1978, 4). Reilly argues that the presence of ethnicity in ethnic literature should be interpreted as a matter of strategy, not only of identity. He reminds us that, whereas identity "can be assumed without reflexion", ethnicity entails a conscious choice, a "*statement* of identity" (Ibid., 3). Finally, it is worth emphasising that when writers do choose to feature ethnicity in their writings, they do so in a variety of ways. As we have seen in Chapter 5, "Gypsiness" is not always portrayed in the same way. Romani authors may opt for a representation of their identity in traditional celebratory terms, they may choose to portray themselves as victims of the non-Roma or they may choose to be active in addressing oppression and discrimination by producing counter-narratives of Romani identity. Romani literature thus cannot be dismissed as mere "protest writing", or as a direct expression of Romani ethnic identity, but should be approached as an affirmative tool for cultural representation that contributes to creating new forms of Romani identities that are not necessarily racialised or politicised.

In short, the use of the ethnic label may lead some readers to oversimplify and unduly homogenise the range of purposes served by Romani literature, which, as we shall see, are not only counter-hegemonic but relate to ongoing identity-building processes within Romani communities. Defining Romani literature as ethnic might also create the impression that all Romani writers exhibit a strong ethnic consciousness, and that Romani writing is an *ex-post-facto* manifestation of Romani ethnicity. Romani literature unquestionably includes a considerable number of texts that can be read as being connected to ethnic themes. This does not mean, however, that the authors' choice to engage in ethnic writing precludes their ability to write literary texts *tout court*. By choosing to prioritise the ethnic component in Romani writing, we run the risk of undermining the efforts of those Romani authors who do not wish to be labelled as "ethnic authors", but aspire to be recognised as authors *per se*, regardless of their ethnic affiliation, and operate within well-established national literatures.[4]

ROMANI LITERATURE VIS-À-VIS MIGRANT LITERATURE

The expression "migrant literature" refers to a literary production that arises from, and is inextricably associated with, the experience of migration. Over the past fifty years, migrant literature, initially located at the margins of the literary establishment, has received increasing critical attention and, to a certain extent, has been acknowledged as belonging to the literary canon (King, Connell and White 1995; Seyhan 2001; Ponzanesi and Merolla 2005; Simonsen and Stougaard-Nielsen 2008).

Migrant literature criticism generally encompasses two main interpretations of the migrant experience. The first interpretation views migration as a cause of loss and displacement and portrays migrant literature as a form of "aesthetic alienation". A second interpretation is based on a positive interpretation of migration as "a mode of being in the world" (King et al. 1995, xv).

A poignant manifestation of the first perspective on migration is represented by so-called exilic and diasporic literatures, that is, literatures produced by diasporic communities from a "perspective of displacement" (Kandiyoti 2009, 38). For these communities, displacement is not a matter of choice, but is often the direct result of expulsion. Diaspora can be described as a (forced) movement away from one's homeland.[5] Likewise, the main theme in diaspora literature is that of the loss of the homeland in which memories of the migrant's former self are rooted. This displacement does not categorically exclude the possibility of a much hoped for homecoming. However, the migrant writer is conscious that he/she will never be able to reclaim the homeland that was lost, but only to recreate a fictional homeland (Rushdie 1991, 10). If the possibility of finding oneself at home in one's homeland has been lost, the migrant writer often laments the impossibility of feeling at home in the host country. The homeless condition of the migrant writer is essentially exilic.[6]

Within the second perspective, the main focus of migrant literature is neither on departure nor on arrival, but on movement and transit. Migrant writing is perceived essentially as writing about borders, and more specifically about the crossing of national and cultural borders. This blurring of national boundaries and fixed identities caused by migration stimulates in the migrant subject/author the search for a new, dynamic identity, a form of identity that "[has] no longer to do with being but with becoming" (Mardorossian 2002, 16). Such a view of the migrant experience is often associated with a postmodern celebration of transnationalism, homelessness and cosmopolitan rootlessness.[7]

The relationship between literature and migration, interpreted as either a liberatory experience or an alienating one, is not transparent, but is culture-bound. It also reflects a sedentary perspective based on the assumption that the migrant will be allowed to embrace a "new" identity in the host country, and that he/she will be accepted. Unfortunately, this outcome varies considerably according to the receiving country's approach to migration, and depends on the time of migration[8] and the ethnicity of the migrant. To put it differently, the successful outcome of what is known as the "migration project" does not depend solely on the migrant's will and intentions, but also depends, crucially, on the host society's attitude towards him/her.

A key aspect of migrant and diasporic identities is their status of "in-betweenness", that is, their being situated at the symbolic intersection between different languages and cultures. Closely associated with the migrant writer's condition of "in-betweenness" are multilingualism and hybridity: migrant literature can be considered as hybrid from both a linguistic and cultural point of view. Although hybridity in itself is not inherently progressive, the hybrid features of migrant writing are often coupled with a high level of artistic experimentation. From their transcultural, transnational perspective, migrant writers are in a privileged position to engage in a powerful critique of host societies and cultures.

Due to their long history of migration, Romani authors ought to be in an ideal position to engage in migrant writing, and their literary creations are often subsumed under the migrant category. Indeed, Romani writing shares several features of migrant literatures as both are centred on movement and characterised by the following features:

- A high degree of linguistic and cultural hybridity;
- a reliance on translation (conceived as both linguistic and cultural translation);
- a sense of alienation and loss for a past way of life (although Romani authors tend to refer to a nomadic past, rather than to a particular homeland);
- the expression of an exilic consciousness;
- the writer's critical awareness of the "invented" nature of his/her identity, which is heightened by the experience of displacement (Rushdie 1991).

Despite the similarities between Romani and migrant literatures, a number of distinctions need to be drawn. First, the Roma's status cannot be simply conflated with that of ordinary economic migrants. It is necessary to emphasise that the Roma have lived among the non-Roma for five hundred years and, while retaining their separate ethnic and cultural identity, they also consider themselves as part of the national community where they reside. Over the centuries, a number of Romani groups (especially in central and Eastern Europe) have been forcibly settled, while those who wish to lead a nomadic way of life are often prevented from doing so: a real paradox at a time of great transnational mobility of people, commodities and capital. In addition, when applied to the case of the Roma, the migrant label is not only a strategy for marking them out as different from the local population, but also to exclude them from their own home countries. This has often led to a situation whereby even Roma who have embraced the linguistic and cultural features of the majority society are still viewed as "foreign" and often mistakenly defined as immigrants.

A second major objection to the inclusion of Romani literature in the migrant paradigm relates to the specific structural features of migrant literature. Critics such as Rose Basile Green (1974) and King, Connell and White (1995) have outlined a developmental model of migrant writing and identified four different phases:

- Testimonial and documentary literature consisting of autobiographies, memoirs, diaries, poetry, songs and oral narratives;
- texts aimed at the immigrant community;

- texts of various kinds, characterised by reflexivity and experimentation with genre and by the attempt at establishing a dialogue with the literary tradition of the host country;
- "post-migration" literature.[9]

This model seems compelling, especially in relation to migration literature in Europe and America. However, it is also highly problematic because it implies that there is a sort of linear development of increasing complexity underpinning migrant literature. Furthermore, this model seems to imply that the first phase of migration writings is confined to autobiographical and documentary texts, and that "genuine" literature should appear only at a later stage. Such a model does not apply to Romani writing, which is extremely varied and characterised by a strong self-reflexive component and a conscious attempt to enter into dialogue with the majority society. In a sense, the development of Romani literature is diametrically opposite to the model outlined above, as it is aimed primarily at a non-Romani readership and only in the second instance at the Roma themselves.

Although the experience of migration plays an important role in Romani literature, it is nomadism, rather than migration, which features at the centre of the Roma's literary efforts. There is clearly a significant overlap between migration and nomadism, but there are also important differences between the two phenomena. As anthropologists explain, while nomadism entails a regular movement from one point to another within a given territory, migration is essentially the act of leaving one's country to live in another.

The nomad and the migrant have radically different perceptions of space. As Deleuze and Guattari point out in their *Treatise on Nomadology*:

> The nomad is not at all the same as the migrant; for the migrant goes principally from one point to another, even if the second point is uncertain, unforeseen or not well localised. But the nomad goes from point to point only as a consequence and as a factual necessity; in principle, points for him are relays along a trajectory. Nomads and migrants can mix in many ways, or form a common aggregate; their causes and conditions are no less distinct for that. (Deleuze and Guattari 1988, 380)

The nomad's trajectory follows a different spatial logic from that of the migrant, as the nomad lives in space rather than moving from place to place.[10] The distinction between the nomad and the migrant is particularly evident from the etymology of the word "nomad", which derives from the Greek *nomos*, for law, and originally referred to a mode of distribution of people and goods "in a space without borders or enclosure" (Deleuze and Guattari 1988, 380). From this point of view, the *nomos* stands in opposition to the *polis*, the city as a space of enclosure.

In principle, both migrants and nomads experience displacement and its effects. The nomad's experience, however, is one of deterritorialisation,[11] whereas the migrant tries to resettle in a new territory (a process called "reterritorialisation"). In the Roma's case, deterritorialisation is absolute as there is an element of coercion to it. For the Roma, migration is seldom a matter of choice. It often takes the form of forced migration due to discrimination, social exclusion and human rights abuses. Roma who would be willing to settle are prevented from doing so and are *a priori* rejected by the members of the sedentary population as the radical "Other".

To sum up, Romani writing should be distinguished from migrant literature because it is more radically deterritorialised. Romani literature arises from a permanent condition of displacement that is closely connected to the treatment of the Roma as a "pariah group".[12] Moreover, Romani literature seems to express a general "poetics of movement", based on a different perception of space and place, which sits in opposition to the sedentarist mindset of the non-Romani population.

ROMANI LITERATURE AS MINOR LITERATURE?

Famously, Franz Kafka defined Czech and Yiddish literatures as "Literaturen der kleinen Nationen", the "literatures of small peoples", as opposed to the "great" or "dominant" European literary traditions. Based on this definition, Deleuze and Guattari categorised these literatures as "minor" literatures.

According to Deleuze and Guattari (1986, 18), minor literature is characterised by three main features: (1) linguistic deterritorialisation; (2) political immediacy; and (3) a form of collective enunciation.

The first feature appears particularly useful to the study of Romani literature. Strictly speaking, linguistic deterritorialisation is the appropriation of a major language by an ethnic minority and, in the case of Romani literature, deterritorialisation is both a necessity and a resource. It is a necessity because, to be heard by the dominant group, Romani writers need to address a wide readership that extends well beyond their own group. Moreover, the strong emphasis placed by Romani authors on counter-hegemonic writing means that Romani texts are largely aimed at non-Romani readers. This explains why so many books by Romani authors are published in non-Romani languages or in both majority and minority languages. In a sense, Romani poets are doomed to be at least bilingual and bicultural. For the Roma—a people living at the margins—continuous shifting between multiple linguistic and semiotic codes is not just a pragmatic necessity, it is a crucial skill.

Generally, Romani writers consider the use of majority languages as an opportunity, rather than an imposition. Writing in majority languages enables them to make themselves "known" to the dominant group, while at the same time challenging and relativising the boundary between the Roma and non-Roma. This implies a continuous manipulation of linguistic borders that also occurs within the text, as can be seen in the following poems:

Atzinganoi: the Greek
(from *Athinganoi*: "heretic")
Zigeuner (German)
(as in: "zig-zag"
as in: "wanders up and down")
Tsigan, Gitane,
Gitano, Gypsy
from *Egyptian*
(as in: "dark-skinned,
foreign, stranger"—
a mistake
appearing first
"the most persistent tag"
in Byzantine poetry)
[. . .]
Synonym: *Roma*
From the Indic *Rom*
for: "married gypsy man"
also their language:
Romany
(the joke: "because we always roam")
[. . .] *Sinti and Roma*
to the Nazis
(as in: numbered, photographed
as in: rounded up and hanged)
—*rom*anticised
Romantic, as in: "not conforming
to classical conventions".[13]

[. . .] When I was twelve year old I wrote
A poem about the sea, and never mentioned boats
But I did mention "Gypsum": It's a stone, a frost-white crystal.
What was Gypsum like? I didn't know back then, I guessed.
But I thought it was crystalline, and, like the sea,
Possessed of a frosty, foamy zest (good guess, I says
To meself, ta-divves- Now, today).
So that's what mandi wrote:
"The shore receives its cleansing Gypsum glaze".
"This works, perhaps, a little obscurely",
Scrawled the jinnapen-mush upon the page
In jinnapen-mush's (oops, "a teacher's") lolli (ah: "red" ink), so you
    would think
He meant it very surely.
I never told him "Gypsum" was a special word for me

Though it comes from Gypsos (chalk, in Greek, you see)
Especially
Because it sounded like the English word "Egyptian"
(And our special, shorter version, "Gypsy")
That refers
In ethnic terms
To me, and to
my family.[14]

These poems are good examples of linguistically hybrid texts within which the dominant language is destabilised through using key Romani words endowed with deep symbolic resonance. On a linguistic level, the juxtaposition of two different linguistic codes has the effect of decentring the majority language. It highlights tensions and ruptures within the hegemonic discourse and constitutes, in Deleuze and Guattari's words, "an intensive utilisation of language".

As maintained by Deleuze and Guattari, the second feature of minor literature is that of being inherently political. As we shall see in the following chapters, much of Romani literature has a political edge. Many Romani authors are committed to denouncing the persistent discrimination and social marginalisation of their people and fighting against the lack of recognition of their linguistic, cultural and ethnic specificity. The role of Romani written literature in the process of political mobilisation of the Roma has proved fundamental. However, this is not to say that all Romani literature is political. For sure, the autonomisation of a Romani field of literature[15] has not yet been achieved, but this is hardly surprising. Being confronted with the constant attempt, on the part of the dominant group, to control and assimilate their group, a large number of Romani authors consider the quest for literary autonomy as intertwined with an active engagement in the political sphere. How can an autonomous field of Romani literature possibly emerge while the Roma are still denied basic recognition as cultural and linguistic minorities? How can the Roma ever aspire to become autonomous writing subjects if they are not recognised as autonomous subjects in the first place? Another important question is whether the political use of Romani writing can be seen as the first step towards its literary autonomisation within the broader field of transnational or "world" literature.

In listing the third major characteristic of minor literature, Deleuze and Guattari state that "in it everything takes on a collective value", and that such literature "produces an active solidarity in spite of scepticism" (Deleuze and Guattari 1986, 17). This position seems to echo the reductive view of ethnic literature as entirely focused on the collective manifestation of ethnic identity. Furthermore, Deleuze and Guattari go as far as maintaining that within minor literature "there isn't a subject; there are only collective assemblages of enunciations" (Ibid.).

To a certain extent, Romani literature seems to fit Deleuze and Guattari's model of "deterritorialised", "minor" literature. However, some problematic aspects of their theory require careful consideration. In particular, the emphasis on the political and collective value of minor literature seems excessive. Implicit in Deleuze and Guattari's claim that everything within minor literature works as a form of collective enunciation is the suggestion that the role of the minor author, as the voice of his/her community, is to minimise the group's internal differences. While it is true that commitment is important to Romani authors, and that many of them choose to deal with collective rather than individual issues, such a commitment does not undermine their right to individual authorship. In particular, the existence of Romani female literature demonstrates how Romani authors succeed in the difficult task of balancing individual and collective claims and perspectives on both Roma and non-Roma societies.

ALTERNATIVE CATEGORISATIONS OF ROMANI LITERATURE

Romani Literature as "Literature with no Fixed Abode"

An alternative definition of Romani literature could centre on the notion of "literature with no fixed abode", which has recently been introduced by German literary critic Ottmar Ette (2003). According to Ette, "literatures with no fixed abode" emerged on the World Literature scene after the Holocaust, produced by displaced individuals with no stable association with a particular national or cultural group. They can be seen as "writing-between-worlds", and are transnational, transcultural and translinguistic systems (Ette 2005, 36). Examples of literatures with no fixed abode include Holocaust literature and diasporic and exilic literatures (Sebald 1997, 2001; Bachmann 1978; Kann 1986, 1998). In view of its transnational and translinguistic features, Romani literature can be included in this literary typology (Kovacshazy 2009). One should bear in mind, however, that for the Romani people homelessness and statelessness are constitutive of their identity as a people. In so far as they are a pariah group, their homelessness is "structural" and therefore Romani literature and culture cannot but reflect this. Perhaps an even more apt category to describe Romani literature is that centred on the notion of "decentralisation".

Romani Literature as "Decentralised" Writing

Displacement and decentralisation are important features of Romani literature and operate at different levels. At the structural level, the decentralised nature of their literature means that it had no synchronous development, but evolved over several periods and was influenced by a range of socio-political factors operating in different geographical contexts. Thus, while in some areas Romani literature has met with favourable conditions to emerge and flourish, in others it has yet to develop fully. Second, no central knowledge of Romani literature is yet available, and currently there are no significant attempts at systematising such knowledge among the Roma.[16]

Furthermore, displacement and decentralisation constitute ongoing processes that are inherent to the formation of Romani literature. As demonstrated in Toninato (2006), such literature relies heavily on translation and on the interweaving of motives and tropes from both major and minor literary traditions. Moreover, Romani literature has been used as a vehicle for cultural translation by Romani authors, who constantly "translate themselves" and their culture to increase knowledge and understanding of Romani cultural practices among the non-Roma and other Romani groups.

Related to the notion of Romani literature as decentralised writing is a relational model of literature. Romani writing is centred on what Édouard Glissant (1997) called a "poetics of relation". It is inherently comparative and committed to dialogism and heterodoxy, which are precisely the principles underpinning other so-called "emergent" literatures.

Romani writing is an example of radically deterritorialised literature within which everything is constantly translated, negotiated and decentralised vis-à-vis the dominant culture. It is a site of syncretic linguistic and cultural practices where the monologic and monolingual features of the dominant literary field are destabilised and new discursive spaces for transcultural dialogue become accessible.

Romani Literature vis-à-vis the World Literature Canon

Another possibility is to look at Romani writing within the broader frame of World Literature (Damrosch 2003; Prendergast 2004; Casanova 2004; Moretti 2005; Piser 2006; Thomsen 2008; D'haen, Damrosch and Kadir 2011). Romani literature embraces the two fundamental principles of world literature: translation and polyglottism (Meltzl 1973, 61). Furthermore, the inclusion of Romani literature (together with American Indian, Aboriginal and other "indigenous" literatures) within the canon of World Literature is instrumental to the creation of a canon that is truly representative of the complexity of our world and that may serve to counterbalance the heavily Westernised version of the canon (Spivak 2003b; Magris 1979; Krupat 1989). Romani literature could inspire a model of literary canon that has no centre and no periphery, no inner hierarchy based on distinctions between "major" and "minor" languages, or between literatures of the First World and "Third World" (Jameson 1986). Within it, borders and boundaries do not cease to exist, but operate as sites of cultural exchange and creative hybridity.

TEXTUAL APPROACHES TO ROMANI LITERATURE: THE NOTION OF HYBRIDITY

The attempt at assessing Romani literature using theoretical macro-categories inspired by the study of ethnic, migrant and minor literatures is certainly a valuable exercise. However, it is equally important to investigate the mechanisms that characterise Romani writing at the textual level, and in doing so the notion of hybridity is particularly useful.

The concept of hybridity is characterised by a long and complex history. It was first used in the biological sciences to describe the cross-breeding of two different species to form a new species. Later, the concept was deployed in philological studies and subsequently "migrated" into contemporary cultural theory. In modern-day postcolonial theory, the notion of hybridity refers to the process of ethnic and cultural mixing that occurs in a colonial context and gives rise to a whole range of new cultural dynamics.[17] Its current use in cultural and literary theory has been influenced by Mikhail Bakhtin's notion of "linguistic hybridity", which he applied to his analysis of the novel as a hybrid site where different voices and languages are set against each other dialogically ("heteroglossia").

One of the main appeals of the Bakhtinian notion of hybridity is its creative and subversive potential vis-à-vis dominant cultural and linguistic structures. The subversive character of hybridity is exemplified by Bakhtin's idea of the "carnivalesque". In his work on Rabelais, Bakhtin describes carnival culture as the "temporary suspension of all hierarchic distinctions and barriers among men and of the prohibitions of usual life" (Bakhtin 1984, 15). The ambivalence characterising the carnival leads to a subversion of established conventions and hierarchies. According to Keith Nurse, carnival:

> Employs an "aesthetic of resistance" that confronts and subverts hegemonic modes of representation and thus acts as a counterhegemonic tradition for the contestations and conflicts embodied in constructions of class, nation, "race", gender, sexuality and ethnicity [. . .]. Carnival is theorised as a hybrid site for the ritual negotiation of cultural identity and practice between and among various social groups. (Nurse 1999, 663)

The subversive potential of hybridity has been further explored by key exponents of postcolonial theory such as Homi K. Bhabha, who developed his notion of "cultural hybridity" (Bhabha 1990b, 1994) to characterise the encounter between colonisers and colonised populations. Processes of cultural hybridisation in the postcolonial context are subversive in that they unleash forms of resistance to colonial authority. They are also considered as highly creative processes, involving the opening up of a "Third Space" or a space "in-between" in which new, hybrid forms of identity are being negotiated. For Bhabha, hybridity is a highly ambivalent condition, which unveils the tensions and conflicts arising from the colonial encounter but also points to new avenues through which the colonised subject is able to subvert dominant discourse through mimicry, repetition and displacement. The notion of hybridity is also central to Stuart Hall's anti-essentialist theorisation of cultural identity (Hall 1990, 1996). For Hall, cultural hybridisation is a crucial mechanism of identity formation characterising diaspora identities, that is, identities that are defined "not by essence or purity, but by the recognition of a necessary heterogeneity and diversity; by a conception of 'identity' which lives with and through, not despite, difference; by *hybridity*" (Hall 1990, 235). In theory, hybridity should pave the way for the emergence of a new consciousness based on a critical self-awareness of identity as constructed through a negotiation of difference (Nederveen Pieterse 2001, 239). According to this critical perspective, borders and boundaries between cultures are always shifting and contingent. The continuous crossing over of boundaries does not produce any particular cultural synthesis, but a temporary syncretic unit: the hybrid cultural text.

Clearly, the concept of hybridity represents an important heuristic tool to analyse the cultural processes triggered by transcultural encounters, allowing one to step away from a purely oppositional definition of the coloniser/colonised relationship and highlight the active role of the colonised subject in reshaping this relationship. Despite its explanatory potential, however, hybridity remains a contested notion. This is mainly due to its biological legacy and enduring ambivalence, which gave rise to a whole range of theoretical aporias. Finally, a serious limitation of the hybridity concept lies in its frequently decontextualised use.

Critics warn us against ahistorical, decontextualised celebrations of hybridity (Young 1995; Werbner 2001; Nederveen Pieterse 2001; Spivak 2003a). They stress the need to approach hybridity in all the complexity of its underlying power structure by including in discussions of hybridity cases of cultural mixing resulting from acts of coercion. Others argue that a macrological approach to hybridity (such as Bhabha's) fails to consider what Gayatri Spivak called the "micrological texture of power" (Spivak 1988, 279). To be theoretically useful, the notion of hybridity requires an accurate contextualisation. In the following section I will therefore focus only on a textual discussion of hybridity within the context of Romani writing.

Within the domain of literary creation, the creative potential of hybridity has been described by Salman Rushdie in relation to his novel as follows:

> *The Satanic Verses* celebrates hybridity, impurity, intermingling and the transformation that comes of new and unexpected combinations of human beings, cultures, ideas, politics, movies, songs. It rejoices in mongrelisation and fears the absolutism of the pure. *Mélange*, hotchpotch, a bit of this and a bit of that is *how newness enters the world*. (Rushdie 1991, 394)

In a work of art, creativity and "newness" seem to arise from a syncretic process of cultural and linguistic *bricolage*.[18] Hybrid texts are characterised by a multiplicity of voices, languages and intertextual connections. Hybridity is not a static mixture, but is transformative and contestative: through their hybrid energy, these texts openly challenge well-established master narratives and problematise traditional notions of the text as a homogeneous, closed system.

At the textual level, hybridity entails a certain degree of agency. A hybrid text is not the passive reflection of the author's multicultural identity: within it, the eclectic mixture of linguistic and cultural elements is not arbitrary but a matter of purposeful selection. In Bakhtinian terms, hybrid texts are characterised by a high degree of "intentional hybridity" (Bakhtin 1981, 358–359). Bakhtin pointed to two different forms of hybridisation: "organic" hybridisation, which is unconscious and unintentional, and "intentional" hybridisation. He defined organic hybridisation as "one of the most important modes in the historical life and evolution of all languages" (Ibid., 358). Organic hybridity is the "mixing of various 'languages' co-existing within the boundaries of a single dialect, a single national language, a single branch" (Ibid., 358–359). Bakhtin distinguished this form of hybridity from the "conscious", intentional hybridisation, by which "two points of view are not mixed, but set against each other dialogically" (Ibid., 360), a process whereby a form of "double consciousness" is created.

I will refer to Bakhtin's notion of intentional hybridity to describe the dialogic mixing of different literary forms detected in a number of works by Roma, and link the notion of hybridity to that of intertextuality to study Romani cross-cultural texts.[19] Following Terry Eagleton (2002, 3), it is possible to distinguish between two main usages of intertextuality: a traditional, conventional usage, which corresponds to literary influence, and a postmodern meaning, as formulated in particular by Julia Kristeva (1981) and Roland Barthes (1968). The crucial distinction between the two lies in the role attributed to the subject/author as far as the authorial intention in the writing process is concerned. While the conventional interpretation of intertextuality-as-influence presupposes "conscious" quotation, in the postmodern rendition of the concept—exemplified in its most extreme form in Barthes' essay "The Death of the Author"—writing becomes an end in itself, a "tissue of quotations" (Barthes 1977, 146), thus relegating the author (and the socio-cultural context where he/she operates) to a secondary role. My approach to intertextuality occupies the middle ground between these two positions. I regard Romani intertextuality not as the direct, mechanical influence of one text upon another, but in terms of cross-cultural interference (not necessarily conscious) and (mostly conscious) hybridisation between different texts.[20]

Hybridity and Intertextuality in Romani Literature

Within Romani literature, intertextual hybridity takes a variety of forms. First, intertextuality operates as transposition of the oral tradition into written literature ("intersemiotic" hybridisation). In this case, hybridised are not just texts and motifs from the oral tradition but also oral modes of narration. Second, intertextuality concerns texts borrowed from both Romani and non-Romani literary traditions and subsequently hybridised ("intertextual" hybridisation *tout court*).

As for the first form of intertextuality, Romani literature (especially at the time of its first appearance in Western Europe) is characterised by the coexistence of different semiotic systems. The transposition of Romani oral texts into written form was largely carried out by the non-Roma (see Chapter 4) who first gave impulse to the transcriptions of autobiographical and fictional narratives and lyrical ballads. These early texts, most of which were meant for oral performance, may be considered as semiotically hybrid. Later Romani texts display another, less straightforward form of hybridisation between the oral and written modes.[21] Such texts, aimed at challenging misleading images and anti-Romani stereotypes, are characterised by a dialogic structure and are studded with direct forms of address, rhetorical questions, widespread use of indexical terms and frequent examples of hyperbolic language.[22] Finally, one may observe the presence of ordinary, colloquial language in the texts, which is an attempt at decentring and subverting dominant modes of literariness conventionally associated with poetic language.

In the two poems presented below the use of the oral mode fulfils a number of different textual functions. The degree of verbal violence conveyed in these texts is a direct echo of the violence suffered by the Roma and serves as a powerful denunciation of the lack of intercultural communication between the Roma and non-Roma. In this way, such texts, presented as monologues in which the authors vent their impotence and frustration, seem to re-enact the problematic features of the Roma/non-Roma relationship. Despite their predication on an oppositional structure, these texts often reveal, on closer examination, an underlying dialogic pattern structured around the counter-punctual interplay between two conflicting points of view. The following poems by Charlie Smith and Mansueto Levacovich are clear examples of this dialogic pattern:

> Up go the barricades, barricades of hate
> Tall wire fences with barbs atop
> Rubble and clay piled high
> Concrete posts block all ways
> Deep deep trenches, mounds of earth
> Defend this land this pleasant land
> Green and pleasant land
> Land of the free
> This land of democracy
> Beware the invaders—free-loaders
> Plagues of drop-outs, riff-raff
> Work-shy, didikois—Gyppos

No space, no space to stop round here
Spoil our views, caravans, children, dogs
Polluting our lands with their presence
Man the barricades of hate
How much does it cost to dig the ditch
Build the fences, tip the rubble.
How many sites could have been built[23]

Gagio, and you *gagi*,
you who follow our way
preaching love and peace
without really knowing what they mean.
We, the Rom, are humiliated and persecuted,
beaten up, squashed, tired and hungry.
We beg you to stop.
Our sufferings are many, so many . . .
No Gypsy, no Gypsies.
We are your destiny.
Our ancestors have persecuted your ancestors,
and we persecute you.[24]

The dialogical structure underlying the poems gives rise to a "hybrid" voice whose mixed ethnic connotations are emphasised by the shift of perspective and the use of Romani words (for example the recurrence of the terms *gagio* and *gagi* in Levacovich's text).

Another instance of textual hybridisation is represented by the apparent mimicking of Gypsy images and themes originally produced by the Gadže. Especially prominent among these themes is that of Gypsy nomadism, which constitutes one of the main instances of textual hybridisation in Romani literature. Images of the Roma as "free spirits" and "sons of the wind" are highly evocative of popular stereotypes of Gypsies as the embodiment of free will. This is particularly evident in the following texts:

I, son of the wind
Father of the long journey . . .
The vast plains of grass my back has touched,
the breath of powerful horses
and the sweet song of birds
my ears have heard.
Green trees have guided
my never ending walk,
and waters and lands
and skies and sun
and light and heat

the days I've lived;
a tent was my home:
I felt free![25]

The Gypsies stop only
to die,
because the road is their life.
On the road we are born,
On the road we live,
At the end of a road death
Will catch us.[26]

The texts clearly evoke hegemonic representations of Gypsy nomadism. Can we talk here of straightforward repetition? Is this a case of "unconscious hybridity" or even a form of literary "self-colonisation"? I would rather put forward two possible readings of these texts. First, they can be seen as an example of cross-cultural textual *bricolage*. As already remarked, *bricolage* should not be understood as uncritical borrowing or straightforward repetition (Okely 1999). In other words, when Romani poets reuse and hybridise images originally created by the dominant group, they do not simply replicate such images but rather critically re-examine them and invest them with new meaning. The second possible reading is based on the notion of mimicry, which produces an uncanny feeling in the reader.[27]

Romani poets have skilfully revisited, manipulated and reappropriated stereotypical images of Gypsy nomadism by deploying a wide range of metaphors, anaphoric repetition, alliteration, exclamation and rhetorical questions. The use of these rhetorical devices could be interpreted as a conscious textual strategy on the part of the author to warn the reader against the risk of accepting at face value what is commonly presented as "the Gypsy way of life", thus challenging the widespread aestheticisation of Romani nomadism. At the same time, their texts deconstruct dominant stereotypes of nomadic Gypsies that have no empirical legitimation.[28] The result is a powerful critique of the dominant view on Romani identity.

The final example of textual hybridity discussed here refers to the syncretic encounter between Romani tradition and mainstream literary traditions. I shall focus on examples taken from the body of Italian Romani literature.

Italian Romani authors find inspiration in the oral tradition of their group and in the poetry of other Romani authors.[29] However, their writing is heavily influenced by the Italian literary canon, both stylistically and thematically. By their own admission, even when producing bilingual texts, Romani authors tend to write in Italian in the first instance. However, the Italian literary tradition is by no means the only source of inspiration for these authors, who also draw from a wider European literary canon. Despite this complex intertextual relationship with other literatures, Italian Romani authors rarely acknowledge the influence of any specific author or literary current in their works. Their aim is not to align themselves with any specific school or artistic trend, and instead they seem to deploy intertextuality with the main aim of creating an aura of literariness in their texts. In other words, they regard non-Romani literature as a whole as a source of literary prestige.[30] Nevertheless, it is possible to detect specific intertextual interferences between Romani and Italian literary traditions, and instances of literary "calques" and variations on traditional Gypsy themes. In texts dealing with extreme violence and expressions of grief (exemplary in this regard are the poems devoted to the Holocaust), Romani authors may adopt expressionistic language and the surrealist method of *écriture automatique*. The use of figurative and symbolic language features prominently in texts where authors engage in a sort of dialogue with nature and its elements. The technical features of Romani texts are equally diverse, as free verse is mostly used, together with the prosaic metre, although some authors seem to privilege formal verse such as the sonnet (see Spinelli).

A further instance of textual *bricolage* is provided by Santino Spinelli's poem *Meribbè* (Death):

Never again shall I listen
to the graceful song
of free birds,
nor shall I feel
the familiar warmth
of the fire
on my dark skin;
I shall no longer see
in my carefree life
the joyful light of the white moon
and of the little stars,
and the sweet melody
of the ancient violin
will not comfort my quiet nights around the fire.
It will cross my threshold
and take away my ancient name,
to carry it away
into the eternal, dark nothingness.[31]

Spinelli's text is influenced by Italian pre-Romantic and Romantic poetry. The incipit of the poem recalls the opening line of the famous Zacynthos sonnet *"Nè più mai toccherò le sacre sponde"* (Nor shall I touch again the sacred shores), and in the epilogue there is a clear reference to the Foscolian "*nulla eterno*" (eternal nothingness). The image of the "dark nothingness"[32] taking away the name of the dead brings to mind the closing lines of Giacomo Leopardi's *Bruto Minor*: "*E l'aura il nome e la memoria accoglia*" (Let the wind receive my name and memory; line 120).

In this textually hybrid poem, Spinelli succeeds in blending images arising from the Romani oral tradition—the fire, the violin and the idealisation of nature—with motifs taken from the written tradition: the notion of death inspired by materialistic philosophy and embraced by poets such as Foscolo and Leopardi. By doing so, the author effectively opens up the Romani cultural repertoire to include elements from non-Romani literary and philosophical sources.

To sum up, the notion of textual hybridity provides an appropriate frame for the analysis of Romani literature. Hybrid Romani texts incorporate images and tropes from different literary and cultural traditions, both oral and written and "high" and "low". These texts can be classified along a virtual intertextual continuum. Spinelli's poems occupy the extreme end of this continuum and are representative of texts that draw heavily from canonical literatures. At the opposite end are texts that could be defined as deliberately "unpoetical" and which are often characterised by the insertion of spoken and informal language into the written text. In the latter case, the use of poetic images and rhetorical devices is avoided in favour of realist language, which can be considered as a rhetorical move in its own right.

There seems to be a recurrent pattern underlying the use of intertextual sources by Romani authors. As already remarked, instances of textual hybridisation are more frequent in socially and politically engaged texts. In these texts the non-Roma are often addressed explicitly and act as interlocutors with whom the Romani poet engages in intense verbal exchanges. Moreover, Romani writers carefully select hybrid textual images—especially those allegedly encapsulating the Gypsy way of life—to bring to light controversial issues concerning the Roma/non-Roma relationship. By utilising linguistic and cultural structures that are familiar to or clearly identifiable by the non-Roma, Romani authors are able to "get the message across": in other words, to target readers directly and effectively. From this viewpoint, poetic language is regarded by Romani authors as a specific code to gain access to a non-Romani readership. This important use of literacy as a tool for inter-ethnic communication will be further explored in the following chapters.

How should one reassess notions of intertextuality in light of Romani cross-cultural literary practices? Earlier, we distinguished between two main ways of looking at textual hybridity: a more traditional notion of intertextuality as influence and a postmodern reading of the concept. A close analysis of Romani texts has highlighted limitations in both interpretations. The traditional notion of intertextuality is not entirely adequate in characterising Romani literature because it remains rooted in the idea of a hierarchical relationship between "high" and "low" literatures. Yet as we have seen, Romani authors do not approach canonical texts within a hierarchical framework, but instead freely appropriate—and often subvert—images and motifs of the dominant literary tradition. A strictly postmodern understanding of intertextuality is equally inadequate, as it fails to capture the author's intentionality and the social context in which he/she operates. Instead, a reading of Romani texts in terms of intentional hybridity would enable one to conceptualise them in dialogic terms, that is, as an integral part of the complex relationship between dominant and minority groups of which Romani writing is often an epiphenomenon. It is only by carefully contextualising the textual hybridity detected in Romani written literary production, however, that its creative and subversive potential can be fully appreciated.

CONCLUSIONS

In this chapter we have assessed the applicability of a range of literary concepts and categories to the study of Romani literature. By adopting a comparative perspective we were able to identify several analogies—and a number of important differences—between Romani literature and so-called "ethnic", "minor" and "migrant" literatures. Similar to the exponents of these literatures, Romani authors have a clear choice to prioritise difference and heterodoxy over continuity and orthodoxy. From their seemingly marginal position, these writers are able to circumvent linguistic and national borders, thereby challenging the centre-periphery model of literature. We have also suggested alternative categorisations of Romani literature as "literature with no fixed abode", as "decentralised" writing and as part of the broader *Weltliteratur* system, where Romani literature occupies a position comparable to that of American Indian, Aboriginal and other "indigenous" or "emergent" literatures.

What is peculiar to Romani literature is a poetics of movement, which is inextricably linked to the Roma's nomadic *Weltanschauung* and the radically deterritorialised features of Romani writing. Furthermore, Romani authors embrace an outsider's perspective towards more "canonical" literary traditions. This has two main implications. First, these authors produce texts that are less bound by the canon and instead based on a free interplay (*bricolage*) of literary themes and motives originating from both Romani and non-Romani traditions. Second, in their texts Romani authors often challenge the canon by openly opposing traditional Gypsy stereotypes. In view of these peculiar features we have argued that Romani literature should be seen as inherently comparative and characterised by an all-pervasive deterritorialised structure.

To conclude, existing theoretical categories are methodologically useful in the study of Romani literature, but they should not be rigidly applied.

In particular, the definition of Romani literature as *a priori* "political" is problematic as it overlooks the complex textual and linguistic strategies adopted by Romani authors. A closer analysis of the texts has revealed that, from their interstitial position, Romani writers do not simply oppose majority culture but are able to dialogise it from within by critically appropriating elements of the dominant culture and rearticulating their meaning. This particular textual approach can be seen as part of a wider political use of Romani writing, which will be the focus of the next chapters.

Part III
The Politics of Romani Writing

7 The Political Use of Romani Writing and the Rise of an International Romani Intelligentsia

The political use of writing is a relatively recent phenomenon among the Roma. It is interconnected with the formation of an international Romani intelligentsia and the rise of Romani political organisations. The first evidence of political mobilisation among the Roma can be traced back to Eastern Europe at the beginning of the twentieth century. At that time there was no coordinated Romani political movement as such. Over the past few decades, however, the field of Romani politics has gradually evolved into a global phenomenon.

A main precondition for the emergence of Romani political writing has been a rise in literacy levels among the Roma. Although most of them continue to rely heavily on the oral medium, this chapter demonstrates that alphabetic writing is spreading beyond the domain of a Romani literate elite and being used for a diverse set of purposes. The chapter opens with some remarks on the Roma's cultural attitudes towards writing before it distinguishes the two main uses of Romani writing for political purposes, which are associated with the academic and political spheres.

As the chapter emphasises, Romani activists and academics are able to "reappropriate" the field of Romani studies through writing. Their texts enhance the credibility of works written by Roma within the academic community and provide a major source of legitimation for their political struggle. Furthermore, the political use of writing by Romani authors constitutes a means of talking back at the dominant group and reclaiming "ownership" of their Romani identity. In doing this, the aim is to overcome the paradoxical situation whereby the only real Roma accepted and recognised by the dominant group are the fictional Gypsy characters that populate European art and literature. Besides challenging and deconstructing anti-Gypsy stereotypes, Romani writing and the Romani language in particular play a major role in the current identity-building process and in establishing a diasporic Romani nation.

TERMINOLOGICAL ISSUES

Before proceeding, a few remarks on the terminology used in this chapter are in order. Expressions such as "Romani intellectuals" and "Romani intelligentsia" require clarification, as they are not universally accepted by the Roma. In particular, they regard the term "intellectual" as biased by a Western perspective, a view confirmed over the course of several interviews I have carried out over the years with Romani writers who are reluctant to embrace the denomination of intellectuals.

The term intellectual is considered typical of Western societies, where it refers to highly educated individuals devoted to some kind of abstract mental activity, rather than of non-Western, so-called "traditional" societies, which tend to be characterised by a less complex division of labour. This study adopts an anthropological definition of the intellectual, encompassing any individual engaged in the preservation, transmission and critical appraisal of his/her cultural heritage. Based on this broader definition, Romani teachers, scholars, journalists, artists, writers and poets could all be defined as intellectuals.

The term "intelligentsia", originally derived from the Latin word *intellegentia* (from *intellegere*, meaning to perceive or understand), is borrowed from Russian (in mid nineteenth-century Russia the term was used to describe a small educated minority particularly active in the public sphere). I use this word in a broad sense to refer to an organised international movement of Roma devoted to the study and transmission of their culture and traditions. The term intelligentsia is increasingly being used by Romani activists in their self-definitions.[1]

Finally, the definition of Romani writing as "political" requires explanation as Romani political writing can be distinguished as "political writing" *per se* and as "political use" of writing. Romani political writing includes the writings by activists that form a major part of their political engagement. These publications are characterised by a "mobilising-rallying function" (Matras 1999, 496) and are committed to the political struggle of the Romani people. Romani writing for political purposes in general is a broader phenomenon, which may include not only writings by activists but also by Romani authors and academics. Clearly, Romani academic writing is not *per se* political, but it fulfils a political function in aiming to challenge stereotypical and non-scientific views about Gypsies that have hitherto hindered the recognition of the Roma as a group with a distinct cultural and linguistic heritage. Another crucial function of Romani political writing is its use for identity-building purposes, which is particularly prominent among Romani political activists.

In analysing the political use of writing it is necessary to consider the political and social context in which it takes place. Romani writing is fundamentally shaped by a configuration of power relations within which Roma and Sinti are placed in a subaltern position vis-à-vis the dominant group. As a result, writing is viewed by Romani authors as a political act in itself, a means of openly asserting their ethnic affiliation. There is a close connection between Romani writing and recent efforts by Romani activists and intellectuals to claim recognition as an ethnic minority. The "ethnic awakening" of the Romani people (Gheorghe and Mirga 1998, 1) is evidence of an ongoing process of ethnogenesis among the Roma.

The term "ethnogenesis" was introduced in the Romani context by Romani sociologist and political activist Nicolae Gheorghe. He described it as a process whereby:

> A social group, previously occupying a despised and inferior position, moves from this position to some kind of respectability with a sort of equality with other social groups in the hierarchy of social stratification on the basis of a revised perception of their identity. (Gheorghe 1997, 158)

The concept of ethnogenesis highlights the main aspects of the socio-political context where the identity-building process takes place, in particular socio-economic inequality, stigmatisation and discrimination. As we shall see, these issues are—directly or indirectly—at the core of the political use of Romani writing.

THE RISE OF A TRANSNATIONAL ROMANI INTELLIGENTSIA

The emergence of a Romani literate elite operating in the international political arena constitutes a new feature within the Romani social system. To understand the radical newness of this phenomenon it is necessary to contextualise it within the internal power structure of Romani communities. Such a structure is not characterised by a hierarchical socio-economic stratification but rather is fluid and decentralised (Piasere 1986). In her study of the Slovenian-Croatian Roma in northern Italy, Dick-Zatta defined them as "an informal association of nuclear families related by kinship" (Dick-Zatta 1985a, 1–2). Within this "informal association", each nuclear unit enjoys considerable autonomy and may leave at any time to join another group of Roma. It is also possible to characterise the Romani social system as "acephalous", or "chiefless", that is, as a society without a centralised political system (Mair 1962). The absence of a centralised system of authority in Romani society is counterbalanced by internal cohesiveness, maintained by close family ties and strong collective pressure to conform to the group's rules and customs. In the event of a dispute or conflict some key members of the group may occasionally act as mediators, although their role does not grant them any tangible power over the other Roma.[2] It is thus the group as a whole that exerts coercive power over its individual members. Although Romani mediators have no effective authority, they are held in great honour and do enjoy a certain degree of moral authority, which explains why they often act as representatives of their group in interactions with the non-Roma. The social and political role of Romani writers and intellectuals can be compared to that of such traditional mediators, and the socio-political implications of their mediating role will be further discussed in Chapter 8.

The first Romani organisations emerged in the late 1920s in the then Soviet Union.[3] During that period, the first Romani associations were also being established in countries like Romania and Greece. The creation of an international federation of Romani organisations dates back to 1967, when the *Comité international tsigane* was founded. The post-World War II period—especially the years following the fall of the Berlin Wall (1989)—saw the spread of Romani associations all over Europe, and during recent years Romani organisations have grown exponentially throughout Europe (Gheorghe and Mirga 1998; Kovats 2003). Currently, one of the main contributing factors to the rise of Romani activism is the range of Roma-related projects and activities supported by European institutions such as the Council of Europe, the Organisation for Security and Cooperation in Europe (OSCE) and the EU, and the increasing concern in Europe over issues related to minority rights protection.[4]

The first World Romani Congress (WRC) took place in London in 1971 and chose as its president the poet Slobodan Berberski. In addition, some crucial symbols of *Romanestan*—the Romani "nation"—were introduced, including the Romani flag[5] and the anthem *Djélem djélem*, and 8 April (the first day of the Congress) was proclaimed as "International Romani Day". The second WRC—held in Geneva in 1978 and attended by more than one hundred delegates—saw the foundation of the International Romani Union (IRU), a non-profit, non-governmental organisation recognised by the UN.[6] In 1990 the writer Rajko Djurić was elected president of the IRU, while at the WRC held in Prague in 2000 Emil Ščuka (Czech Republic) was elected president. In 2004 the WRC was held in Lanciano (Italy), where Stanisław Stankiewicz (Poland) became the new IRU leader. Stankiewicz was reconfirmed as IRU president at the seventh WRC held in Zagreb in October 2008.

Besides the IRU, another major actor in the international political arena is the Roma National Congress (RNC), an umbrella organisation including several Romani NGOs operating in Europe and beyond. The RNC was founded "to help protect and represent Roma who have become stateless or de facto stateless" because of political transition processes taking place in Eastern Europe.[7] Its main aim is to lobby European governments and institutions to devise effective policies not only for the improvement of the Roma's living conditions but for the protection of their civil and human rights. The group is also active in the political representation of the Roma, and its members argue that the Roma should be recognised as a European non-territorial nation. The RNC was among the first organisations to develop the idea of a European Charter on Roma Rights including freedom of movement, freedom of cultural and political organisation and the right to receive native language instruction and vocational training.[8]

At present, Romani organisations are characterised by extreme fragmentation and a highly diverse nature. According to Bársony and Daróczi, Romani NGOs may include "local or national cultural organisations and clubs; civil rights organisations; political and human rights organisations; national umbrella organisations representing Romani political interests; 'showcase' Romani organisations (created and financed by the state); groups organised on the basis of kin links, representing various interests (including economic) and formations with religious orientations".[9]

The fragmentation of Romani organisations is mirrored in their wide sphere of action, with their scope constantly expanding to include issues such as human rights protection and political representation, and the preservation and diffusion of Romani culture. Romani activists and intellectuals—among whom there are a considerable number of writers—are particularly active in supporting the creation of a common literary language and the establishment of a written literature in Romani. For them, literacy constitutes an indispensable tool to promote the Roma's self-awareness and knowledge of their history and culture. In the school context, as will be seen later, this entails receiving instruction about Romani history and culture in the Romani language.

The Intellectuals' Approach to Literacy and Schooling

Romani intellectuals and activists tend to have a favourable attitude towards the schooling of Romani children. To echo the poet Leksa Manuš, they believe that "strength is in literacy", not in its avoidance.[10] Romani intellectuals are also aware of the potential risks related to the Roma's involvement in mainstream education. This is why most activists argue that it is preferable the teaching of Romani subjects be performed by Romani teachers and Romani teaching assistants, or at least by teachers with specific expertise in Romani culture (ACERT 1993, 149). Romani activist Ronald Lee has expressed this view as follows:

> It is important for young Romani students to be able to learn about their own history and culture. The learning tools they need can only be created by fellow Roma and preferably in the Romani language. This is being accomplished by the growing number of educated Roma.[11]

There are several reasons why specific Romani subjects should be taught by Romani teaching staff. First, as Lee states, Romani teachers have an insider's competence and first-hand knowledge of these subjects—in other words, the relevant cultural capital—which is particularly difficult to achieve due to the overall isolation and marginalisation of the Romani people. Moreover, Romani teachers may set a positive example for other members of their ethnic group who still fear that educational attainment may come at the expense of maintaining one's ethnic and cultural identity. Finally, Romani teachers are in the best position to activate a process of mediation from within Romani communities.[12]

Despite the scepticism that still surrounds the teaching of the Romani language and culture at school,[13] the support of the intellectuals in this regard signals a dramatic shift in the attitude of the Roma towards the non-Roma's educational system as described earlier. The formal school system, which for a long time posed a threat to Romani cultural identity, is now perceived as potentially beneficial. This drastic change of attitude can be explained by the Roma's remarkable ability to adapt to their circumstances. As Hancock wrote:

> It must be remembered that Gypsies have survived by constantly adapting to the changing environment—indeed by staying a couple of steps ahead of the society around them, while maintaining the linguistic and cultural core to which the ethnic identity is anchored. If staying ahead means acquiring literacy, this will be accommodated as needed. (Hancock 2000, 20)

The shift in the Roma's attitude towards the acquisition of alphabetic literacy can indeed be interpreted as an attempt to adapt to recent social, political and economic changes, of which literacy constitutes a central component. However, this change should not be seen as a mechanical response to modified living conditions but rather the result of active cultural processes currently taking place within Romani society, namely the development of an ethnic self-consciousness centred on the idea that the Roma need to take a more proactive public role, and on the understanding that literacy (especially in its form of "critical literacy") may help them in their endeavours.

To conclude, Romani activists regard literacy as a means to achieve autonomy and self-determination. As Matras and Reershemius emphasise, "Romani literacy is now emerging as a function of changing attitudes toward cultural and political needs, trying to promote political and cultural self-organisation in the various countries and in Europe as a whole [. . .] and it correlates with nationalist or rather with civil rights activities" (Matras and Reershemius 1991, 110). Given the strong connection between writing and activism, our definition of the intellectuals' use of literacy as "politically engaged" seems justified.

Instances of engaged Romani writing include academic writing and strictly political writing. In what follows I will first concentrate on the work of a number of Romani scholars who for some time have committed themselves to Romani cultural politics and the field of Romani studies.[14] I will later discuss instances of Romani writing that are directly linked to the current ethnic awakening of the Romani community.

THE CASE OF ROMANI ACADEMIC WRITING

As seen in Chapter 1, since the late fourteenth century written and visual representations of Romani groups have drawn on a number of recurrent Gypsy stereotypes, some of which remain part of the collective imagination of contemporary Western societies. A central factor in explaining the rise and diffusion of such stereotypes is the general lack of information about the Romani people as an actual ethnic group. Gypsy myths and stereotypes are in fact not built on first-hand contact with the Roma, but derived mainly from books and other written sources regarded as authoritative. However, this cannot be the only reason for the persistence of Gypsy myths. According to Romani intellectuals, the root of these myths is the deeply ingrained belief that Gypsies are a secretive group, a belief that, as Hancock explains, has itself become a myth (Hancock 2002, 65). The result of this process of fictionalisation has been, as Ralph Sandland cogently put it, the colonisation of the real by the hyper-real and the consequent "death of the referent", that is, the reality of the Romani people themselves (Sandland 1996, 387). Claiming the right to name and define who is a "Gypsy", the non-Roma have confined the Roma to a fictional image. This is exemplified by the careless use of the word "gypsy" (with the lower-case letter), instead of the word "Gypsy" (with a capital "G"), not to describe the member of an ethnic group but simply to add an exotic flavour to a work of fiction.

After being displaced for centuries into a fictional world, the real Roma have become invisible on the socio-political stage, while their Gypsy persona seems to have acquired a life of its own. The fictionalisation of Romani identity has led to the paradoxical situation whereby some Roma and Gypsies find it necessary to point out that the Roma are a real people:

> When I am asked if I am a "Real Gypsy" my answer is this: I am flesh and blood, I feel pain, I feel joy, I love, I hate, cut me I bleed, I am a real human being living in today's world who happens to be a Gypsy. Not some stereotype that fits misinformed peoples' ideas of what a Gypsy should be.[15]

The displacement of Romani identity is a widespread cultural practice that has devastating consequences for the Roma population. In some cases it culminated in the demotion of the Romani people to a "subculture" or a people who have embraced "a nomadic lifestyle".[16] Perhaps the most severe consequence of the symbolic displacement of the Roma has been their erasure from official history. A case in point is their exclusion from official accounts of the Holocaust.[17]

A number of Romani academics have devoted their efforts to unmasking and deconstructing persisting Gypsy stereotypes. In particular, the scholar Rajko Djurić is concerned with the different manifestations of Gypsy stereotypes in European culture.

Rajko Djurić

According to Djurić, the prominent role played by fictional Gypsy characters is evidence of the deep fascination of European society with regard to
the Roma through the ages, and more specifically points to the legacy of
Romani culture within the body of European literary and artistic heritage.
However, he also emphasises that these images are too often the result of
a distorted representation of Romani identity. Djurić praises writers such
as Cervantes, Pushkin and Lorca for having positively contributed to combating anti-Gypsy views (Djurić 1993a). Nonetheless, he acknowledges
that non-Romani authors in general were not immune to the influence of
stereotypes, prejudice and inaccuracies involving the people from whom
they drew inspiration. In fictional works, the roles played by Romani
characters are usually limited and confined to the category of the exotic.
Particularly in the works of Romantic authors, the Roma are invariably
portrayed in a way that reflects the popular image of the Gypsies as fas-
cinating wanderers of the world, leading a poor but happy life, endowed
with extraordinary musical and artistic talent and whose women possess
an irresistible, sensual beauty.

Djurić views the Gypsy theme not only as a literary motive, but also
as a socio-historical and cultural phenomenon. He points out that "prejudices expressed in a literary work, regardless of its autonomy, are never
neutral from an ethical point of view" (Djurić 1996, 58). Once they have
been given aesthetic form, stereotypical images may become a vehicle
for racist and nationalist ideologies. Despite (or rather because of) the
presence of such dangerous stereotypes, Djurić encourages the Roma to
become active readers of European literature and specifically to acquaint
themselves with the manner in which their people have been portrayed
in literary works with a Romani inspired theme. As *homines lectores*,
argues Djurić, the Roma would be in a position to read textual representations with a Romani theme critically. Such a critical reading would
not only offer them the opportunity to uncover and denounce cases of
anti-Gypsism within the body of European literature, it would also enable
them to see themselves through the eyes of the non-Roma and, in some
cases, provide them with an important source of information on how
the situation of the Romani people in Europe has evolved through time
(Djurić and Courthiade 2004, 115). For this reason, non-Romani literary
texts—even when they are openly biased—should not be ignored or dismissed. Instead, such texts should be approached as constitutive of a possible dialogue to be established between the Roma and non-Roma. The
knowledge acquired from reading non-Romani literary works on Gypsies,
Djurić maintains, can in fact be used "to get to know one another better
and favour improved understanding between the Romanies [. . .] and the
majority" (Djurić 1996, 60).

Ian Hancock

In addition to uncovering and deconstructing the main Gypsy stereotypical images in non-Romani culture, Romani academics investigate the socio-political dynamics underpinning such images. Ian Hancock, Professor of Linguistics at the University of Texas at Austin, argues that Romani identity has always been at the centre of a power struggle between the Roma and non-Roma, and that the latter have so far monopolised the Romani image for their own benefit. He argues that a reappropriation of this image is necessary to bring some measure of reality to Romani identity:

> It has always been the case that non-Gypsy specialists have attempted to control and define Romani identity. [. . .] In order for things to change, the Gypsy image must be deconstructed, and a more accurate one put in its place—in the bureaucratic structures as well as in the textbooks.[18]

Hancock's work is devoted to investigating the extent to which anti-Gypsism permeates European culture, and he analyses how anti-Gypsy stereotypes and attitudes were instrumental in legitimising the centuries-old persecution of the Roma. In his book *We are the Romani people/Ame sam e Rromane džene* (Hancock 2002) he rejects misleading appellations (such as "Gypsies", *Zigeuner, Gitanos, Zingari, Heiden, Cigani*, etc.) with which the Roma are labelled. He insists on using the term "Romani" ("Romanies" in the plural) to restore the dignity of the Roma as a people:

> The first thing to remember when interacting with Romanies is that we are a people just like you. When the slave owners said we didn't feel pain as much as you do, and that we could stand the cold much better than you do, and that we valued life less than you do, they were wrong. When cartoonists depict us as preferring to live in filth, they are wrong; we feel the same pain and joy and fear as you, we want the best for our children, and we want a comfortable home—just like you. (Hancock 2002, 91)

Hancock's rewriting of Romani history involves a number of scientific approaches that include sociolinguistics, history and genetics. His writings aim ultimately at establishing a unitarian sense of Romani identity. During the 1980s Hancock developed the notion of *Jekhipè* (oneness), the idea that, despite their differences, all Romani groups share the same history, similar cultural traditions and a common language (Hancock 1987). In his view, the history of the Romani language provides the necessary evidence to prove the Indian origins of the Roma. For him, it is the Indian-influenced traits characterising Romani populations worldwide—above all their language—that are the most powerful catalysts of a common

Romani ethnic identity and that should be recognised by the different states where the Roma live, in particular by the school system.

Santino Spinelli

Musician, singer and songwriter, but also poet, teacher and member of the *Centro studi zingari* (Centre for Gypsy Studies) of Rome, Santino Spinelli (pen name "Alexian") is a leading exponent of the international Romani intelligentsia. In 1990 Spinelli established the cultural association *Thém Romanò* based in Lanciano, Chieti (Abruzzi). His interests and activities are concerned with the study of Romani literature and culture, especially the Romani musical tradition. He has also been a member, between 1991 and 2004, of the Pedagogic Group for the Education of Gypsy Children in Europe.[19]

There are three main aspects of Spinelli's work: his artistic endeavour, his political engagement and his production as a writer and academic. Spinelli taught Romani language and culture at the Universities of Trieste and Chieti, and his main publications include the books *Prinčkaránǧ/ Conosciamoci* (Getting to Know Each Other, 1994), *Baro Romano Drom* (The Long Romani Road, 2003) and *Rom, genti libere* (Roma, Free Peoples, 2012).

Similar to other members of the Romani intelligentsia, for Spinelli the Romani language is the main instrument to establish the truth about Romani history, "outshining the darkness of mistaken beliefs and assumptions" (Spinelli 2003, 34). He admits that reconstructing Romani history is a difficult task, mainly due to the lack of written documents and testimonies, but he also states that "a 'true' history [of the Rom, Sinti Manouches, Kale and Romanichals] will never exist unless they write it themselves, analysing the documents written by others about them" (Ibid., 7). In his books, Spinelli documents the increasing number of bans issued against the Roma since the sixteenth century, highlighting that the Romani people, who "did not arrive in Europe either with hostile intentions, nor with weapons in their hands [. . .] were forced to live in hiding and were deprived of any rights" (Ibid., 37–38). This led to a situation of social marginalisation that persists today. Spinelli devotes particular attention to the forgotten Romani Holocaust. He denounces the fact that the memory of this event has been intentionally removed from history, and warns his readers against ongoing forms of oppression and persecution against his people, which are more subtle but not less harmful as they are based not on physical violence but on misinformation and ignorance.

So far, Spinelli argues, the Roma have chosen to adopt a strategy of "passive resistance" vis-à-vis the dominant group. Such a strategy is based on the strengthening of bonds of kinship and group solidarity, and on the preservation of Romani language and culture, but it can involve resorting to thieving, lying and self-marginalisation. This is why, regrettably, this strategy of self-defence has worsened conditions for many Roma. Spinelli maintains that it is crucial to provide the public with accurate information about the Roma to overcome the barriers that have hitherto prevented constructive communication between the Roma and non-Roma (Ibid., 64). Against the traditional strategy of passive resistance and social invisibility, Spinelli embraces a strategy centred on cultural exchange and reciprocal knowledge. From this perspective, the work carried out by Romani activists in their attempt to battle ignorance and prejudice is crucial. As Spinelli maintains:

> The Romani *Intelligentsia* is growing, rising out of the darkness of silence with the firm intention of affirming the Romani voice with pride and courage in response to the dual stimulus of constructive confrontation, on the one hand internally, within the Romani world, and on the other hand externally, with sensitive, receptive Gadj[e]. (Spinelli 1997, 11)

Within this logic of "reciprocal confrontation", the mutual exchange of knowledge between the Roma and non-Roma constitutes a real alternative, a "third way", as Spinelli defines it, "through which Gypsies will be active and fulfilled within majority society without losing their culture, and which falls between the paths of self-marginalisation and assimilation" (Spinelli 1997, 11).

Vania De Gila-Kochanowski

Vania de Gila-Kochanowski (1920–2007), whose literary work was discussed in Chapter 4, was a Romani activist who established himself as an authority in Romani studies. He authored a number of books, including *Parlons Tsigane* (1994) and *Précis de la langue romani littérature* (2003, co-authored with Huguette Tanguy and Jean Mégret).

Kochanowski used his work to "debunk public opinion" and "restore the offended dignity of the Gypsies" (Kochanowski 1994, 23). According to him, the key to explain the present condition of the Roma is to be found in their past. As Kochanowski remarked, despite the great amount of research being carried out on Romani topics (by both the Roma and non-Roma), no serious attempt has yet been made to explain the historical reasons behind the persecutions suffered by the Roma in Europe:

> At all congresses and meetings of Gypsies and non-Gypsies, organised by Gypsies or non-Gypsies, I have repeatedly pointed out that none of the authors of the incredible number of books and articles written on the recurrent persecution and attempts at extermination of the Romanies, particularly in Western Europe, has taken the trouble to offer valid reasons for these persecutions and to propose workable solutions that would bring them to an end. (Kochanowski 1983, 13–14)

In his work Kochanowski aimed to fill this significant gap. Consequently, he investigated the historical and sociological root of the persecution of the *Romané Chavé* by non-Romani authorities, in particular the Church. He argued that, despite the fact that they were accepted by the European aristocracy and lived "fundamentally in accord not only with Christianity but with every religion in the world" (Kochanowski 1983, 13–14), the Roma in Europe were subjected to a witch-hunt carried out by ecclesiastic authorities based on accusations of heathenism and sorcery.

Another major focus of Kochanowski's research was reconstructing the origin of the Romani people. Like Hancock, Kochanowski retraced the migration routes taken by the Roma on their way out of India using linguistic and historical evidence (Kochanowski 1968, 1990, 1994). He argued that, against common belief, the Roma were not originally a pariah group from India but had for centuries been members of a warrior nobility, the Rajputs. Upon their arrival in Europe, however, the Roma *became* a pariah group through the imposition of "impossible" or "unacceptable" conditions and obstacles (such as the protectionist attitude of the guild masters) that ultimately prevented their successful integration into European society.

Kochanowski's investigation into Romani history is inextricably linked to the attempt to stimulate a sense of critical self-awareness among the Roma. In this respect, his academic efforts have a deep political significance. He urged the Roma to "look around and understand" the true nature of the policies adopted by state and church authorities towards them, and tirelessly reminded them of the dangerous implications of the denial, on the part of the non-Roma, of their real origin, stating that "peoples who don't have a past cannot pretend for the future" (Kochanowski 1981/1982, 25).

THE POLITICAL WRITING OF ROMANI ACTIVISTS

The second instance of Romani writing analysed here consists of the political writings of Romani activists. These include texts written in Romani and other languages, including political periodicals, internet publications, pamphlets, statuses, political manifestos and various official publications. Such writings are instrumental in nature and serve the explicit political purposes of spreading ideas and facilitating mobilisation. At the same time they serve to establish a sense of common belonging among Romani groups previously isolated and under-represented. To put it in Benedict Anderson's terms, they help to create "unified fields of exchange and communication" (Anderson 1983, 44) that enable members of dispersed multilingual communities to communicate with each other via the written word and to become part of the same "imagined community". In this respect, Romani political writing is linked to a specific political project: the awakening of a Romani national consciousness.

Initially, the political project of forming the Roma into a nation seems contradictory. As already seen, the Roma and Sinti are widely dispersed ethnic groups who appear not to constitute "one people" and are scattered across the world. This great dispersion of Romani groups, in conjunction with their deterritorialised way of living, has recently led a number of Roma to formulate their pan-Romani identity as diasporic.[20]

What are the main components of diasporic identities? According to the widely quoted definition proposed by William Safran, the key components of the classical diaspora paradigm are:

- Dispersal from a homeland;
- collective memory of the homeland;
- lack of integration in the host country;
- a "myth" of return and a persistent link with the homeland. (Safran 1991, 83–84)

The Roma undoubtedly share some crucial features of the classical diaspora model. As already remarked, they are a widely dispersed and internally varied group (see point 1 of Safran's definition), and their great dispersion is mirrored in the inner diversity of the Romani language (Bakker et al. 2000; Matras 2002) and in the variety of terms and ethnonyms used by Romani groups in defining themselves. Furthermore, the Romani diaspora is characterised by a difficult relationship between Romani communities and their host countries (see point 3 of Safran's definition). Despite these shared elements, however, diaspora scholars emphasise that the Roma also lack some key diasporic features, such as a strong link with a homeland[21] and, crucially, a strong diasporic consciousness.

It is certainly true that the condition of being widely dispersed does not necessarily entail the development of an awareness of living in a diasporic condition, and this can be said of the Roma. However, in recent years we have witnessed the rise of autochthonous diasporic discourses,[22] especially among Romani activists and intellectuals.[23] The emergence of Romani literacy in combination with the growing use of writing for identity-building purposes is a major factor behind the establishing of recent Romani diasporic discourses. Romani scholars and writers in particular play a fundamental role in initiating and promoting diaspora discursive and political practices. They aim at fostering a sense of belonging to a common diasporic identity, and to achieve this they promote the notion of Romani diasporic unity.

The following poem by the Romani political activist Jorge M.F. Bernal[24] illustrates the path of progressive *prise de conscience* that leads from diasporic condition to diasporic consciousness:

I am a Rom, I have always been aware of that,
and a Kalderàs since I was born,
I also knew this.
But there were a lot of things I did not know,
I saw a Bojas, I thought he was not a Gypsy, to me he was a gagò;
I met a Spanish Rom, I mistook him for a gagò,
I met a Rom Xorxanò, I despised him.
What kind of language did they speak?
Where did these people come from?
Are we Rom, Xitanuria, Romà
or Ludàr?
We are nobody.

The preceding text describes the negative consequence of diaspora, which is synonymous with displacement, isolation, marginality and, ultimately, identity loss. Scattered among the non-Gypsies and increasingly threatened by vexing policies and a lack of communication, Romani groups face a constant threat to their unity as a people. This negative side of diasporic identity evokes the traumatic experiences associated with the Jewish and the Black diaspora. However, there is another aspect of the diasporic experience to which the poem seems to refer:

I was a fool
I did not want unity,
I did not accept my people.
What have you done? Did you expel your brothers
When we are the same people?
Ashkenazi, Sefardites!
North-South, up-down!
Oh Manuśa, I will never do it again!
We are Roma, remember!
I have learnt that we are the same people.
I have learnt what I did not know.[25]

Here the author hints at a higher level of unity among the Roma, a unity that, although it may not be immediately evident, can be achieved regardless of inter-group differences. This sense of common identity, the poem seems to suggest, needs to be constantly reaffirmed to foster a sense of self-awareness among the Romani people. Within the text such self-affirmation is marked by the shift from the first person used at the beginning of the poem (*I* am a Gypsy) to a collective "we" (*We* are Gypsies!), and through emphatic repetitions ("my people", "we are Roma", "we are the same people"). This performative act of self-determination is precisely what lies at the root of the political project aimed at establishing a Romani nation.

Building the Romani Nation

Djélem djélem lungone drômènsa
Maladílem báxtale Rromênsa
Ái Rromale, kátar túmen áven
Le tsêrènsa báxtale drômènsa
Vi-man sas u bári familíya
Thai mudardya la E Kali Lêgíya
Ái Romale, Ái Shavale
Áven mánsa sa lumiyáke Rroma
Kai putáile le Rrománe dróma
Áke vryámya, úshte Rrom akána
Ame xutása míshto kai kerása
Ái Rromale, Ái Shavale.

I have travelled over long roads
I have met with fortunate Roma
Oh Roma, from wherever you come
With tents along fortunate roads
I too once had a large family
But the Black legion murdered them
Oh Romani adults, Oh Romani youth
Come with me, Roma of the world
To where the Romani roads have opened
Now is the time—stand up, Roma!
We shall succeed where we make the effort
Oh Romani adults, Oh Romani youth. (Lee 2005, 197)[26]

The idea of a diasporic Gypsy nation was first introduced by Ionel Rotaru, a Romanian-born writer (known in France as Vaida Voevod, the "supreme chief" of the Romani people) who called it *Romanestan*: the "country of the Roma". In 1959 he founded a Romani group, the *Communauté Mondial Gitane* ("World Gypsy Community", later called *Comité International Tsigane*), which relied on "a nucleus of followers among French Kalderaš and Yugoslav Roma living in the *bidonvilles* of the capital" (Puxon 2001, 95). Rotaru tried to finance his project with the help of German war crimes reparations that never materialised. At one stage he demanded land near Lyon from the French government on which to establish Gypsy villages. In another initiative he pleaded with the UN to allocate territories in Somalia for the Gypsy state and even issued his own passports for the future state (Hancock 2002, 119–120). The idea of *Romanestan* was reintroduced in the 1970s by the activists who organised the first WRC, which was partially financed by the Indian government. In 2000 the IRU issued the *Declaration of a Nation*, a document of great significance calling for the recognition of the Romani people as a "non-territorial nation":

Individuals belonging to the Roma Nation call for a representation of their Nation, which does not want to become a State. We ask for being recognised [*sic*] as a Nation, for the sake of Roma and non-Roma individuals who share the need to deal with new challenges. We, a Nation of which over half a million were exterminated in a forgotten Holocaust, a Nation of individuals too often discriminated, marginalised, victim of intolerance and persecution, we have a dream, and we are engaged in fulfilling it. We are a Nation, we share the same tradition, the same culture, the same origin, the same language: we are a Nation.[27]

The reference in the declaration to the forgotten Romani Holocaust is of particular significance. The Holocaust is considered by Romani activists as the founding event of the Romani nation that, together with the reference to a common language and heritage, is shared by all Roma. As Hancock remarks, the Holocaust unified European Gypsies "like no other factor, not even slavery, has managed to do" (Hancock 1983, 12). In a similar vein, Gheorghe and Mirga (1998) argued that "the experience of the *Porrajmos* played an important role in providing the Romani diaspora with its sense of nationhood". In this respect, Romani activists share the view expounded in Walter Benjamin's *Theses on the Philosophy of History* (1955) that their future imagined community should be based on the memory of the atrocities of the past.

As already seen in the case of Romani academics, Romani activists do not regard the Holocaust as an isolated event but as a particularly horrific episode in the ongoing persecution suffered by the Roma and Sinti. From this perspective, suffering and trauma are invested with a collective symbolic meaning providing a binding factor for the establishment of a Romani nation whose boundaries transcend national political borders.

The Roma's strategy of claiming victim status carries some potential risks. As highlighted by Jennifer Hohschild:

> While claims of victim status may be effective in getting something out of the dominant society and eliciting resources from the state through manipulation of guilt and social responsibility, there is a very real danger that the disadvantaged group may come to believe in them, to internalise victim status as an unchanging reality of life. (PER Report, 1992, 20)

The claims of Romani activists, however, do not focus exclusively on victimhood. Within these claims a dual interpretation of the Romani nation can be detected: one that conceives the Romani nation as bound together by a common experience of persecution and discrimination, and another presenting the Roma as a nation whose members share a common "project identity" (Vermeersch 2001).

While remaining firmly anchored to a past of common persecution, the Romani nation is therefore oriented towards the future. This explains why the IRU's Declaration is also characterised by a deep-rooted utopian vision associated with a particular political project. "We have a dream", maintain the Romani activists of the IRU, echoing the words of Martin Luther King: that of "being recognised as a Nation". The belief that the Roma constitute a nation is not exclusive to the IRU but widely shared by the members of the international Romani intelligentsia and clearly pre-dates the IRU's Declaration of 2000. For example, one of the fundamental principles on which the RNC was established in the 1980s is that "the Roma are a European nation" and that the Roma's emancipation "needs to draw on common roots and common perspectives beyond national considerations, citizenship, group affiliation or country of residence".[28] However, what Romani activists mean by "nation" is not entirely clear.

There is a contradiction at the root of the activists' concept of Romani nationhood. On the one hand, the IRU associates the idea of the Romani nation with structures (a president, a parliament and a government) and symbols (the flag and the national anthem) comparable to the traditional symbols of European nation-states. On the other hand, the IRU endorses a concept of nation that is clearly distinct from the dominant international system and maintains that: "We have never looked for creating [*sic*] a Roma State. And we do not want a State today, when the new society and the new economy are concretely and progressively crossing-over the importance and the adequacy of the State as the way how [*sic*] individuals organise themselves". Here, the activists of the IRU establish a clear distinction between nation and state, thus distancing their political project from a narrow nation-state paradigm.

In that it does not involve any specific territorial claim, the Romani nation to which the activists refer differs greatly from the traditional idea of a nation, which is based on "a definite, compact territorial homeland" (Smith 1994, 188). Rather than being founded on a territorial paradigm, the idea of a Romani nation is based on the idea of a shared language and culture and on the link with a historic homeland. It is thus closer to the ethnic model of the nation as "a community of culture and history, with a bond of solidarity that resembles the familial bond" (Smith 1994, 188).

Amari Chib: The Key to the Indian Origin of the Roma

Narratives of common origin play a central role in forging a group's identity. As Anthony Smith puts it, "'who we are' is a function of 'whence we came' in time and space; character is determined by origins" (Smith 2001, 29). For diasporic groups such as the Roma (and of course the Jews) the notion of shared origins retains an even more important function.

Romani activists are aware of the great symbolic significance of sharing a common ancestral homeland: India. As mentioned earlier, the link with India was officially acknowledged at both the first and the second WRC. The second WRC saw the participation of delegates from India and was characterised by the mutual recognition of the Romani intelligentsia and the Indian government.

Like Romani academics, Romani activists see the Romani language as key to establishing the Indian origin of the Romani people, and they use evidence gathered by researchers in comparative linguistics, physical anthropology and population genetics (Gresham et al. 2001). As established in Chapter 4, Romani is an Indo-Aryan language, a fact known in the late eighteenth and early nineteenth centuries. Romani linguists and historians argue that their ancestors left northern India in the eleventh century or later (Lee 1998; Hancock 1998).[29] They also argue that the study of the Romani language offers clues as to what position the Roma used to occupy within the Indian societal system, although this claim is controversial. Some maintain that the Roma originated in a caste of metalworkers, commercial nomads and musicians, while others support the idea of a warrior origin (Kochanowski 1968; Hancock 1995, 1998).

The historical evolution of Romani provides an indication of the path of Roma migrations through the centuries. In particular, linguistic borrowings help reconstruct the route taken by Romani groups leaving India. What emerges from the historical and linguistic study of Romani migrations is a complex scenario. This complexity pre-dates the migration from India and confirms that the Roma were an ethnically various population from the beginning.[30] Subsequent migrations out of India have increased this diversification, and when the Roma first appeared in Europe they were divided into several groups (Fraser 1995). Over time, as the Roma started to interact with several European populations this fragmentation increased, and the Roma today constitute a mosaic of groups scattered across the world. Romani intellectuals tend to highlight that, despite the inner fragmentation of Romani populations, what unites them is their common Indian heritage, of which the *Romani chib* is the main component:

> It is our speech which is the greatest part of that heritage, and even among those populations whose Romani has been reduced to only a vocabulary, as in England or Spain or Scandinavia, it remains a powerful ingredient in Romani ethnic identity. Today, the Romani language, like the Romani people and Romani culture, remains at heart Indian, despite being modified through contact with others over the years. (Hancock 1998, 18)

The Romani language represents the unmistakable mark of Romani identity, as it can only be learnt directly from other Roma (incidentally, this is why so many Roma are still reluctant to extend the use of the Romani language outside their group). Its very existence is testimony to the resilience of the Romani people who have managed to survive despite being oppressed and discriminated against throughout their history.

THE USE OF WRITTEN ROMANI IN THE PUBLIC SPHERE

If spoken Romani has always been a powerful influence on Romani identity, written Romani has recently emerged as a vital tool in pursuing a higher degree of unity among Romani groups. This political use of Romani has been embraced by Romani intellectuals and activists, for whom Romani is essentially a language of rights and of public debate in the political arena. There are, however, some problematic aspects in the use of Romani in the official sphere. The fragmentation of the Romani language (despite the persistence of a linguistic "core" shared by all speakers of Romani) is at the origin of serious problems of inter-comprehension that have been tackled through a process of standardisation and unification. Such a process is at its root a political process, since Romani activists consider the lack of communication among Romani groups dispersed worldwide as "perhaps the greatest obstacle in achieving political and cultural unity" (Hancock 2010, 118).

The proposal for a common Romani language emerged at the first WRC and led to the inauguration of a Linguistics Commission of the International Romani Union, which had the complex task of standardising Romani. The work of the commission came to fruition when the fourth WRC, held in Serock (Poland) in 1990, adopted the standard Romani alphabet proposed by Marcel Courthiade. This has since been deployed in publications of various nature and purpose (from educational material to linguistic research), but its use is currently restricted to a small minority of Romani intellectuals. Despite these recent codification efforts, the phonetic normalisation of Romani is only a small step towards the creation of a standard language. For the time being, the dominant trend is that of a decentralised standardisation process (Matras 1999) in which Romani speakers may opt for a certain degree of adjustment to local majority languages. This has led to the creation of a multiplicity of Romani writing systems.

The other main issue faced by Romani intellectuals striving to create a common language is that of recognition. As already mentioned, Romani is recognised by the European Charter for Regional or Minority Languages as a non-territorial language that should be covered by special language provision. However, special legislation is seldom applied to Romani and its use is not actively encouraged. Despite this there is ample evidence that Romani is increasingly used in the public sphere, where it acts as "a language of public debate and public negotiation"

(Matras 2005a, 13). This includes the use of Romani as a vehicle of oral communication in formal and semi-formal exchanges at international conferences and public events, and its use in a range of publications arising from these events (e.g., articles, bulletins and periodicals).[31] Although, as Matras observes, the readership of these texts is limited, they fulfil an "emblematic" function (Ibid., 12), demonstrating that the use of written Romani is possible, and enable Romani users to claim a space for themselves in the public arena. A particularly meaningful example of the emblematic value of writings in Romani is that of texts commemorating the Romani Holocaust, such as those placed at Bergen-Belsen and at the Documentation Centre on German Sinti and Roma in Heidelberg:

> I Rikerpaske ap u Sinti de Roma, mare Mulenge, gei weian maschke 1933 de 1945 mardo an u Manuschengromarepen
>
> In memory of the Sinti and Roma, our dead, who were murdered in the Holocaust between 1933 and 1945. (Matras 1999, 496)

At present, Romani is used in a wide range of media, from print to electronic and broadcast media (Halwachs 2011). There are a number of radio and television broadcasts in Romani, which, in countries such as Macedonia and Serbia, began in the 1980s (Friedman 1999; Kenrick 2001). Additionally, Romani is widely employed as a means of communication on the internet (in e-mail exchanges, mailing lists and chat rooms). Finally, Romani is also acquiring new acrolectal functions in the educational sphere.

Until recently, Romani has not been a vehicle of instruction but instead perceived as a hindrance to the education process. As Halwachs remarks:

> It was only in the course of the self-organisation, a result of the Roma's quest for emancipation and of the multilingualism and intercultural awareness which became more important in the second half of the twentieth century as a reaction to migratory movements, that Romani was perceived in an integrative manner—if only in a peripheral way—by the educational establishment. (Halwachs 2005, 162)

Nowadays, the Romani language appears in texts introducing children to reading and writing in Romani (readers/primers, collections of poems and fables, etc.). Teaching materials in Romani are regularly produced in countries such as Romania, and in Austria, Finland, Sweden and Bulgaria. Romani as an object of study and research is offered as part of undergraduate and postgraduate programmes in Romania (Bucharest University) and the Czech Republic (Charles University in Prague),[32] while courses in Romani linguistics have been offered at the universities of Manchester, Amsterdam and Barcelona (Matras 2005a, 14). In 1993 the "Romani-Project", an academic project in Romani linguistics, was launched at the University of Graz, in Austria. The project provides a range of fact sheets and educational material on Romani language, literature and culture, and ROMLEX, a lexical database covering a variety of Romani dialects. In 2006 the Manchester "Romani Project", coordinated by Professor Yaron Matras, was established at the University of Manchester. In 2007 a "Curriculum Framework for Romani" (CFR) was developed to support the teaching and learning of the Romani language in schools across Europe and to provide Romani children with "equal quality opportunities to learn" and "the right to Romani mother tongue tuition and functioning plurilingualism" (Little and Lazenby Simpson 2008, 4).

CONCLUSIONS

Romani writing for political purposes has two main uses, which are associated with the academic and political spheres. The political use of writing by Romani scholars aims to reshape the agenda of the field of Romani studies, which has long been the exclusive domain of non-Romani scholars. In this chapter I have argued that the significance of the work of Romani academics such as Djurić, Hancock, Spinelli and Kochanowski lies, on the one hand, in its powerful critique of anti-Gypsy stereotypes (anti-hegemonic function) and in its identity-building function on the other. Their writings provide the cultural foundations for the development of a political consciousness among the Roma, and encourage them to embrace their own history and cultural heritage. Crucially, by publicly challenging deeply ingrained anti-Gypsy stereotypes, these academics contribute to creating a revised perception of Romani identity among members of the dominant group, thereby promoting a better understanding between the Roma and the majority population.

The second use of Romani writing for political purposes is associated with the Roma's political activism. In this context, Romani writing has a crucial role in the political struggle for the recognition of the Roma as an ethnic group. It makes visible and increases public awareness of the conditions in which the Roma live. As a result, Romani issues are on the political agenda internationally and, although in some cases the Roma are not yet recognised as a separate ethnic group, human and civil rights violations against them are more readily denounced and sanctioned.

There is no denying that Romani writing is still in the hands of a relatively small elite of literate Romani activists. The majority of Roma remain unaware of their efforts or even question the authority of those who claim to speak in their name. Moreover, the use of Romani writing for political purposes is mired in conflicts between traditional intellectuals, who still favour spoken Romani and oppose linguistic codification, and the new generation of Romani intellectuals who use writing daily, mainly in interactions with the non-Roma. Given these conflicts, the extent to which Romani writing for political purposes has already increased awareness of the lack of political legitimation and democratic participation among the Romani people is promising.

8 The Mediating Role of Romani Literacy

At this point we must take stock and reiterate that the field of Romani literacy and writing is expanding. Initially confined to instrumental uses in school contexts and other institutional settings, it now includes literary efforts and Romani writing contributing to debates in the public sphere. Alphabetic literacy has been appropriated by Romani writers, academics and activists for counter-hegemonic and identity-building purposes. As already noted, and within the school system in particular, literacy has been used by the non-Roma as a tool for control and assimilation. However, Romani authors demonstrate that alphabetic literacy can also be appropriated as a tool of resistance to assimilation and, most importantly, as an instrument to overcome tension and conflict.

In this concluding chapter I consider the positive attempts of Romani authors in relation to mediation between the Roma and non-Roma. The argument developed is that Romani writing is a central instrument in the establishment of proper forms of inter-group communication to facilitate mutual understanding. I shall analyse two main areas in which Romani writing acts as a mediating tool: the domain of literary writing by Romani female authors and the use of intercultural literacy practices in the classroom environment.

ROMANI WRITING AS A TOOL FOR MEDIATION: CONFLICT RESOLUTION THROUGH CULTURAL TRANSLATION

Romani writing can be seen as a tool to support communication between the Roma and non-Roma, and in this way it can offer a means of conflict resolution. In socio-legal terms, conflict resolution is a form of managing disputes that occurs either on a bipartite or on a tripartite basis. The most prevalent form of bipartite conflict resolution is negotiation, which is a process involving communication between two parties to reach a settlement through consent. Negotiation usually involves a compromise from both sides and requires a joint agreement. Tripartite forms of dispute resolution differ according to the degree of third-party intervention, and two forms of third-party intervention are particularly relevant to our case: conciliation and mediation. Conciliation is a process whereby parties are assisted by a conciliator who acts as go-between in attempting to reach a mutually satisfactory agreement to the dispute. The role of the third party is merely to facilitate negotiation and encourage the parties to recognise each other's position while appreciating and accommodating their differences. A successful conciliation is one in which the parties themselves are willing to cooperate and reach an agreement that takes into account their respective needs and different backgrounds. In contrast, in mediation the third party plays a more active role and intervenes in the dispute by making concrete proposals that the parties either accept or reject.

The socio-legal notion of mediation is certainly pertinent to our case, but is confined to individual conflict resolution. A cultural understanding of mediation broadens this view to include more generalised forms of conflict, such as those arising in inter-ethnic situations and characterised by tension and a lack of effective communication. Moreover, in the case of cultural mediation there is no conclusive and permanent agreement to be reached. Nevertheless, both processes (voluntary conflict resolution *strictu sensu* and cultural conflict resolution) share common features: they view conflicts as manageable—no solution can be reached without the voluntary, active participation and mutual agreement of all parties involved—and third parties support the disputants without imposing solutions.

In the cultural domain, the need for mediation arises when communication between groups and individuals from different ethno-cultural backgrounds is hampered by linguistic and cultural barriers and power imbalances. An extreme case of cultural conflict occurs in the colonial setting, characterised by an ideology of cultural and racial supremacy on the part of a dominant culture and the use of policies of forced assimilation of colonised minorities. In this context, the unilateral imposition of a cognitive divide separating native "primitive" cultures from the "civilised" colonisers effectively prevents the use of cultural mediation, which requires openness and some form of mutual recognition. Cultural mediation aims to overcome cultural binarism in favour of a dialogic exchange in which both "dominant" and "subaltern" cultures are granted equal status. Most crucially, it is based on a willingness to step beyond the bounds of one's own culture to "understand" another culture. In this context, the role of translation is vital.

In broad terms, translation relates to the transfer of meaning—the word "translation" derives from the Latin term *translatus*, past participle of *transferre*, and literally means "carried across"—from a source language (SL) to a target language (TL). But how are the source language and target language affected in the course of this process? What processes of cross-cultural transformation, and what cross-cultural interference, does this semantic transfer trigger? It is possible to distinguish between four approaches in theorising the processes of translation. For a long time, the dominant approach predicated that the best translation is one that "mirrors" the original text as far as possible. The task of the translator, according to this approach, is to unlock the "essence" of the original text. The emphasis is on the source text, while the target text is considered a mere copy of the original in another language. A second approach views translation as a linguistic transfer from one national context to another. It privileges the target language over the source language and makes the source text conform to the conventions and the style of the target language. This can mean a "rewriting" of the original text (Lefevere 1992), which is "appropriated" for the benefit of the target culture. The translator's efforts are expected to efface any trace of foreignness and "domesticate" the original text.

While the first and the second approaches focus on the linguistic aspect of translation, contemporary approaches privilege cultural over linguistic aspects. Exponents of the so-called "cultural turn" in translation studies (Bassnett and Lefevere 1990) and postcolonial translation theorists (Nirañjana 1992; Spivak 1987, 1993; Tymoczko and Gentzler 2002) emphasise the context in which translation takes place, the importance of issues of power and how these reflect on the translated text. However, these approaches are also limited and confined to textual understandings of translation. What is required is the inclusion of the practical dimension of translation as a mediating tool between source culture and target culture. An important practical context is education, where translation facilitates intercultural exchanges and creative learning. A fourth approach, which will be dealt with later, views translation as a two-way transformative process, one that affects both source and target culture and stimulates a critical redefinition of both.

As discussed previously, mediation is a form of conflict resolution. Unlike mediation, translation is not inherently linked to conflict resolution but can be deployed for this purpose. Translation, if used to transfer cultural meaning, can become a medium for establishing communication and can be used as part of mediation processes to solve inter-cultural conflict. In this context, translation can be conceptualised in terms of "cultural translation" (Asad 1986, 1995) as practised by anthropologists. Cultural translation aims to "explain" the social practices and modes of thought of remote groups in a way that makes them accessible (both culturally and linguistically) to a Western readership. An important methodological aspect of this anthropological process is that it treats the other's culture as a text that can be read. However, critical questions can be raised as to the usefulness of considering traditional societies—often non-literate societies—as "texts". As Asad points out, "society is not a text that communicates itself to the skilled reader", but is rather formed by subjects who are themselves producers—and not simply carriers—of cultural meaning (Asad 1986, 155). Furthermore, members of traditional societies may become aware of textual representations of which they are object and engage critically with such representations by producing alternative self-translations.

As I demonstrate in the following section, the endeavours of Romani writers often entail an act of self-translation, which I propose to define as the outcome of a process of negotiation of meaning across dominant and minority cultures. Unlike the socio-legal notion, in this case negotiation is confined to mental processes in the mind of the writer. Nevertheless, the ultimate goal of both definitions of negotiation is similar. In the case of negotiation in the literary context, the aim is to generate a positive response in the readers and to initiate a dialogue with them to overcome inter-ethnic tension triggered by stereotypical assumptions, cultural misunderstandings and misrepresentations of Romani culture. Moreover, the act of translation performed by minority authors ultimately involves a transformation of the source culture, which becomes an object of conscious scrutiny and criticism. Within this lies the mediating function of Romani literature.

THE ROMANI WRITER AS MEDIATOR

Due to their knowledge of writing and their familiarity with non-Romani communication technologies, Romani writers and intellectuals are natural intermediaries between the Roma and non-Roma.[1] Before we discuss their mediating role vis-à-vis the non-Roma, however, it is necessary to consider the implications of their status as literate individuals on their social position.

First, it is important to state once again that Romani writers are not granted positions of power and authority within their group due to their knowledge of literacy. Far from being an advantage, Romani writers' literacy skills are often the object of disapproval on the part of fellow group members. What is the reason for this mistrust?

Although encounters with the non-Roma are necessary and thus actively sought after by the Roma, they are also regarded as a potential source of assimilation and therefore carefully restricted. This is why Romani individuals who work alongside the non-Roma are regarded with an ambivalent attitude: there is a perceived element of risk attached to their cultural hybridity and their continuous crossing of ethnic boundaries. As Dick-Zatta (1986, 1990) maintained, the Roma believe that relying heavily on alphabetic literacy makes them potentially vulnerable and dangerously exposed to the lies of the non-Gypsies. In extreme cases, the Roma's involvement in writing practices can determine their exclusion from the group, as in the case of the female Romani poet Papuśa,[2] who was expelled from the Polska Roma due to her association with the Polish poet Jerzy Ficowski. It is important to note that in this particular case the reason for the expulsion was not the use of alphabetic writing *per se* but the misuse of her work on the part of the non-Roma to support the Polish government's policy of compulsory sedentarisation of its Romani population. Similarly, the use of writing by Romani intellectuals is not rejected *a priori*: it is its decontextualised and potentially assimilationist use that is contested. It is not surprising, then, that the activities of the Romani intelligentsia, centred as they are on literacy and writing, are often criticised by ordinary Roma and Sinti who advocate a more traditional approach to written communication.

Earlier in this book I referred to the notion of hybridity to describe the structural features of Romani literature, and the textual strategies adopted by Romani writers to oppose anti-Gypsy stereotypes and renegotiate their image. Here, I wish to focus in particular on the socio-political implications of hybrid literary practices and especially on their mediating function. Romani authors operate in a specific social space: the border zone where Romani and non-Romani languages and cultures come into contact. To clarify the social context within which these writers operate, it is useful to recall Fredrik Barth's groundbreaking conceptualisation of the ethnic boundary (Barth 1969).[3] He sees boundaries between cultures not as pre-existing entities demarcating a particular "cultural space" but as something across which contacts and interactions between cultures occur. Thus what characterises boundaries between cultures is their porous configuration. Barth emphasises that these boundaries exist not despite, but through, constant intercrossing. It is precisely a dynamic cross-cultural and linguistic exchange that characterises border writing (Hicks 1991). However, the porosity of the border has its limitations. For example, intercultural exchange taking place across contiguous borders between dominant and minority cultures is hampered by factors such as unequal power relations, social inequalities, illiteracy, discrimination and racism (Pratt 1992).

So far, contact across the Roma/non-Roma cultural border has been confined to a number of ritualised situations and practices, including economic transactions (often carried out by women), dealings with public authorities and non-Roma bureaucracy, and limited school attendance aimed at obtaining basic literacy skills. In other words, this contact has been limited to instrumental purposes and has not led to any substantial cross-cultural exchange. With the advent of a written Romani literature, however, new spaces of cross-cultural dialogue have been created. Like other border writers, Romani writers are culturally well equipped to explore these avenues due to their bicultural and bilingual (or even multilingual) competence.

It is arguable that Romani authors (especially Romani female authors) occupy, to use another anthropological concept, a "liminal" space.[4] They are neither "here" nor "there", but inhabit a hybrid place situated between their culture and the dominant culture. The position of such authors can be interpreted as a privileged site from which they can challenge and renegotiate existing cultural meaning relating to their own and the other's culture. However, it can also be perceived as a highly ambivalent position that carries with it advantages and considerable risks. The intrinsic ambiguity that characterises the liminal subject has been emphasised by Victor Turner, who applied Van Gennep's notion of liminality to the study of the ritual among the Ndembu of Zambia (Northern Rhodesia at the time), with whom he lived from 1950 to 1954. According to Turner:

> The attributes of liminality or of liminal *personae* ("threshold people") are necessarily ambiguous, since this condition and these persons elude or slip through the network of classifications that normally locate states and positions in cultural space. Liminal entities are neither here nor there; they are betwixt and between the positions assigned and arrayed by law, custom, convention and ceremonial. (Turner 1969, 95)

In Turner's view, this status of ambiguity may even engender feelings of fear among members of the social group, feelings that can be defused and neutralised through a complex range of symbolic and ritualised behaviour.[5] As in the case of Romani writers and intellectuals, the activities performed by liminal subjects are often regarded with scepticism or even fear. Besides the risks, however, there are a number of potential benefits to the liminal condition. Through their textual representations, Romani writers manage to make their otherness, that is, their modes of life and their "modes of thought" (Lienhard 1954) understandable to non-Romani readers. In this respect, it could be said that they are engaged in a process of cultural self-translation.

The role of cultural translators is not automatically granted to Romani writers by virtue of their ethnic identity, but there are a number of enabling factors that make self-translation possible. Among these are the acquisition of literacy skills and the ability to "feel at home" in more than one language, while the location of these writers "on the border" is another crucial factor. Self-translation is a deliberate act that requires a reflexive process on the part of the Romani writer. As Anthony Cohen (1998) explains, the act of crossing boundaries implies and stimulates in the individual his/her self-awareness, a kind of deeper consciousness of his/her position. In the case of Romani writers, such enhanced awareness may result in an increased self-reflexive involvement in a redefinition of the image that the non-Roma have of the so-called Gypsies.

Negotiation is a key element in the process of self-translation described above. It highlights the role of the writer as a mediator between different cultures and contributes to define the act of cultural translation as an ongoing attempt at mediating between different cultural points of view. How does this process operate within a text? A poem by Romani author Šemšo Advić may help illustrate it:

> I sit and watch the Gypsy caravans
> it is dark,
> a fire is burning in front of each cart.
> Everybody runs and smiles carelessly.
> You can hear the violins
> playing melancholic Gypsy songs.
> The people who listen are amused
> but they do not know that we, the Gypsies
> in every song we cry

we express our sadness.
They will never know
that they take pleasure from our sadness.[6]

The poet posits himself at the margins of the poetic frame and tries to provide a description of an idyllic scene that is immediately recognisable by a non-Romani readership. In this case, the text presents an image of nomadism that is strikingly similar to the opening scene of one of the most influential texts on Gypsies, Pushkin's *Tsygany*:[7]

Today over the river, long,
They're lodging in their tents, worn out.
Like freedom their night-resting is—
And peaceful sleep the heavens under.
Between the wagons' tired wheels,
Covered with rugs, long-used in wonders,
A fire's flamed. A family's
Preparing, round it, a dinner;
A horse is gazing in the fields,
Is sleeping, free, a teamed bear-thriller.

At first glance, Advić's text seems to reproduce a conventional, romantic interpretation of nomadism based on a number of literary *topoi* largely deployed by non-Romani writers: the fire, the carelessness and cheerfulness of Gypsy life, the melancholic music of the violin. However, by projecting this highly conventional scene onto a poetic frame, the Romani poet is able to detach himself from it, thus uncovering its fictional, constructed nature. Only outsiders (i.e., non-Roma), due to their limited knowledge of Romani culture, are likely to mistake the medium of this representation (i.e., the poetic frame) for the reality beyond that frame (the Roma's suffering). The similarities between the two poems are in fact only superficial. Pushkin's interpretation of Gypsy travelling hinges on a monologic structure (the Gypsies' point of view is absent and the author remains invisible), which generates an essentialist image of the Gypsies as absolute "Others". In contrast, Advić's text dialogises this structure by including the point of view of both the observer and the observed. Through an act of cultural mediation, the Romani poet succeeds in presenting Romani nomadic life in a way that is linguistically and culturally familiar to non-Romani readers, while at the same time encouraging them to acknowledge the point of view of the Roma.

Acting as translators and interpreters of their own culture vis-à-vis the non-Roma enables Romani poets to point to instances of mistranslation of Romani identity and denounce the imbalance of power relations that makes mistranslation possible in the first place. It also enables them to reflect on the cultural politics of translation, and in particular on the use of translation as a tool of cultural assimilation. In contrast with an understanding of translation as a site where the otherness of the source culture is constructed in oppositional terms and subsequently appropriated by the target culture, self-translation in a Romani context is not based on an oppositional logic but relies on a process of cross-cultural hybridisation. Again, the border status of Romani writers plays a crucial role in this as it enables them to shift between different languages and representational repertoires, enhancing their ability to adopt a critical stance and engage in a social critique of the dominant order. This critical act is not only directed at the non-Roma. The critical rewriting of the "Gypsy" image vis-à-vis the majority group may in fact extend to the other side of the cultural border within which Romani writers move. The case of Romani women writers is enlightening in this respect.

The Mediating Role of Romani Women's Writing

Within Romani society, women are border subjects *par excellence*.[8] Their socio-economic role entails a continuous crossing of cultural and ethnic boundaries as they are expected to interact with the non-Roma almost on a daily basis. This generates a permanently displaced identity characterised by a high degree of ambiguity, as Judith Okely has highlighted:

> There is a paradox embedded in the Gypsy woman's role. Within her own society she is hedged in by restrictions, expected to be subservient to her husband and cautious with other men. Yet nearly every day she is expected to go out to "enemy" territory, knock on doors of unknown men. (Okely 1975, 58–59)

On the one hand, Romani women are perceived as "dangerous" by the members of their own group. This is why the symbolic space where they move is limited by a number of taboos and restrictions aimed at protecting the ethnic boundaries against the risks of assimilation implied in the constant contact with the non-Roma. On the other hand, Romani women are regarded with suspicion by the non-Roma, who tend to project onto them a plethora of stereotypical representations centred on their allegedly promiscuous and mysterious nature.[9] As a result, Romani women are caught between two hostile cultures that are unwilling to communicate with each other.

Due to their double marginality (as women and as members of an ethnic minority), Romani women are unable to feel at home in the cultures across which they move. This has at least two consequences: these women are forced to inhabit a symbolic "no-place", a borderline, and this is at the root of their condition of "unhomeliness":

> How can one situate oneself on the border? What kind of space characterises it? In theory, and effectively in practice, borders are neither

inside nor outside the territory they define but simply designate the difference between the two. They are not really spaces at all; as the sites of differences between interiority and exteriority, they are points of infinite regression. (JanMohamed 1992, 103)

However, the borderline status of Romani women presents another, potentially positive, aspect: their ability to operate *across* different discursive practices. The textual manifestation of Romani women's in-between position consists of a "polyphonic" text (Bakhtin 1981) that includes a multiplicity of voices, thus moving away from the rigid monologism of hegemonic discourses.

From her position of "insider-outsider", the Romani woman/writer is able to find alternative ways to express herself and renegotiate her identity through a number of different strategies, as the following example illustrates:

> Romani woman,
> Woman of loneliness,
> suppressed dreams.
> Romani woman,
> Woman of loneliness,
> you dream of being free,
> you only find reproaches
> you do not understand them
> they do not understand you.
> Is there anywhere in time
> a place of your own
> where you can be yourself
> inside and outside yourself?[10]

The direct expression of the female "I" here is partially eluded through its replacement with a generic third person. Such metaphoric displacement is reinforced by the use of abstract images of loneliness and isolation to typify the female condition (e.g., the suppressed dreams, the torn wings and the pairing Woman-loneliness). This textual strategy can also be found in Paula Schöpf's poems, which are dominated by key words such as *amarezza* (bitterness), *confusione* (confusion), *stanchezza* (tiredness) and *rassegnazione* (resignation). Textually, women's direct self-expression is tempered by the referential ambiguity of the enunciating subject and the use of abstract, figurative language. In some cases, however, women writers openly refer to an act of rebellion:

> I went against the tide
> [. . .] I broke free from the bonds
> I broke the chains of customs and traditions.[11]

It is important to point out that Romani women's writing does not focus only on the conflict characterising the experience of Romani women, although this is certainly one of its crucial functions. There is also a constructive function of their writing that should be acknowledged. As already remarked, Romani writers strive to oppose the stereotype of the Roma as a people "without history". In the case of female poetry, their endeavour is not just to shed light on Romani history but also to disclose individual life stories usually overshadowed by collective history. In addition to the history of their people, female poets give voice to another unheard story, a silence that is not the result of a lack of meaning but has been imposed on them by a male-dominated society. It is a silence that carries with it an alternative discourse on the dominant society, as Rasy points out:

> [Women's] silence [. . .] has two faces. [. . .] It is the sign of the impossibility to communicate, and therefore of subjugation to men; but is also a different kind of communication, another way to express herself.[12]

Romani women writers, in being engaged in the exploration of their repressed selves, undermine the Gadže's ethnocentric notion of their group's identity as a compact "whole", within which the individual's identity is replaced by the generic label of Gypsies. In addition, as already mentioned, the use of writing by women contributes to problematise and diversify oversimplified representations of Romani culture as "ethnic" and the view that in so-called minor literature "there are only collective assemblages of enunciation" (Deleuze and Guattari 1986, 18).

To conclude, Romani women authors, due to their double marginality, are able to perform a dual act of renegotiation of their identity. On the one hand, writing—which in Romani society is still a marginal practice—seems to grant them an uncharted territory, a space where they are relatively free to rewrite and symbolically renegotiate their selves away from patriarchal schemes. On the other hand, it enables them to resist the imposition of a faceless, depersonalised identity while also dialogising and renegotiating their difference vis-à-vis the dominant group. Most crucially, Romani women are in a better position to mediate between the Roma and non-Roma than many Romani men. In their daily encounters with the non-Roma, these women are more likely to face the harsh reality of racism and exclusion. At the same time, however, this encounter may reveal an opportunity to establish a dialogue with the dominant group. This is probably why, as we shall see in the next section, Romani women are particularly active in the field of Romani school provision, where their role as cultural and linguistic mediators is crucial.

THE MEDIATING ROLE OF ROMANI LITERACY AT SCHOOL

The other main domain where the mediating role of Romani literacy could play a crucial role is school. In Chapter 1 we saw that literacy practices aimed at the Roma have historically been a site of social struggle. In this section I aim to demonstrate that they can potentially facilitate a productive encounter between the Roma and non-Roma. However, for this to occur, a reconceptualisation of literacy education aimed at the Roma should take place. Literacy activities should be inclusive, flexible, internally diversified and driven by students' needs and specific cultural backgrounds.

The first step towards such reconceptualisation is recognising the power imbalance underlying literacy practices, and how this affects Romani, Gypsy and Traveller pupils. In the formal school environment, asymmetric power relations are replicated through the marginalisation of Romani minorities within mainstream education, and through the exclusion of their culture from the curriculum. Such marginalisation manifests itself in what has been described as the "invisibility" of Romani and Sinti pupils at school, that is, their tendency to withdraw to the margins of the classroom, to remain silent and often hide their ethnic identity. Unfortunately, this attitude is usually dismissed by teachers as an expression of their "difficult" and "problematic" behaviour, when it should instead be addressed as symptomatic of the atmosphere of inter-ethnic tension characterising the wider social context.

Second, it is important not to identify alphabetic schooled literacy as literacy *tout court* to be aprioristically imposed on students. As already emphasised, there is no such a thing as a single literacy, rather a multiplicity of literacies and literacy practices that may vary considerably depending on one's cultural and ethnic affiliation. A pedagogic approach based on such a pluralistic notion of literacy should not regard students as if they were culturally *tabula rasa* or, to use Freire's expression, "empty vessels" (Freire 1985, 30) to be filled with standardised cultural content. Instead, their specific literacy practices should be acknowledged—together with the cultural factors behind them—and form an integral part of pedagogic practice. In other words, literacy should be seen as something that has to be constructed in collaboration with the students through a bottom-up approach.

Third, literacy should not be regarded as a decontextualised technology or a set of techniques (as the exponents of what Street defines as the "autonomous" model of literacy argue), but as a communicative practice that enables social actors to engage in meaningful dialogue. The dialogic potential of literacy is particularly crucial in an ethnically diverse context, where literacy may act as a mediating tool through which different learning styles and approaches can be explored and negotiated. This would give rise to a hybrid literacy space where students from different cultural and ethnic backgrounds interact and actively participate in the learning process.[13] In the following section I will consider two ways in which this space can be created through concrete educational practice: the use of cultural and linguistic mediators and the use of hybrid literacy and intercultural textual practices. I shall focus on the Italian context and pay particular attention to examples of good practice I have observed first hand.

Romani and Sinti Cultural Mediators: The Italian Case

Generally, cultural mediation can be interpreted as a broad notion embracing "understanding, explication, commenting, interpretation and negotiating various phenomena, facts, texts, behaviour, situations, feelings, emotions, etc. between people belonging to different cultures or subcultures" (Irishkanova et al. 2004, 103). In the field of education it may be useful to refer to the notion of cultural mediation as defined in the Common European Framework of Reference for Languages, where mediation relates to the use of language activities to "make communication possible between persons who are unable, for whatever reason, to communicate with each other directly" (CEFR 2001, 14).

Cultural mediators in Italy are generally members of immigrant or minority groups with expertise in Italian language and culture and with some knowledge of Italian administrative structures. They are responsible for explaining school rules and procedures to pupils and assisting them during their first encounter with the school system by providing interpretation and translation. They also assist teaching staff in assessing the background and existing competencies of the students and in gaining useful information about their families. Most crucially, they facilitate meetings between parents and teaching staff and contribute to cross-cultural dialogue.

The work of Romani and Sinti linguistic and cultural mediators is based on the following premises: the acknowledgment of a separate Romani culture, the mutual recognition of the role of the mediator by both Roma and non-Roma, and a continuous process of inter-group interaction. The role of the mediators extends across three main levels (Nigris 1996). On a practical level, they assist Romani children and help them understand precisely what is expected of them and how they can achieve it. They also have a fundamental role in liaising with the families of Romani pupils, providing information about the school, its structure and educational activities. Finally, mediators perform an important educational function.

The first training course for Romani and Sinti cultural mediators was established in 1993, organised by the association *Opera Nomadi* and the Institute of Pedagogy of the State University of Milan. This initiative was a clear response to the Circular Directive no. 205, issued in July 1990, in which the Italian Ministry of Education first introduced the notion of "intercultural education" into the Italian school system. The course was attended by women (12 out of 13 participants), mostly Slovenian-Croatian Romnia, a significant fact that confirms the important mediating function of women and their higher level of scholarisation in this group. After two years, during which the use of mediators was limited to a number of primary schools in the Milan area, this initiative was extended to the rest of the country.[14]

The presence of cultural mediators has had a positive impact on the school attendance of Romani pupils, promoting a positive attitude towards school and learning among the Roma. However, their work presents a number of challenges. While they cannot be expected to solve all tensions and difficulties characterising the relationship between the Roma and non-

Roma at school, their role is multifaceted. They have to perform a difficult balancing act between the needs, fears and expectations of Romani pupils and their families, and the requests and expectations of the teaching staff. This sometimes creates confusion as to what precisely the tasks and duties of a mediator should be. To carry out their work successfully, mediators need to be provided with adequate support materials and specific guidelines, and vitally they need suitable preparation and permanent training.

Despite the difficulties it is worth emphasising that the role of Romani cultural mediators goes well beyond providing valuable help with practical and bureaucratic issues. They carry out a crucial mediating function between schools and Romani communities, helping to foster dialogue between teachers and the families of Romani pupils. Within the school, they mediate between Romani pupils and teachers, promoting successful communication and better teaching provision. Additionally, cultural mediators are in a position to achieve a number of important objectives at a personal level (acquisition of professional expertise, self-esteem), group level (creation of authoritative figures and positive role models for Romani pupils, new jobs, dissemination of Romani culture) and inter-group level (opportunity for the non-Roma to become acquainted with a culture that is often marginalised and misunderstood).

Use of Hybrid Literacy and Textual Practices with Romani and Sinti Pupils: Examples of Good Practice

In this section I shall report on examples of good practice in which the use of hybrid literacy had a positive effect on the learning process of both Romani and non-Romani children. During the scholastic year 2000–2001 I conducted structured and semi-structured interviews and carried out non-participant observation in three primary schools in north-east Italy (in Friuli Venezia-Giulia and in the Veneto region) as part of the wider *Opre Roma* Project.[15] These schools relied on support teachers (*insegnanti facilitatori*) to promote the active inclusion of Romani pupils in mainstream classroom activities. Although they were taught in the general classroom, Romani children attended additional classes aimed at reinforcing their literacy and linguistic skills.

The interviews with the teachers revealed that the main difficulties faced by Romani pupils are evident from the moment they enter the school. For them—the teachers reported—the school environment is extremely unsettling as they are exposed to a range of communicative strategies and behavioural codes very different from their own. In the classroom environment, verbal communication dominates and alphabetic literacy is given priority. Teachers consider the achievement of a satisfactory level of Italian language proficiency as the basis for school success, and the language in which learning occurs is exclusively Italian, which for Romani pupils is often a foreign language.

The spaces used and times allocated for teaching and learning are rigidly organised. Great emphasis is placed on discipline and students are expected to comply with the rules. Such a normative concept of education is centred on the teacher, rather than on the students' issues and needs, and this vision of the school system clearly penalises Romani children and practically "erases" their cultural diversity. As seen in Chapter 2, within the Romani understanding of the education process the child occupies a central role. Conversely, Romani children in the formal school setting are not allowed to establish with their teachers the close, dynamic relationship they long for. Resultantly, they develop a sense of inadequacy that negatively affects their motivation to succeed.

From their first day at school Romani pupils perceive the existence of a gap between themselves and their fellow students, a gap they are unable to bridge because they have not yet attained the necessary cultural tools. Their reactions to this situation are usually described in negative terms by teachers, that is, as "non-participation", "lack of interest" or "lack of understanding" of the surrounding environment. After the initial cultural shock, Romani students tend to "exclude themselves" from classroom activities. One teacher summarised Romani pupils' attitude by defining them as "transparent" children, that is, children who try to make themselves invisible to the eyes of the teacher.[16] In subsequent years, when their knowledge of the world of school has somehow consolidated, this behaviour tends to evolve into extreme isolation or open hostility. Such behaviour is usually dismissed as "deviant", and few educators consider it as indicative of inadequate teaching strategies and/ or a result of the different learning styles of Romani pupils. This cultural misunderstanding triggers a vicious circle whereby teachers adopt a disciplinary approach towards Romani students, insisting that they should first follow the rules of the school and "behave properly". School discipline thus becomes the main objective of educating Romani children, with educational attainment considered of secondary importance.

The urgency to devise teaching methods more conducive to the needs of Romani pupils is seldom acknowledged. This is far removed from the guidelines provided by the New Primary School Programs (*Nuovi programmi didattici della scuola primaria*, 1985), which urged teachers to regard ethnic and cultural diversity not as a "problem" but as a positive contribution to the main goals of the scholastic institution, that is, to value diversity and help children overcome an ethnocentric view of the world. By contrast, and as observed in the case studies of good practice, the presence of Roma and Sinti students at school was welcomed as an opportunity to increase pupils' awareness of different ethnic groups and deal positively with their cultural identity. The focus was not placed on disciplinary matters but on devising specific measures to facilitate regular school attendance and integrate the pupils into the life of the school. Particular importance was placed on learning objectives that could be achieved by both Romani and non-Romani pupils, such as critical self-awareness, socio-linguistic competence and appreciation of their cultural heritage. In addition, further learning objectives were identified for Romani students, such as the consolidation of literacy and oral communication skills and the development of linguistic proficiency in the Italian language. Literacy was placed at the centre of the education process and regarded as a crucial tool for increasing the students' self-awareness. However, literacy activities were carried out in a non-hierarchical fashion, that is, they were moderated, not dominated, by the teacher. The "open structure" characterising these activities enabled students to participate in the learning process and use their existing literacy skills. This was achieved through the adoption of a hybrid understanding of literacy.

Teaching and Learning Romani Culture and Language through Hybrid Literacy Practices

Linguistically hybrid classroom activities included the use of bilingual (Italian/Romani) texts and narratives to which both Romani and non-Romani children were exposed. In this context, Romani students were allowed to

Figure 8.1 Nursery rhyme in Romani. In this activity, the child provides a written description (in Italian) of the meaning of a Romani nursery rhyme: "We use this nursery rhyme when a child loses one tooth: he holds the tooth in his hand, recites the poem, and then throws the little tooth behind him".

Table 8.1   Romani Chib: The Romani Language. Research Project by Romani
Students for their Final-year Exam

OUR RESEARCH
ROMANI CHIB: THE ROMANI LANGUAGE

The language of the Rom has its roots in India. It is divided into several dialects
because each territory crossed by the various Romani groups left a trace on the
language: one can thus find in it words of Iranian origin (concerning travel, strength,
luck, the sea) and words of German, Greek, Italian and Slavic origins [. . .]

We know many languages: together with *romanes* we have learnt the Slavic
language, the dialect spoken in the areas where we stop for longer periods and
finally Italian because of the school. Many of us go to school, but change school
frequently, and it is difficult to learn properly in these conditions. The first words
we have learnt when we were little were in the Romani language, which in a way
forms the basis of all Gypsy languages. These are among the most common words:

Rom	Gypsy man
Romnì	Gypsy woman
Gagio	non-Gypsy man
Gagì	non-Gypsy woman
Dej	Mother
Dat	Father
Chavoro	Son
Chavora	Daughter
Phral	Brother
Phen	Sister
Babo	Grandfather
Grast	Horse
Kampina	Caravan
Lacio drom	good journey

play the role of linguistic and cultural mediators, actively collaborating
with the teacher in producing an Italian translation of the text and providing the basic cultural coordinates to interpret it. The example illustrated in
Figure 8.1 is taken from the project "Italian as L2" for Romani children,
devised and implemented by teacher Paola Gavagnin in a primary school in
the city of Mestre (Venice) in 2001–2002.

The use and production of intercultural material allow Romani pupils
to develop a sense of participation in the school process. By actively contributing to teaching activities, Romani pupils feel they are no longer passive recipients of formal instruction. Moreover, the positive recognition of
the ethno-cultural background of these students is likely to increase their

self-esteem and further develop ethno-cultural self-awareness in the class-room context. In some cases, the Romani language played an important role alongside the dominant language, and it sometimes became a subject of study and research, as the activities carried out by Gavagnin with final-year primary students demonstrate. At the end of the scholastic year Romani students produced a booklet illustrating the origins of the Romani language and its main features. This included poems translated into Italian with facing-page Romani text, sections on Romani history and traditions and a short Italian/Romani glossary (Table 8.1).

A specific section of the booklet reported the students' views on their learning experience at school, again placing particular emphasis on the Romani language and its different uses. This enabled students to develop metacognitive knowledge about their language skills and to assess their progress.

QUESTION: How many languages and dialects can you speak?
ANSWER: I can speak Sinto and Italian, and I understand the *extrex-aria* dialect. I am also learning English at school.
QUESTION: What language do you speak when you are at home with your family?
ANSWER: When I speak to my mum and dad I use the Sinto dialect.
QUESTION: When you are at school, do you have the opportunity to speak your own language? If yes, when and with whom?
ANSWER: At school I speak my language when the teacher is out and during the breaks. I also speak Sinto when I attend the supplementary course, or when I am with my friends.
QUESTION: Did you know that Romani children have difficulty in learning Italian because for them it is a foreign language?
ANSWER: No, I did not know that Romani children have difficulty in learning Italian. However, I think that if they attend school they will be able to learn Italian.
QUESTION: In your opinion, can the fact that Romani dialects are not written make it difficult for a Gypsy child to learn to write in Italian?
ANSWER: I think that if your language is not a written language, this makes it difficult for you to learn to write in Italian.

Hybrid Romani and non-Romani literacy practices were also implemented during the 1990s by primary school teachers in the province of Padua (Dick-Zatta 1992). These consisted of the use of texts taken from the Romani oral tradition, which were transcribed and translated by the pupils themselves. Dick-Zatta described the textual and linguistic analysis of a folktale, *Mro dat i cora hravati* (My father and the Croatian bandits), as particularly successful. The text was studied by both Romani and non-Romani pupils, who were introduced to key aspects of Romani culture and encouraged to appreciate the importance of the oral tradition. Romani children were asked to read, understand and translate a folktale into Italian. The Italian translation of the text was then used by the entire class to initiate a range of reading comprehension activities. The structure of the text was discussed with non-Romani students, together with its stylistic features. Finally, students were asked to identify the sequence of events in the story and illustrate individual episodes through drawing. All of the children, Dick-Zatta reported, welcomed the activities with enthusiasm:

> The reaction of all the children, both Gaje and Rom, was of great enthusiasm, and much importance was given to the fact that the stories are actually true. The material was extremely motivating for the Rom children, and writing exercises based on these stories were always willingly accepted, something that is not always the case. (Dick-Zatta 2000, 206)

Among the specific benefits of the use of Romani texts in the classroom, Dick-Zatta included "an improvement in the usage of Italian especially on the part of those children who show the greatest interference between Italian and

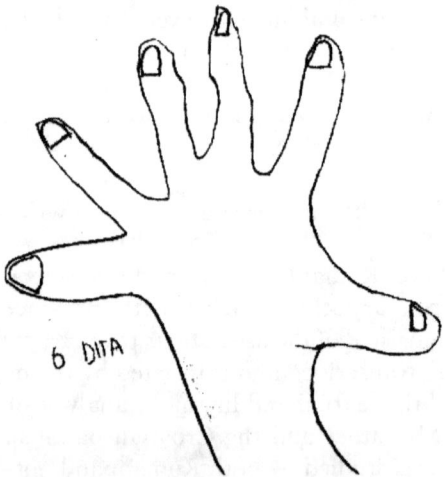

Figure 8.2 Teaching maths to Romani pupils: "What would have happened if humans did not have five fingers?" (Ignazi and Napoli 2004, 121).

Romanes" (Dick-Zatta 2000, 206). This is in line with the experience of bilingual education in California, which showed that "correlations between literacy development in the first language and the second language are high" (Krashen 2001, 111) and that knowledge obtained through one's first language is likely to improve second language usage and understanding (Krashen 1996).

A further example of good practice in numeracy and literacy teaching is provided by the activities carried out by educator Paola Zaniboni. Zaniboni developed a range of materials to teach Romani children mathematical concepts, characterised by a practice-led approach to knowledge and learning (Figure 8.2). She suggests teaching maths to Romani pupils using the same channels and criteria according to which learning is organised in their source culture: usefulness, imagination, dramatisation, closeness to the body and to everyday, concrete experience and reference to the oral tradition (Zaniboni 2004, 114).

What conclusions can be drawn after analysing the examples of good practice discussed above? What factors contributed to their success and what indications can be taken from these examples to improve the learning experience of Romani children? First, these cases of good practice point to the need to expand a narrow understanding of literacy as monolingual and monocultural, and firmly position literacy teaching and learning in the wider social context. This is particularly necessary in a multicultural environment, within which cultural and ethnic diversity should not be stigmatised but instead become the yeast of the learning process. The use of hybrid literacy practices seems to be the way forward, and should be extended into adult literacy education. Hybrid literacy increases the level of participation of minority students, encouraging them to express—rather than hide or suppress—their cultural and ethnic background. This contributes to ensuring their school experience is less traumatic and overcoming their marginalisation within the school structure.

Hybrid literacy practices are not only helpful to Romani students but also enrich non-Romani children, promoting their self-awareness and cross-cultural competence. By engaging in these practices, they effectively contribute to forging intercultural educational competencies. It is in this context that the role of Romani literature could play a crucial part. This is why an increasing number of teachers propose expanding the classroom curriculum to include texts by Romani authors, in line with current guidelines on multicultural and intercultural education.

CONCLUSIONS

This chapter has discussed the mediating potential of Romani writing in two domains: the literary sphere and education. Romani writers in their auto-ethnographic texts reflect critically on both source and target cultures, turning the liminal space in which they operate into a site of cross-cultural dialogue. As for the mediating role of Romani literacy at school, we have examined examples of hybrid literacy practices and activities where Romani children were actively involved in the learning process and their non-Romani fellow students were able to appreciate aspects of their culture that were hitherto obscured by prejudice and stereotype. We have argued that these practices should not be confined to remedial and "special" classes but extended to the general classroom context as they benefit both Romani and non-Romani pupils.

The mediating potential of Romani literacy essentially resides in its ability to bridge different cultures and languages by uncovering continuities and connections between them. As shown in this book, what both the Roma and non-Roma seem to share is an interest in literacy and writing. On this basis, it is possible to identify a common ground where Romani and non-Romani literacy practices act as resources that collaboratively strengthen— and do not undermine—each other. Including the Romani perspective on writing, literacy and education into our literacy practices could function as a catalyst for a range of important social and cultural changes.

In education it is essential to increase the level of communication between Romani families and the school, and to allow a certain degree of flexibility to accommodate the needs of travelling Romani groups. As far as the school curriculum is concerned, it is crucial to acknowledge the centrality of the oral tradition in Romani culture and to integrate into teaching and learning practices the Roma's specific ways of learning. This could mark the beginning of a "culture of collaboration" built through hybrid literacy practices (Gutiérrez et al. 1999a).

At the level of cultural representation, integrating the Roma's textual self-images into our representations of the Gypsies is a crucial step towards the dismantling of the ethnocentric paradigm of the "Gypsy-as-Other" (uncivilised, undisciplined, illiterate). This in turn could pave the way for a process of radical rearticulation of the wider Roma/non-Roma relationship based on a non-oppositional logic, that is, a logic founded on the dialogic encounter of two cultures for the benefit of both Roma and non-Roma alike.

Notes

NOTES TO THE INTRODUCTION

1. The terms "Roma" (pl.), "Rom" (m.s.), "Romni" (f.s.) and "Romani" (adj.) are ethnonyms (self-definitions) used by Gypsy groups, especially in southern/Eastern Europe, while the word "Gypsies" is a derogatory term attributed to the Roma by the non-Roma. In this study the term Gypsy is mainly used in opposition to the Roma's self-definitions; however, the word is also used as an umbrella term to refer to Romani groups in general. Other ethnonyms used by Gypsies are *Romanichals* in England, America, Australia and New Zealand, *Sinti* in Germany, Austria, central and northern Italy and southern France, *Kalé* in Spain and *Manuš* in France. The term used by the Roma to define the non-Roma is "Gadźe", also spelled *Gaje* or *Gage*.
2. In contemporary discussions about literacy, the term "illiteracy" is often replaced with the expression "non-literacy" due to its negative connotation. For a critical application of the notion of non-literacy to the specific case of Gypsies, see Okely (1997).

NOTES TO CHAPTER 1

1. One possible reason why the first groups of Roma were called "Egyptians" (of which the term Gypsy is the shortened form) is that they said they came from what was known as "Little Egypt", a region in the Peloponnese (Fraser 1995).
2. The word "exile" derives from the Latin *extra solum*, which means "outside the (native) country". For an interpretation of the term exile, see Isidore of Seville's *Etymologies* (2006).
3. As for the Jews, people in the Middle Ages relied on Biblical exegesis to account for the diasporic condition of the Gypsies. At the time, the main explanation for the wandering habits of the Gypsies was that they were the victims of a divine curse. In contrast with this belief, see the Roma's reinterpretation of this "curse" as the result of social exclusion (see Chapter 5).
4. The use of safe-conducts and letters of protection—whether authentic or forged—was relatively common among the itinerant population of the Middle Ages, and the Gypsies were no exception to this practice.
5. See Cornerus in Eccard (1723, vol. 2, col. 1225).
6. Sigismund (1368–1437), King of Hungary since 1387, became the official Holy Roman Emperor in 1433.
7. The word *voivoda* means "local ruler".

8. As noted by Fraser, the rendition *waynoda* (spelt with an "n" rather than a "v") is probably due to a mistake in the manuscript (Fraser 1997, 293).

9. Andreas Ratisbonensis Presbyter, *Diarium sexennale*, in Oefelius (1763, 21); English translation by Fraser (1997, 293).

10. On the instrumental approach of the Roma towards writing, see Chapter 3.

11. In medieval times, "ugliness" did not merely represent an aesthetic quality. It was an integral part of the ontological structure of every being, and considered the external manifestation of internal qualities. The classical ideal of beauty was characterised by a close connection between phenomenic reality and transcendental qualities, an ideal encapsulated by the expression *kalos kai agathos* (beautiful and good, contracted to *kalos kagathos*). The Middle Ages inherited this ideal of beauty as closely related to goodness and moral perfection and it was thus based on a moral judgment. Whereas physical beauty was interpreted as a clear sign of the soul's beauty, physical deformity was considered a manifestation of evil. If the Gypsies were defined as "the ugliest people ever seen", perhaps it was because they were subject to some generalised form of moral contempt.

12. The alleged link between the black colour of the Gypsies and their "dirty habits" is confirmed by later authors such as Grellmann, who states that "the dark colour of the Gipseys [*sic*], which is continued from generation to generation, is more the effect of education, and manner of life, than descent" (Grellmann 1807, 13–14). Grellmann also argues that the Gypsies "would, long ago, have been divested of their swarthy complexions, if they had discontinued their filthy mode of living" (Grellmann 1807, 13).

13. Cornerus in Eccard (1723, vol. 2, col. 1225).

14. *Journal d'un bourgeois de Paris (1405–49)* (237). In a later text (Spelman 1626, 239), Gypsies are portrayed as "a people hideously black, burnt by the sun, filthy in their clothing, and dirty in all their habits" (*homines nigredine deformes, excocti sole, immundi veste, & usu rerum omnium foedi*).

15. In opposing this belief, Romani writers tend to portray their blackness in positive terms, and consider the issue of colour as closely related to their social marginalisation.

16. On the magical powers often attached to Gypsies and other marginal groups in medieval and early modern Europe, see Roek (2004).

17. See Genesis (9, 24–25).

18. Due to the terrible sin they had inherited, it was thought that Gypsies deserved to be treated as slaves, a belief that was later exploited as a theoretical justification of slavery.

19. In the Roma's version of this tale (as testified by the oral tradition) the Gypsies remove one of the nails from the Cross, which is why they were allowed to steal with impunity.

20. For more detail on the Roma's occupations through history, see Mayall (1988), Fraser (1995) and Vaux de Foletier (2003).

21. This seems to have happened in France—where a special decree issued in 1682 threatened to strip aristocrats of their lands if they were sheltering Gypsies (Kenrick and Puxon 1995, 15)—Italy (Zuccon 1979), Spain and Scotland (Fraser and Vaux de Foletier 1972).

22. The trope of the deceitful nature of the Roma's practices gained great resonance in Western folklore and literature (from Miguel de Cervantes' *Gitanilla* to Henry Fielding's *Tom Jones*, from Teofilo Folengo's *Baldus* to George Eliot's *The Spanish Gypsy*), and still permeates popular perceptions of Gypsy identity (there is even an English slang term, "to gyp", meaning "to cheat"). It is as *Cerretani* (charlatans) that the Gypsies were increasingly known in early modern Europe: tricksters, masters in the art of deceit,

always ready to take advantage of the gullibility and simple-mindedness of the herd. Literary and pictorial representations of Gypsies as tricksters were much more than a mere *jeu littéraire*. They were in fact symptomatic of a substantial change in the official attitude towards the Gypsies, and helped forge an image that formed the basis of the effective criminalisation of the Roma's entire way of life.

23. The itinerant way of life of the Gypsies was seen as a typical manifestation of their idleness. If in medieval times idleness was strongly disapproved of, as it was considered a sign of moral degradation, during the sixteenth century it was condemned by both Catholic and Protestant ideology, according to which it had to be eradicated.

24. As shown by Jacques Le Goff, in the medieval West there was a hierarchical classification of professions, characterised by a rigid bipartition between the "licit" and the "illicit". What was the distinguishing criterion underlying this bipartition? At that time, the social acceptability of an occupation was related to the rural structure of Western European society. On the one hand, occupations connected with the cultivation of the land were considered "opportune", appropriate and blessed by God. On the other hand, occupations such as the innkeeper, the butcher, the minstrel, the magician-sorcerer, the alchemist, the physician, the surgeon and the prostitute were condemned, as it was believed they involved committing one of the deadly sins: "[Lust] was the basis for condemnation of innkeepers and bathkeepers, whose premises were frequently notorious, as well as jongleurs, [. . .] tavern keepers; [. . .] avarice, or greed, was in a sense the professional sin of both merchants and men of the law—lawyers, notaries, judges. The condemnation of gluttony naturally led to the condemnation of cooks. Pride and avarice no doubt added to the condemnation of soldiers. Even sloth could be used to justify the presence on the index of the beggar's profession" (Le Goff 1980, 59–60).

25. Quoted in Liégeois (1994, 131).

26. As already remarked, the Gypsies were thought to come originally from Egypt, the cradle of astrology, and this reinforced the belief in their magic powers. Such a belief was still widespread in eighteenth-century Europe: Voltaire identified the Gypsies as the descendants of ancient priests and priestesses of Isis.

27. Forging was also considered an activity that lingered perilously on the fringes of the occult sciences, since blacksmiths and coppersmiths (like alchemists) were thought to imply the use of magic or even the invocation of diabolic entities.

28. In the centuries following the European voyages of exploration and encounters with American natives, while some continued to stigmatise the customs of the natives as feral and uncivilised, some began to regard them as closer to an original state of nature on which Western civilisation had a corrupting influence. In particular, during the eighteenth century the notion of the savage was replaced by the notion of the primitive and the belief that primitive people were the last survivors of a mythical Golden Age. This shift in attitude paved the way for the rise of the Noble Savage myth, which was to reach great popularity during the Romantic period.

29. Despised by public authorities, Gypsies and other marginal groups were raised to the status of privileged artistic subjects, featuring in literary works and low-life genre painting. Gypsy encampments, nomadic scenes and cultural practices (from Gypsy music to fortune telling) became recurrent objects of representation. For an overview of the role of the Gypsy image in European literature, see Djurić (1998, 2004), Trumpener (1992), Nord (2006), Glajar and Radulescu (2008) and Saul and Tebbutt (2004).

30. The image of the savage Gypsy is highly ambivalent. If early modern European culture produced a negative view of Gypsy primitivism—especially during the eighteenth and nineteenth centuries—the romanticised depiction of the Gypsy as a good savage later began to emerge (Mayall 1988, 2004; Sonneman 1999; Nord 2006).
31. The notion of "dangerous classes" is taken from Chevalier (1973). On the notion of Gypsies belonging to the dangerous classes, see Kaprow (1991).
32. The uniformity characterising anti-Gypsy legislation can be seen in the terminology used to address the Gypsies. Despite the variety of names used in different countries to define them (*Cingari* in Italy, *Egyptians* in England, *Bohémiens* in France, *Gitanos* in Spain and *Zigeuner* in Germany), in legal terms they always appear dangerous and alien to the settled population.
33. Reported in Fraser (1995, 89); Vaux de Foletier (2003, 88).
34. See Vaux de Foletier (1961, 51); English translation by Fraser (1995, 95).
35. *Records of the Parliaments of Scotland to 1707*, A1593/9/14.
36. The first English Vagrancy Act was issued in 1597.
37. The first instance of anti-Gypsy legislation implemented in England targeting "Aegyptians" or "pretended Aegyptians" dates back to the "Egyptian Act" of 1530 (Ribton-Turner 1972, 677).
38. In Muyart de Vouglands (1780, 411). Reprinted in Wellstood (1911–1912).
39. From an edict issued in Milan by the Prince of Ligne; in Colocci (1889, 88).
40. "Possiendo etiam li detti Cingani, così huomini come femine, che saranno ritrovati nelli Territori Nostri esser impune ammazzati, sì che li Interfettori per tali homicidij non habbino ad incorrer in alcuna pena". Extract and translation of this edict taken from the *Journal of the Gypsy Lore Society* (1), 1 (1890–91), 358–359.
41. For many Roma/Gypsies this situation continues today, as the expulsion of hundreds of Romanian and Bulgarian Roma from France during the summer of 2010 showed. These Roma, who under EU law have the right to move between and reside freely in member states, will probably try to return to France or another EU member state due to the harsh living conditions in their home countries.

NOTES TO CHAPTER 2

1. On the ambivalent perception of Gypsy nomadism, see Chapter 1.
2. In 1788, the Spanish King Charles III also forbade Gypsies to use their name, speak the Romani language, practise their traditional occupations and marry other Gypsies.
3. In that same year, Charles III issued a Pragmatic Sanction in line with Joseph II's policies regarding Gypsies.
4. For example, in early twentieth-century England, the 1908 Children Act made school attendance compulsory for Gypsy and Traveller children. Parents who refused to send their children to school incurred a severe penalty and risked losing their children, who could be sent to "a place of safety" (Children Act, section 118, subsections 1–2).
5. See in particular the case of the Swiss *Jenische* mentioned in Chapter 4 and Chapter 5.
6. De Schutter (2007); my translation.
7. Official texts dealing specifically with the Roma as a minority include the Framework Convention for the Protection of National Minorities (Council of Europe 1995; see article 6), the European Charter for Regional or Minority

Languages (1992) and, more recently, the Communication of the European Commission on an "EU Framework for National Roma Integration Strategies up to 2020" (European Commission 2011).

8. When Karpati refers to Gypsies in her work, she is generalising her observations about the Sinti of northern Italy.

9. Karpati's notion of degeneration derives to an extent from biological theories developed by race scientists such as Robert Ritter and in particular Hermann Arnold, whose study *Vaganten Komödianten Fieranten und Briganten* (Arnold 1958) she refers to in her dissertation.

10. Unless otherwise indicated, all translations of Karpati's insights are mine.

11. Karpati's views on Gypsy education were influenced by a Catholic view of education. In particular, she was inspired by the work of Spanish scholar and clergyman Andrès Manjón, founder of the Ave-María Schools that provided free instruction to Gypsy children.

12. Literally "Nomad Works", a non-Romani organisation founded in 1963 by a priest, Bruno Nicolini, which became a national organisation in 1965 and mediates between the Italian government and Romani communities.

13. An organisation founded by volunteers in 1970 and renamed in 1991 "Gypsy Council for Education, Culture, Welfare and Civil Rights".

14. It is also worth mentioning the activities carried out by the Council of Europe's Council for Cultural Cooperation (CDCC) in the area of Gypsy school provision. The CDCC was formed in 1961 as a committee of governmental representatives within the Council of Europe. Following Resolution 125 (1981), the CDCC organised a series of seminars for the training of teachers of Romani children, and published the book *Gypsies and Travellers* (Liégeois 1987a), which was updated in 1994 (Liégeois 1994).

15. Other relevant projects are the "Decade of Roma Inclusion" (2005–2015), an initiative of the World Bank and the Open Society Institute that involves twelve countries: Albania, Bosnia and Herzegovina, Bulgaria, Croatia, the Czech Republic, Hungary, Macedonia, Montenegro, Romania, Serbia, Slovakia and Spain. Its aim is to improve the welfare of the Roma, and its key areas of intervention are education, employment, health and housing. Other important initiatives are the "Roma Participation Programme 2" (OSI-RPP), the "Roma Education Fund" (REF), established in 2005 within the framework of the Decade of Roma Inclusion, and the Council of Europe's awareness-raising campaign "*Dosta!*", aimed at fighting anti-Roma prejudices.

16. The Copenhagen criteria urged these countries to address Roma issues as a priority and to ensure equality of access to quality education.

17. Surrey City Council's Hurtwood School. See Bowen (2004).

18. These include the duty to provide accommodation for Gypsy caravans on authorised sites, as stated in the Caravan Sites Act (1968), thus making it possible for Gypsy children to attend school. On this issue, see the Department for Education and Science's paper *The Education of Travellers' Children* (DES 1983), which was the first government publication entirely devoted to Gypsy education.

19. See the latest reports of the European Commission against Racism and Intolerance (ECRI) on Italy (ECRI 2006, 2012).

20. See for example the study by Lloyd and Norris (1998).

21. See Chapter 3.

22. As Liégeois points out regarding the situation of Romani pupils in Europe, "up to 80 per cent of all Gypsy children may be in classes for the 'socially handicapped' or 'mentally retarded'" (Liégeois 1994, 216); he refers to this phenomenon as "integration-by-handicap".

23. The general lack of recognition of the cultural identity of Romani children manifests itself in the ethnocentric features of the national curriculum, as evidenced by Karpati (1962), Piasere (1986) and Liégeois (1987a, 1987b).
24. Also stated by Liégeois (1994, 206).
25. As highlighted in recent reports, some schools and pre-schools tend to enrol children whose parents are both in employment (Council of Europe 2012, 117).

NOTES TO CHAPTER 3

1. On the stigma of disability imposed on Romani children at school see, among others, Liégeois (1994, 216) and the results of the "*Opre Roma* Report" (2002, 85–93) mentioned in Chapter 2. The belief in the psychic deficiency of Romani students (a belief closely connected to the stereotype of the "savage Gypsy" discussed in Chapter 1) has led to a situation whereby Romani children are routinely classified as having learning disabilities.
2. Liégeois himself avoided this risk and urged readers not to dwell exclusively on the conflicting aspects of the two educational approaches, but to find possible points of convergence between "the desire to provide schooling and the [Roma's] desire to be schooled" (Liégeois 1987b, 169).
3. *Märchen* is the German term for "folktale". In this particular context, the term refers to the "magic" or "wonder folktale". See Dégh (1972, 62–65).
4. See in particular: Heinrich von Wlislocki (1880, 1886); John Sampson (1891–1892); F.H. Groome (1899); and T.W. Thompson (1914–1915), and the publications of: Diane Tong (1989); Milena Hübschmannová (1985, 1987, 1996); Mozes Heinschink, Mirella Karpati and Giulio Soravia, who transcribed and published the narratives of Rasim Sejdić (Soravia 1978, 1980); Jane Dick-Zatta (1985, 1986); Patrick Williams (1986); and Jelena Čvorović (2009). See also Mode and Hübschmannová (1983).
5. Ginny Lapage has defined the contribution of English Romanichal Gypsies to the English folktale corpus as "massive" (Lapage 1997, 28).
6. On the notion of *čače romane lava*, or *čače rromane lava*, see Hübschmannová (2009). See also the notion of "true speech" (*čači vorba*) discussed by Michael Stewart in relation to the songs of the Hungarian Vlach Gypsies (Stewart 1989).
7. See the bans against the use of Romani introduced in Spain during the fifteenth and sixteenth century, and the persecutory measures introduced in Hungary during the eighteenth century by Maria Theresa of Austria. The persecutory attitude towards the use of the Romani language in the public sphere is not confined to the distant past. As reported by Hübschmannová (2002, 67), in the former Czechoslovakia Romani children had their heads shaved for using Romani at school.
8. I refer in particular to features such as skin colour and itinerant occupations, as discussed in Chapter 1.
9. This observation seems to apply to the case of other Roma and Sinti groups. See for example the case of the Sinti in northern Italy, analysed by Tauber (2002, 2003).
10. For more detail on the notion of peripatetics, see Chapter 5.
11. Tauber explains that there is an important difference in the way Romani and Sinti children use Romani in a classroom situation: while Romani children speak Romani loudly and with no inhibitions, Sinti children tend to speak Italian in the presence of the teachers and turn to Romani when no teacher is around (Tauber 2003, 15).

12. As anthropologists point out, different cultures have different views about what constitutes "literacy" and "illiteracy", and in some contexts—as the case of the Roma seems to confirm—illiteracy may even be regarded as a value (Smith 1986, 265).

13. On the social and cognitive implications of literacy see: Vygotsky (1962); Bruner et al. (1966); Goody and Watt (1968); Cole et al. (1971); Scribner and Cole (1974); Luria (1976); Goody (1977, 1986); Hallpike (1979); Scribner and Cole (1981); Olson (1994); Olson, Torrance and Hildyard (1985); and Cook-Gumperz (2006).

14. See the evidence gathered by: Karpati (1962); Okely (1983); Piasere (1986); Liégeois (1987); Gomes (1998); Kiddle (1999); Toninato (1999); Tauber (2003); Bhopal (2004); Derrington and Kendall (2004); and Danaher, Coombes and Kiddle (2007).

15. The fundamental link between literacy acquisition and securing a livelihood has also been detected among other non-literate societies. See in particular the case of the Vai of Liberia, studied by Sylvia Scribner and Michael Cole (Scribner and Cole 1981).

16. Nonetheless, when referring to the Roma, the non-Roma tend to regard their high illiteracy rate as an indication of their supposed "primitive" nature.

17. Ruth Finnegan rightly contends that "the idea of pure and uncontaminated 'oral culture' [. . .] is a myth" (Finnegan 1977, 24).

18. On the specific impact of schooled literacy on minority cultures, see Ogbu (1987, 1990) and Ferdman et al. (1994).

19. Pivotal instances of early NLS include the already mentioned work by Scribner and Cole (1981) and studies by: Shirley Brice Heath (1980, 1983); Graff (1979); Street (1984, 1993); Cook-Gumperz (2006 [1986]); James Gee (1990); and David Barton (1994). For more recent research in the area of NLS see for example: Barton and Hamilton (1998); Barton (2007); Barton at al. (2000); Collins and Blot (2003); Gee (2004); and Martin-Jones and Jones (2000).

20. See Gmelch (1986a) and Stewart (1997). On the notion of a redistributive economy, see Polányi (1957) and Sahlins (1972).

21. See Weyrauch (2001); see also Chapter 8 on the role of mediators within Romani society.

22. The Roma do not follow a specific religion, but tend to adopt the religion of their "host" cultures.

23. As reported by Fraser (1967).

24. For an in-depth discussion of the Roma as a "peripatetic group", see: Berland and Rao (2004) (on the Gypsies in general); Piasere (1987) (on the Xoraxané Roma); Gmelch (1977) (on the Irish Travellers); Salo (1979); and Salo and Salo (1982) (on the Romanichal Gypsies in America).

25. A number of authors have commented on how the Roma have managed to survive in a hostile environment by hiding their identity, thus "making them selves invisible" to the non-Roma; see Sutherland (1975), Lee (1971), Hancock (1987) and Piasere (1991).

26. A typical example of the Roma's secretiveness is a careful avoidance of using their "true" Romani name (*nav romano*) in public, instead using their non-Gypsy name (*nav gajikano*) that is used only with non-Roma and meant to hide their true identity (Sutherland 1975; Okely 1983; Piasere 1984; Williams 1997).

27. See for example Clébert (1963).

28. The expression "Court of Miracles" refers to a refuge for beggars, vagrants and criminals, not unlike the *Cour des Miracles* memorably described by Victor Hugo in *Notre-Dame de Paris* (1831).

29. I refer here to the textual mechanism by which the Roma are "demoted" from ethnic group to social underclass.

30. The same applies to letters or postcards sent to family members in/from prison.
31. The model proposed here uses categories such as "Roma" and "non-Roma" only for heuristic purposes, and does not necessarily reflect the position of all Romani groups towards writing.

NOTES TO CHAPTER 4

1. A remarkable exception to the fictitious representations of the language of the Gypsies is the seventeenth-century comedy by Florido De Silvestris, *Signorina Zingaretta*, where Romani is authentic; see Piasere (1994).
2. The European Charter for Regional or Minority Languages was adopted by the Committee of Ministers of the Council of Europe on 25 June 1992 and came into force on 1 March 1998. Its aim is twofold: to "protect and promote regional and minority languages as a threatened aspect of Europe's cultural heritage", and enable "speakers of a regional or minority language to use it in private and public life". The Charter defines as "regional or minority languages" those languages that: (1) are used "within a given territory of a state by nationals of that state who form a group numerically smaller than the rest of the state's population"; (2) are "different from the official language(s) of that state"; and (3) "include neither dialects of the official language(s) of the state nor the languages of migrants" (see http://www.coe.int/t/dg4/education/minlang/aboutcharter/default_en.asp).
3. However, as of August 2013, the Charter has only been ratified by twenty-five Member States of the Council of Europe.
4. On the political use of Romani writing, see Toninato (2011).
5. For further information about Communist policies concerning Roma/Gypsies in Eastern Europe see Crowe and Kolsti (1991), Crowe (1996), Barany (2000, 2002) and Guy (2001).
6. A case in point is that of the Roma in the former USSR during the 1920s and early 1930s. At this time, the study of Romani language was encouraged and the first texts in Romani were published; the Moscow Romani Theatre was founded in 1931. Roma in Russia were granted the status of a "national minority" in 1925, although this was later revoked.
7. Other Romani authors from Poland include Edward Debicki, Teresa Mirga and Edward Grof Glowacki; see Djurić (2002, 109).
8. For the following survey I am indebted to Djurić (2002). For an updated overview of Romani publications worldwide, see Bakker and Kyuchukov (2003).
9. See Seton (1935), Kafanova (1972) and Lemon (1991, 1998). For a recent ethnographic study of the Roma in Russia, which includes fieldwork with Moscow Romani Theatre performers, see Lemon (2000).
10. Kalinin also translated the Bible into Baltic Romani.
11. The Republic of Macedonia has a large Romani population, which is mainly concentrated in the capital Skopje (in particular in its satellite town Šuto Orizari, home to one of the largest Romani communities in Europe).
12. The earliest known Romani author from the former Yugoslavia is, according to Rajko Djurić, the Serbian female poet Gina Ranjicic. Other well-known Romani authors, whose achievements are described by Djurić in his history of Romani literature, are Milan Begović, Nikolaj Velimirović and Velimir Živojinović-Masuka (Djurić 2002, 52–55). More recent authors include Seljajdin Salijesor, Iljaz Šaban, Lumnia Osmàni, Rudzija Sejdović, Demir Ljatif, Rasim Sejdić and Šemšo Advić.

13. Berberski (1919–1989) published several collections of poetry. Alongside his work as a poet, he was a prominent political leader and elected president of the first World Romani Congress in 1971 (see Chapter 7).

14. The Gurbet Roma are part of a larger *Vlach-Roma* group whose language is heavily influenced by the Romanian language.

15. For a more detailed discussion of Romani literature in Hungary, see Eder-Jordan (2009) and Djurić (2002, 82–83).

16. According to Michael Stewart (1997, 10), there are three main Romani groups in Hungary: the Hungarian Gypsies (the *Romungro* Gypsies, also known as "musician Gypsies"), the *Boyash* (also known as *Beas*) and the Romani-speaking Gypsies (who called themselves *Rom*), also known as *Vlach* Gypsies.

17. Béla Osztojkán is a writer of both poetry and prose. His books include two volumes of poems, a collection of short stories—*Nincs itthon az Isten* (God Isn't at Home, 1985)—and a novel, *Átyin Jóskának nincs, aki megfisessen* (Nobody Will Pay For Átyin Jóska, 1997).

18. For an analysis of József Holdosi's work, see Eder-Jordan (1994, 2009).

19. In these two collections Cioabă wrote the Romani and the Romanian versions of the poems. Beatrice Ungar edited the German translation while Mircea Ivănescu edited the English translation.

20. From the website of the Ion Cioabă Foundation: http://www.icfoundation. ro/index.html.

21. The *Kulturno-prosvetna organizacija na ciganskoto malcinstvo v Bălgarija* (Cultural Enlightenment Organisation of the Gypsy Minority in Bulgaria), established in 1946, the Theatre *Romen* in Sofia and the newspaper *Romano-Esi* (Gypsy Voice).

22. The Democratic Union of the Bulgarian Roma, headed by Mustafa Aliev (Manuš Romanov)—formerly director of the Romani theatre in Sofia—was established in 1990 and in the national elections in June that year the first Roma leaders were elected to parliament.

23. Maximoff's mother was a cousin of the great Romani jazz musician Django Reinhardt.

24. The Roma had been enslaved in the former Wallachia and Moldavia since the fourteenth century (Hancock 1987). In these areas, slavery was officially abolished in the mid-nineteenth century.

25. Sandra Jayat's books include *Herbes Manouches* (1961), *Lunes nomades* (1963), *Moudravi où va l'amitié* (1966), *Kourako* (1972), *La longue route d'une Zingarina* (1978), *Je ne suis pas née pour suivre* (Philippe Auzou, 1983), *El Romanes* (1986) and *La zingarina ou l'herbe sauvage* (2010). Jayat's work will be discussed in the next chapter.

26. Born in Paris 1952, the Sinto Jean-Marie Kerwich is author of *L'ange qui boîte* (2005), *L'Évangile du gitan* (2008) and *Les jours simples* (1997).

27. Alexandre Romanès is author of *Paroles perdues* (2004) and *Sur l'épaule de l'ange* (2010).

28. Lick Dubois is a Sinto from Piedmont who lives in France. He is author of the books *Scènes de la vie manouche* (1998) and *Il était une fois les Bohémiens* (2003), both published by Wallâda.

29. Joaquín Albaicín is author of the novel *La serpiente terrenal* (1993), the book *En pos del sol. Los gitanos en la historia, el mito y la leyenda* (1997)—which focuses on the Roma's Indian heritage—and the volume of tales *La Estrella de Plata* (2000).

30. Other Romani writers who published autobiographical texts include Lolo Reinhardt—author of the memoir *Uberwintern: Jugenderinnerungen eines schwäbischen Zigeuners* (1999)—and Dido Ernst.

31. Otto Rosenberg, a Sinto from Berlin, published his autobiography *Das Brennglas* in 1998. The book was published in English the following year as *A Gypsy in Auschwitz*. Rosenberg's work is discussed by Grobbel (2003) and Rosenhaft (2004).

32. Walter Winter's memoirs, *Winter Zeit: Erinnerungen eines deutschen Sinto, der Auschwitz überlebt hat* (1999), were based on four recorded interviews carried out by historians Thomas Neumann and Michael Zimmermann. They were published in 1999 and translated into English in 2004, published by the University of Hertfordshire Press.

33. Alfred Lessing is author of the memoir *Mein Leben im Versteck: Wie ein deutscher Sinti den Holocaust überlebte* (My Life in Hiding: How a German Sinto Survived the Holocaust, 1993).

34. The *Jenische* are a travelling people who mostly live in Germany, Austria, Switzerland and France. The Jenisch speech is highly dynamic. It is typically based on a German structure and includes words from Yiddish, Romani, Rotwelsch (or "Cant") and French. For further information on the *Jenische*, see Reyniers and Valet (1991).

35. A charitable organisation founded in Switzerland in 1926. Under the "Children of the Road" programme, *Jenisch* children were removed from their homes without parental consent and subsequently institutionalised or sent to foster homes. The children's names were changed, and any contact with their families was forbidden until they had reached adulthood.

36. Mariella Mehr's books have been translated into several languages, including Romani, French, Italian and Finnish.

37. Another pertinent example of a collaborative autobiographical account is Davide Halilovich's diary *Tema sulla mia vita* (An Account of my Life), which appeared in 1999.

38. Massimo Converso is the national secretary of the *Opera Nomadi*, a pro-Roma association founded in 1963.

39. All the works mentioned above have been published in Italian.

40. On the debate over the political function of Romani literature vis-à-vis the issue of literary autonomy, see Chapter 6.

41. Veijo Baltzar—Finland's most prolific Romani author—is a poet, novelist, playwright and theatre director. Among his novels (written in Finnish) are *Polttava tie* (1968), *Mari* (1970), *Musta tango* (Black Tango, 1990), *Käärmeenkäräjäkivi* (1988), *Phuro* (2000) and *Sodassa ja rakkaudessa* (2008).

42. For further details about the association's aims and projects (in particular the Romani Library project), see the IRWA website: www.romaniwriters.com/.

43. From the IRWA website: http://www.romaniwriters.com/library.htm (Accessed 26 July 2012).

NOTES TO CHAPTER 5

1. These key themes of Romani written literature have much in common with the themes and modes of Romani oral traditions. There are, however, some important distinctions. Romani folk traditions and Romani written literature centre on topics of timeless and universal significance, such as love, death, travelling and the lament for lost freedom. On the other hand, Romani written literature is characterised by a closer focus on specific issues and historical events.

2. The concept of peripatetics has been introduced in Romani studies by scholars such as Aparna Rao (1985, 1987), Joseph Berland (1982) and Salo and Salo

(1982). Peripateticism is a mode of subsistence of great adaptive value. Peripatetics are endogamous groups who "employ regular spatial mobility as an economic strategy" (Rao 1987, 1). They occupy a particular peripatetic niche, that is, "a demand for specialised services/goods which sedentary communities cannot, or are unwilling to support on a full-time basis" (Berland 1987, 248), and are providers of goods and services on an itinerant basis.

3. The first attempt to establish a link between nomadism and Gypsies' racial identity was made by Grellmann (1807), whose work greatly influenced nineteenth-century Gypsy representations. The belief that nomadism is a genetic trait of the Gypsies persists today at both the popular and the policy level. As already stated in Chapter 2, Roma and Sinti in Italy are still labelled by the authorities as "nomads", even though they have been sedentary for several generations. In this case, their categorisation as nomads is a means to single them out as "foreign" and exclude them from the body of the nation (Sigona 2005).

4. According to Mary Louise Pratt (1994, 28), an autoethnographic text is "a text in which people undertake to describe themselves in a way that engages with representations others have made of them". As argued by Paola Toninato, Romani authors frequently recur to autoethnography, conceived as a strategy used by the Roma to represent themselves through a constructive confrontation with Gypsy hetero-representations (Toninato 2006, 240–244).

5. From the poem "The Long Road" published in Hancock, Dowd and Djurić (1998, 34), only in an English version.

6. From the poem "Without House or Grave" by Rajko Djurić, published in Hancock, Dowd and Djurić (1998, 143–145) in a bilingual Romani/English version.

7. From the poem "Bi kheresqo bi limoresqo" (Without House or Grave), published in Hancock, Dowd and Djurić (1998, 143–145) in a Romani/English version; translated into English by Siobhan Dowd.

8. From the poem "Phir" (Walk on) by Nada Braidic, published in Spinelli (1996, 23–24) in a Romani/Italian version; my translation into English.

9. From the poem "Av te ğav" (The search for peace) by Ilija Jovanović, published in Spinelli (1995, 34); my translation into English.

10. From the poem "I Was Born in Black Suffering", published in Hancock, Dowd and Djurić (1998, 77) only in an English version.

11. The term *Négritude* was first introduced by Martinican poet Aimé Césaire in the 1930s to affirm the existence of a common identity of all African people worldwide. On its formulation, the concept became the centre of a complex literary and ideological movement in favour of the revalorisation of black identity and culture. Among the leading figures animating the debate about this concept are Frantz Fanon, André Gide, Jean-Paul Sartre, Albert Camus, Léopold Senghor and Édouard Glissant.

12. Unpublished poem; my translation into English.

13. See the poem "Rom … Korov" (Gypsy … Weed), published in Karpati (1993, 201) in a Romani/Italian version.

14. From the poem "Ródm" (The raid), published in Hancock, Dowd and Djurić (1998, 112); translated into English by Minna Proctor.

15. From the poem "Ćori kali morći" (Poor black skin), published in Spinelli (1995, 31–33) in a Romani/Italian version; my translation into English.

16. From the poem "Senza speranza" (Without hope), published in Italian in Levacovich (1991, 37); my translation into English.

17. From the poem "Senza diritti né umanità" (Without rights or humanity), published in Italian in Levacovich (1991, 35); my translation into English.

18. Despite having being singled out, together with the Jews, as "enemies of the race-based state", the Roma's voice was not heard at the post-war Nuremberg

trials. As a result, the Romani Holocaust (unlike the Jewish Holocaust) has largely remained forgotten. Some still try to minimise the effective number of Roma and Sinti victims of the Holocaust. The argument of the "exclusivists" is that the Roma were not targeted for extermination and were not persecuted on racial grounds, but rather due to their "criminal activities". They therefore argue that, since theirs was not a case of genocide, Roma and Sinti should not be included in Holocaust scholarship (Bauer 1980).

19. *Porrajmos* is the term used by the Roma to refer to the Romani Holocaust. It literally means "devouring". Other expressions used to define it are *Baro Porrajmos* ("great devouring") (Hancock 1997) and *samudaripen* ("mass killing").

20. *Gene Expression*, January 17, 2004; http://www.gnxp.com/MT2/archives/week_2004_01_11.html.

21. See for example the Romani Archives and Documentation Center at the University of Texas and the Unites States Holocaust Memorial Museum in Washington.

22. See Hava-Robbins (2004).

23. Published in Stojka (2003, 24); my translation into English.

24. From the poem "Gazisarde romengi violina" (Their feet crushed the Romani violin), published in Sejdić (1987, 16–17) in a Romani/Italian version; my translation into English.

25. From the poem "Bistardi Laida" (Forgotten Holocaust) by Paula Schöpf, published in Karpati (1993, 208) in a Romani/Italian version; my translation into English.

26. Published in Spinelli (1988, 29) in a Romani/Italian version; my translation into English.

27. From the poem "Kusibbè Romanò" (Romani curse), published in Spinelli (1993, 64–65) in a Romani/Italian version; my translation into English.

28. The perception of women as "dangerous" and "polluting" has been pointed out by Okely (1975). On the same topic, see Okely (1983, 206–212).

29. Other Romani female writers whose work is not discussed here include: Katarina Taikon (Sweden); Jane Kieffer (France), author of *Cette sauvage lumière* (1961) and *Pour ceux de la nuit* (1964); Brigitte Lecomte (France), author of *Regards d'une femme manouche*; Esmeralda Romanez (France), author of *Les chemins de l'arc-en-ciel* (Wallâda, 1992); and Hilda Péliné Nyári (Hungary), author of the autobiography *My Little Life* (1996). In the early 1990s, Mossa (France) published, together with Bernard Leblon, a remarkable testimony on the female condition in Gypsy society (L'Harmattan, 1992). The autobiography of Nan Donohue, an Irish Traveller woman, has been published posthumously by American anthropologist Sharon Gmelch (1986).

30. I met Paula Schöpf for the first time in 2002 with the help of the anthropologist Elisabeth Tauber. I was able to conduct a series of formal and informal interviews with her; we also exchanged letters and had a number of telephone conversations.

31. All of these poems are published in Hancock, Dowd and Djurić (1998).

32. From the poem "Amico mio vorrei parlarti" (My friend, I would like to talk to you), published in Schöpf (1997, 66) in Italian; my translation into English.

33. From the poem "La notte non è finita" (The night is not over), published in Italian in Schöpf (1997, 26); my translation into English.

34. See also the poem "Sola" (Alone), published in Italian in Schöpf (1997, 19); my translation into English. On the meaning of silence in Romani poetry, see also the poems devoted to the Holocaust.

35. From the poem "Cercherò" (I will seek), published in Italian in Schöpf (1997, 28); my translation into English.

36. I refer in particular to Nada Braidic and her poems "Ǧiuvli Romani" and "Ćai Romani", discussed in Toninato (1999).
37. See the poem "Mi porto un demone" (I am carrying a demon in me), published in Italian in Schöpf (1997, 32); my translation into English.
38. I refer in particular to Schöpf's poems "Sorella amica prostituta" (My sister and friend prostitute), "Il povero" (The poor) and "Il mendicante" (The beggar), published in Schöpf (1997).
39. Tellingly, the author dedicates her first book *steinzeit* to "all unloved children, to the children of the orphanages, of the institutions [. . .] to those who cannot speak" (Mehr 1995).
40. See in particular the novels *steinzeit* (1981) and *Brandzauber* (1998).
41. Mehr (1995, 194); my translation.
42. From the poem "Not Born to Follow" in Jayat (1995, 47); translated into English by Ruth Partington.
43. From the poem "The Blue Eagle" in Jayat (1995, 38); translated into English by Ruth Partington.
44. On the use of writing as a form of negotiation of Romani identity, see Chapter 8.
45. As seen in Chapter 4, Cioabă's work is highly regarded by contemporary Romanian poets and has received international recognition.

NOTES TO CHAPTER 6

1. Romani intellectuals are not the only ones to appreciate and encourage the publication of literary works in Romani. Giulio Soravia, whose studies on the Romani language have been highly influential, recognised the importance of developing a body of literary works for the unification of the Romani language and remarked: "Even though still confined to a handful of dialects, the publication of literary works in Romani and the propagation of the language in written form may be a first step towards its unification and may lead to a deeper self-awareness among this people in search of itself" (Soravia 2002).
2. The tendency to identify the literary text with a written text is evident from the origin of the term literature, which derives from the Latin word "*littera*" that is, "letter of the alphabet". The idea of text is also closely connected with writing, although, as Walter Ong has pointed out, the term "text"—whose root meaning derives from the verb "to weave"—"is, in absolute terms, more compatible etymologically with oral utterance" (Ong 1982, 13). Despite this, written texts are regarded as more "literary" than oral ones. Written poetry in particular is considered as one of the most refined literary genres *par excellence*. Its technical and stylistic features and the subtle—at times hermetic—symbolism of poetic language have largely contributed to the image of poetry as one of the most sophisticated forms of expression of the human mind.
3. On the distinction between "ethnic cultures" and "minorities", see JanMohamed and Lloyd (1990) and Lloyd (1994, 221–238). For a critique of the notion of "minority", see Brah (1996, 186–190).
4. Romani writers who can be ascribed to this trend include, among others, Matéo Maximoff, Károly Bari, Jorge Emilio Nedich, Joaquin Albaicín and José Heredia Maya (see Chapter 4).
5. For a general discussion of the notion of diaspora, see Safran (1991) and Cohen (1997). For a postmodern interpretation of diaspora, see Hall (1990), Gilroy (1993), Clifford (1994) and Brah (1996).
6. I refer to the notion of exile as defined by Hamid Naficy, who used it to refer to "individuals or groups who voluntarily or involuntarily have relocated

outside their original habitus". These individuals or groups on the one hand "refuse to become totally assimilated into the host society", and on the other hand "they do not return to their homeland—while they continue to keep aflame a burning desire for return" (Naficy 1993, 16).

7. A major criticism of the latter view is that a decontextualised celebration of the migrant's status often fails to take into sufficient account the social conditions in which migrants have to live. Furthermore, the expression "migrant literature" may appear deceivingly straightforward, and is often based on a homogenisation of the migration phenomenon.

8. Second generation migrants in particular seem better equipped to embrace this newness.

9. Adapted from Gebauer and Lausten (2010).

10. A distinction is usually made between notions of "space" and "place". For Michel de Certeau (1988), place "implies an indication of stability", whereas space "is composed of intersections of mobile elements" and has none of "the univocity or stability" of place (de Certeau 1988, 117).

11. The notion of deterritorialisation applies to a range of different phenomena. Deleuze and Guattari use it to refer to the spatial practices connected with nomadism (Deleuze and Guattari 1988) and to the consequences of displacement on language and literature (Deleuze and Guattari 1986).

12. Anthropologists and sociologists such as Weber (1958) and Barth (1969) have identified the Roma as a pariah group, that is, a group actively rejected by the larger society "because of behaviour or characteristics positively condemned" (Barth 1969, 31). In the case of the Roma, the condemned behaviour is their nomadic way of life and their "flagrant violation of puritan ethics of responsibility, toil and morality" (Barth 1969, 38).

13. From the poem "Tsigan" by Cecilia Woloch (2002, 44–45).

14. From the unpublished poem "Words I Like" by Damian Le Bas.

15. According to Bourdieu, the literary field "is constituted as it establishes its autonomy, that is to say, its specific laws of functioning, within the field of power" (Bourdieu 1993, 163). "Literary autonomy", Bourdieu maintains, is the result of a process through which the field of literature gradually becomes independent of—or even opposite to—the dynamics of the economic, the political and the religious field. Despite the persistent exclusion of Romani literature from mainstream literary discussions, the emergence of a Romani literary field has played a crucial role in the process of political autonomisation of the Romani people (see Toninato 2009).

16. With the exception of Djurić's history of Roma and Sinti literature (Djurić 2002), most attempts at systematising Romani literature have been carried out by non-Roma (see for example Eder-Jordan 1993 and Toninato 1997).

17. For valuable overviews of the notion of hybridity, see Young (1995), Papastergiadis (1995) and Mabardi (2000).

18. According to Lévi-Strauss (1962), the *bricoleur* makes use of a pre-existent set of tools, which he is able to employ in a creative and innovative manner. Romologists such as Judith Okely (1986, 77) regard *bricolage* as a key ethnic strategy used by British Traveller-Gypsies in negotiating the relationship between Gypsy and Gorgio (non-Gypsy) cultures.

19. On the theory of intertextuality, see also Bakhtin (1981) and Kristeva (1981).

20. I remain fully aware that my reading of the text is only one possible interpretation, largely dependent on my own cultural background, and that what I perceive as intertextual writing might produce different responses from other readers.

21. I refer in particular to the poems by Mansueto Levacovich and Paula Schöpf analysed in Chapter 5.

22. Hyperbolic language has been recognised as a typical feature of the oral tradition of Romani groups such as the Slovenian Roma (Dick-Zatta 1985).
23. From the poem "Barricades of Hate" by Charlie Smith, published in the collection *The Spirit of the Flame* (Smith 1990, 10).
24. From the poem "Senza speranza" (Without hope) by Mansueto Levacovich, quoted in Chapter 4 in this volume.
25. From Spinelli's poem "Son of the wind", quoted in Chapter 4 in this volume.
26. From Pučo's poem "Destino" (Destiny), published in Karpati (1993, 209); my translation into English.
27. On the notion of mimicry as something that is "almost the same, but not quite", see Bhabha (1994, 86).
28. This is confirmed by the fact that nowadays few Roma actually lead a nomadic way of life. On the widespread fictional representations of nomadism, see also the Gadže's postmodern fascination with the figure of the nomad (Chatwin 1977) and the great popularity enjoyed by travel writing.
29. See the influential works by Papuśa, who remains a constant point of reference for Romani authors, and, more specifically, some instances of cross-referencing among Romani poets as in the case of Rasim Sejdić and his son Aladjn.
30. The positive attitude of the Roma towards the poetic mode should probably be read as a tacit recognition of the "authority" provided by the written medium and by particular textual structures. This perception of poetry is clearly instrumental as it places emphasis on the medium, rather than the message conveyed by the text. On the instrumental use of writing in traditional societies, see Lévi-Strauss (1955, 288–293).
31. Published in Spinelli (1993, 68–69) in a Romani/Italian version; my translation into English.
32. See the *nere ombre* in Leopardi's *Bruto Minor* (line 45).

NOTES TO CHAPTER 7

1. It is necessary to point out that a considerable gap still exists between Romani intellectuals and ordinary Roma. Nicolae Gheorghe, himself a member of the Romani intelligentsia, stated: "We are trying to build now a political identity of being Roma, being Gypsies, working with political institutions. Is this an artificial exercise? [. . .] There exists a stratum of Romani people integrated in our society who are able to maintain a dialogue with the different establishments—political, administrative and academic—who nonetheless suspect that we are not 'true Gypsies' because we no longer live in the traditional conditions which are documented by ethnographers and anthropologists. There is therefore a crisis of legitimacy for our (i.e., Romani intellectuals') own 'ethnic identity', towards our own constituency which sometimes refuses credit and in the questions of the 'Gaje' establishment regarding who exactly we are. Who is the actor promoting this kind of new Gypsy perception? Is it a legitimate actor who does this?" (Gheorghe 1997, 157). On this point see also Derek Tipler (1968, 70).
2. See for instance the role performed by the elderly as mediators among the Slovenian-Croatian Roma (the *phurano dat*, that is, the "grandfather" or "old father" and the *phurani daj*, the "grandmother"), or the roles of the *baro Rom* ("big man") and the *plešnóri* ("peacemaker") among the *Xoraxané* Romà (Piasere 1991). The term "big man" (derived from Melanesian ethnography) is used here to define the leader of a small group who, despite not

holding a position of formal authority, "acts as a focal point for the exchange of goods between local communities" (Seymour-Smith 1986, 24). I use the term mediator in the sense of "peacemaker", that is, a person designated to settle conflicts and resolve disputes within the group.

3. For a discussion of earlier manifestations of the Romani political movement, see Klímová-Alexander (2004, 2005a, 2005b).
4. See in particular the already-mentioned Copenhagen criteria introduced in 1993.
5. The Romani flag was established in 1933 and consists of a blue stripe symbolising the sky, a green stripe representing the earth and a wheel at the centre.
6. This organisation is not only concerned with political and minority rights issues but also promotes research and study into Romani history, arts and language.
7. From the mission statement of the Roma National Congress, published online at http://www.romnews.com/x1.html.
8. Other Romani organisations include the "Central Council of German Sinti and Roma" (*Zentralrat Deutscher Sinti und Roma*), founded in February 1982 and based in Heidelberg, and the "European Roma and Travellers Forum" (ERTF), a non-profit international NGO representing Roma, Sinti, Kalé, Travellers and related groups in Europe. For a full account of Romani international organisations see Barany (1998, 2002b), Vermeersch (2003) and Klímová-Alexander (2004, 2005a, 2005b).
9. Reported in Trehan (2001, 135).
10. Quoted in Hancock, Dowd and Djurić (1998, 12).
11. See Lee's factsheet "Roma and Education" (1998), downloadable at http://www.romatoronto.org/facts_education.html.
12. See Chapter 8.
13. The idea of teaching Romani history and culture at school is highly controversial, even among the activists. According to Romani activists Andrzej Mirga and Nicolae Gheorghe, the attempt at introducing educational programmes specifically aimed at Romani children, while opening up new opportunities for Romani children to improve their social condition, may also trigger a process of change that will affect their self-perception and ultimately their ethnic identity. This is why ordinary Roma tend to reject the idea that Romani children should be taught Romani subjects—and Romani language in particular—in a formal school environment. A particularly critical view on this issue has been expressed by the German Roma and Sinti, who firmly object to any outsiders' attempt to use their language in the public sphere (Bakker 2001, 307).
14. Romani academics and intellectuals who have made important contributions to the field of Romani studies include, among others, the scholars Leksa Manuš, Šaip Jusuf and Andrzej Mirga and the sociologists Nicolae Gheorghe and Brian Belton.
15. From the preface of Charlie Smith's book *The Spirit and the Flame* (Smith 1990, 5).
16. In some European countries (for example Italy), the Roma are not recognised as autonomous legal subjects and are still denied the status of a separate ethnic minority.
17. It took several decades for the Roma and Sinti to obtain recognition as Holocaust victims. In 1963 the West German Federal Court of Justice ruled that their persecution on racial grounds began in 1938 with the issue of Himmler's decree for "Combating the Gypsy Plague". The first public commemoration

of Romani persecution under the Nazis was held in October 1979 at the site of the former Bergen-Belsen concentration camp. From the late 1970s onwards, compensation issues have been intertwined with the wider struggle of Gypsy activists, such as Romani Rose and Rudko Kawczynski, whose initiatives and activities successfully thrust Roma and Sinti issues into the political arena. The enduring presence of anti-Gypsy practices in German society was publicly denounced, and by the 1980s Romani activists began to focus increasingly on civil and human rights issues. It was only in 1985 that the Roma and Sinti were officially recognised as Holocaust victims. Despite this, the Roma remain the most discriminated-against ethnic group in Europe, and anti-Gypsism in Europe is still rampant (FRA 2009). This situation has led some to argue that for the Roma, "the Holocaust is not yet over" (Hancock 1996, 55).

18. Hancock, "The Struggle for Control of Identity", in *Perspectives*, http://www.osi.hu/rpp/perspectives1c.htm.
19. This is known as the *Interface* project, supported by the Centre for Gypsy Research of the University René Descartes and by the European Commission.
20. Despite their extreme geographical dispersion and their fragmentation, the Roma have been engaged for some time in diaspora politics—evidence of a diaspora discourse among the Roma can be traced back at least to the early twentieth century—and they have developed their own autonomous diaspora discourse.
21. Safran for example underlines that the Roma have "no precise notion of their place of origin, no clear geographical focus and no history of national sove-reignty", and that they are a "truly homeless people" (Safran 1991, 86–87). As Barany argues, the Roma "are unique in their homelessness"; for them "every country is a 'foreign' country, a 'country of residence'" (Barany 1998, 143, quoting Liégeois 1994, 225).
22. On the rise of Romani diasporic politics, see Toninato (2009).
23. This confirms Sheffer's assertion that intellectuals "can be quite useful in fostering close contacts between diasporans and their homeland [. . .] and in the creation of incipient diasporas and in their transformation into estab-lished entities" (Sheffer 2003, 167).
24. From Bernal's poem "So ći ʒanàvas me" (What I did not know), published in a bilingual *Romanes*/Italian version in Spinelli (1995, 17–19); my translation into English.
25. In Spinelli (1995, 17–19); my translation into English.
26. The song "*Djélem Djélem*", based on a traditional Serbian-Romani song, was adopted at the first WRC in London in 1971 as the Romani national anthem. The words are by Zarko Jovanović, a Roma Holocaust survivor. English translation by Ronald Lee.
27. The text of the *Declaration* can be found in Acton and Klimová (2001, 216–217).
28. See the RNC's website http://romanationalcongress.webs.com/whoweare.htm (Accessed 9 August 2013).
29. The notion of an Indian homeland dates back to at least the early twentieth century and was upheld not only by intellectuals but also by self-proclaimed representatives such as the members of the Kwiek family, who were able to establish a Gypsy royal line in Poland in the late 1920s. Michal Kwiek II declared in 1934 that it was his intention to create a Romani state on the banks of the River Ganges, which he considered as the place of origin of the Roma. His successor, Mathias Kwiek, renounced the title of king and declared himself "Leader of the Gypsy Nation". Another member of the

Kwiek family, Janusz Kwiek, planned to create a Romani state in Abyssinia. Janusz Kwiek (crowned in 1937 as Janos I) advocated the representation of the Romani people in the League of Nations. After World War II, the members of the Kwiek family emigrated to France from Eastern Europe, carrying with them the project of an independent Romani state.

30. This seems to contradict hypotheses such as Sampson's (1923), according to which the Roma, after leaving their ancestral Indian homeland, arrived in Persia before 900 AD as "a single race speaking a single language".

31. Periodicals using written Romani languages include: *La Voix Mondiale Tzigane*, published by the CIT (Comité International Tsigane); the academic journals *Études Tsiganes* and *Interface* (France); *Roma*, the official organ of the IRU; the *Journal of the Gypsy Lore Society* (since 1888); *Romano Drom*, published by the Gypsy Council; *Travellers Time* (UK); the journal *Lacio Drom*, published by the Centre for Gypsy Studies in Rome; *Thèm Romanó*, published by the homonymous Romani association (Italy); *Zigenaren*, published in Sweden; *Romani Patrin/Roma Blatt*, a bilingual journal published in Austria by the Roma Association in Oberwart; *dROMa*, journal of the Romani organisation *Verein Roma Service* (downloadable at http://www.roma-service.at/droma/droma-2011.shtml); the *Journal des Romano Centro*, a bilingual journal published by the *Romano Centro* association based in Vienna; *Romano Lil* (Romania); the online newspaper *Romano Vodi*; the bulletin *Romano l'il*, published by the Union of Roma (Svaz Cikánù-Romù, SCR); the journal *Romani l'il nevo* (Czech Republic); and the worldwide magazine *O Drom International*. For a comprehensive list of publications in the Romani language, see Bakker and Matras (2003).

32. In 1990 Milena Hübschmannová established the first academic degree programme in Romani Studies at Charles University.

NOTES TO CHAPTER 8

1. Another possible definition of Romani authors is that of "cultural brokers" (Wolf 1956; Geertz 1960; Gentemann and Whitehead 1983). Gentemann and Whitehead define the cultural broker as an actor who is "acculturated in both the mainstream and the ethnic cultures" and an "expert manipulator of cultural symbols, information and people" (Gentemann and Whitehead 1983, 119).

2. For a more detailed discussion of Papuśa's work, see Chapter 4 in this book.

3. I treat the terms "border" and "boundary" as synonyms, although I am aware that they can be analytically distinguished. Richard Sennett, for example, has pointed out that "in natural ecologies, borders are the zones in a habitat where organisms become more inter-active, due to the meeting of different species or physical conditions", whereas the boundary "is a limit; a territory beyond which a particular species does [not] stray". From Richard Sennett, "Quant: The Public Realm", available at http://www.richardsennett.com/ (Accessed 26 July 2012).

4. The concept of liminality was first formulated by the ethnographer Arnold Van Gennep (1960) in relation to the study of the ritual. It generally refers to a special state during which the person undergoing a ritual is separated from the rest of society, a condition marked by the adoption of a series of practices that are in sharp contrast with conventional patterns of behaviour.

5. Clearly, the ritual subversion of social structures is a carefully controlled act that helps to manage violence and social conflict by reasserting, at the end of

the ritual process, the "normal" order of things. What is worth emphasizing, however, is that by casting light on the possibility of another social order, the partial suspension of the conventional order enacted in the ritual may lead to the formulation of social and cultural structures that are alternative to the existing ones (Turner 1969).

6. Published in Advić (1985, 10–11) in Romani and Italian; my translation into English.

7. Pushkin's *Tsygany* was translated into Romani in 1937 by Nikolai Pankov as *Roma*. Translated here by Yevgeny Bonver, 2005, available at http://www.poetryloverspage.com/yevgeny/pushkin/gypsies.html.

8. On the ambiguous role of women as intermediaries, see also the figure of the *Malinche* as discussed by Pratt (1993), Kidwell (1992) and Cypess (1991).

9. See for example Mérimée's *Carmen*.

10. From the poem "Ğiuvli Romani" (Romani woman), published in Romani/Italian in Spinelli (1994a); my translation into English.

11. From the poem by Paula Schöpf "Il mio tormento" (My torment), published in Schöpf (1997, 44); my translation.

12. Rasy (2000, 26); my translation into English.

13. On the notion of hybrid literacy practices, see Gutiérrez et al. (1999a, 1999b, 2001). The idea of hybrid literacy is closely linked to that of creating a Third Space (Bhabha 1994) within the school environment where "alternative and competing discourses and positioning transform conflict and difference into rich zones of collaboration and learning" (Gutiérrez et al. 1999b, 286–287). It is also linked to the Bakhtinian notion of hybridity (Bakhtin 1981) discussed in Chapter 6.

14. A number of initiatives for the training of teachers of Romani children have been introduced at a European level. A recent example is "INSETRom" (IN-SErvice Training for Roma Inclusion), a project funded by the European Commission within the framework of the Lifelong Learning Programme and carried out in eight countries (Cyprus, Italy, The Netherlands, Greece, Austria, Romania, United Kingdom and Slovakia). The project's main aim was to "facilitate school and Roma family partnerships in order to establish an environment of collaboration and shared goals for children's education" (from the project website: http://www.iaie.org/insetrom/). This was to be achieved through the direct involvement of members of the Romani communities in the teaching process and through the training of Roma teachers, assistants and school mediators. It is also worth mentioning the training of Romanian Roma School Mediators (SM) as part of the Roma Education Initiative, as well as the ongoing Council of Europe's ROMED programme for the training of Roma mediators, which was launched in 2011 as part of the implementation of the Strasbourg Declaration on Roma (2010).

15. Namely the primary school "G. Carducci" in Udine and the school district "Virgilio" in Mestre.

16. This is confirmed by Tauber's research on Sinti children in Italian primary schools (Tauber 2002).

Bibliography

A Parisian Journal, 1405–1449. Translated by J. Shirley. Oxford: Clarendon Press, 1968. Translated from the anonymous *Journal d'un bourgeois de Paris*.

Acton, Thomas. *Gypsy Politics and Social Change: The Development of Ethnic Ideology and Pressure Politics among British Gypsies from Victorian Reformism to Romany Nationalism*. London: Routledge, 1974.

Acton, Thomas, and Ilona Klímová. "The International Romani Union: An East European Answer to West European Questions?". In *Between Past and Future. The Roma of Central and Eastern Europe*, edited by W. Guy, 157–219. Hatfield: University of Hertfordshire Press, 2001.

Acton, Thomas, and Gary Mundy, eds. *Romani Culture and Gypsy Identity*. Hatfield: University of Hertfordshire Press, 1997.

Advić, Šemšo. *Poesie*. Edited and translated by Sergio Franzese. Cuneo: Primalpe, 1985.

Advisory Council for the Education of Romany and other Travellers (ACERT), in conjunction with NATT. "Traveller Education—Post-Chester Proposals: Planning and Providing Education for Gypsy, Fairground and Circus Children". Harlow: ACERT, 1986.

Advisory Council for the Education of Romany and other Travellers (ACERT). *The Education of Gypsy and Traveller Children: Action-Research and Co-ordination*. Hatfield: University of Hertfordshire Press, 1993.

Anderson, Benedict. *Imagined Communities: Reflections on the Spread and Origins of Nationalism*. London: Verso, 1983.

Andreas, J. "The Patteran". *Journal of the Gypsy Lore Society* (3), 12, no. 1 (1933): 55–57.

Andreas, Presbyter Ratisboniensis. *Diarium sexennale*. In A. F. Oefelius. *Rerum boicarum scriptores*. Augsburg, 1763, vol. 1.

Andree, Richard. "Old Warning Placards for Gypsies". *Journal of the Gypsy Lore Society* (2), 5, no. 2 (1911–1912): 202–204.

Arnold, Hermann. *Vaganten Komödianten Fieranten und Briganten*. Stuttgart: Thieme, 1958.

Asad, Talal. "The Concept of Cultural Translation in British Social Anthropology". In *Writing Culture: The Poetics and Politics of Ethnography*, edited by James Clifford and George E. Marcus, 141–164. Berkeley: University of California Press, 1986.

Asad, Talal. "A Comment on Translation, Critique, and Subversion". In *Between Languages and Cultures: Translation and Cross-Cultural Texts*, edited by Anuradha Dingwaney and Carol Maier, 325–332. Pittsburgh: University of Pittsburgh Press, 1995.

Augustini ab Hortis, Samuel. *Cigáni v Uhorsku—Zigeuner in Ungarn*. Bratislava: Štúdio dd, 1995[1775].

Bachmann, Ingeborg. *Werke*. Edited by Christine Koschel, Inge von Weidenbaum and Clemens Münster. Munich and Zürich: Piper, 1978.

Bakhtin, Mikhail. *The Dialogic Imagination: Four Essays*. Edited by Michael Holquist, translated by Caryl Emerson and Michael Holquist. Austin: University of Texas Press, 1981.

Bakhtin, Mikhail. *Rabelais and His World*. Translated by H. Iswolsky. Bloomington: Indiana University Press, 1984.

Bakker, Peter. "Romani in Europe". In *The Other Languages of Europe: Demographic, Sociolinguistic and Educational Perspectives*, edited by G. Extra and D. Gorter, 293–313. Clevedon: Multilingual Matters, 2001.

Bakker, Peter, and Hristo Kyuchukov. "Publications in Romani, Useful for Romani Language Education. Preliminary and Experimental Edition". October 2003. Accessed 13 August 2012. http://fc.hum.au.dk/~peter_bakker/00D44EE2–0075824E.-1/romedu-prefinal-november-20.pdf.

Bakker, Peter, and Yaron Matras, eds. *Bibliography of Modern Romani Linguistics*. Amsterdam: John Benjamins, 2003.

Bakker, Peter, et al., eds. *What is the Romani Language?* Hatfield: Centre de Recherches Tsiganes and University of Hertfordshire Press, 2000.

Bancroft, Angus. "'Gypsies to the Camps!' Exclusion and Marginalisation of the Roma in the Czech Republic". *Sociological Research Online* 4, no. 3 (1999). Accessed 13 August 2012. http://www.socresonline.org.uk/4/3/bancroft.html.

Bancroft, Angus. "'No Interest in Land': Legal and Spatial Enclosure of Gypsy-Travellers in Britain". *Space & Polity* 4, no. 1 (2000): 41–56.

Barany, Zoltan. "Orphans of Transition: Gypsies in Eastern Europe". *Journal of Democracy* 9, no. 3 (1998): 142–156.

Barany, Zoltan. "Politics and the Roma in State-Socialist Eastern Europe". *Communist and Post-Communist Studies* 33 (2000): 421–437.

Barany, Zoltan. "Ethnic Mobilization without Prerequisites: The East European Gypsies". *World Politics* 54 (2002a): 277–307.

Barany, Zoltan. *The East European Gypsies: Regime Change, Marginality and Ethno-politics*. Cambridge: Cambridge University Press, 2002b.

Barfield, Thomas, ed. *The Dictionary of Anthropology*. Oxford: Blackwell, 1997.

Bari, Károly. "To Be a Gypsy and a Poet". *The Hungarian Quarterly Homepage*. Spring 1997a. Accessed 11 November 2011. http://www.hungary.com/hungq/no145/p3.html.

Bari, Károly. *Winter Diary*. Translated by Dezso Benedek, Endre Farkas and Laura Schiff. San Francisco: Mercury House, 1997b.

Barnes, Bettina. "Irish Travelling People". In *Gypsies, Tinkers and Other Travellers*, edited by F. Rehfisch, 231–256. London: Academic Press, 1975.

Barth, Friedrich, ed. *Ethnic Groups and Boundaries*. London: Allen and Unwin, 1969.

Barthes, Roland. *Le degré zéro de l'écriture*. Paris: Seuil, 1953.

Barthes, Roland. "The Death of the Author". In *Image, Music, Text*. Translated by Stephen Heath, 142–148. London: Fontana, 1977.

Bartlett, D.M.M. "Münster's *Cosmographia universalis*". *Journal of the Gypsy Lore Society* (3), 31 (1952): 83–90.

Barton, David. *Literacy: An Introduction to the Ecology of Written Language*. Oxford: Blackwell, 1994.

Barton, David, and Mary Hamilton, eds. *Local Literacies: A Study of Reading and Writing in One Community*. New York: Routledge, 1998.

Barton, David, Mary Hamilton and Roz Ivanič, eds. *Situated Literacies: Reading and Writing in Context*. Abingdon and New York: Routledge, 2000.

Bassnett, Susan, and André Lefevere, eds. *Translation, History and Culture*. London: Pinter, 1990.

Bassnett, Susan, and André Lefevere. *Constructing Cultures*. Clevedon: Multilingual Matters, 1998.

Bastide, Roger. "Color, Racism, and Christianity". *Daedalus* 96, no. 2 (1967): 312–327.

Bataillard, Paul. "Beginning of the Immigration of the Gypsies into Western Europe in the Fifteenth Century". *Journal of the Gypsy Lore Society* (1), 1, no. 4 (1888–1889): 185–212; 260–286, 324–345.

Beier, A.L. *Masterless Men: The Vagrancy Problem in England 1560–1640*. London: Methuen, 1985.

Bell, Michael. *Open Secrets: Literature, Education, and Authority from J-J. Rousseau to J.M. Coetzee*. New York: Oxford University Press, 2007.

Benjamin, Walter. "Theses on the Philosophy of History". In *Illuminations*. Translated by Hannah Arendt, 245–255. London: Pimlico, 1999.

Berland, Joseph C., and Aparna Rao, eds. *Customary Strangers: New Perspectives on Peripatetic Peoples in the Middle East, Africa, and Asia*. Westport, CT: Praeger, 2004.

Bernheimer, Richard. *Wild Men in the Middle Ages*. Cambridge: Harvard University Press, 1952.

Bezzecchi, Giorgio. "La mediazione culturale: Incontro-confronto tra culture diverse". In *Il cambiamento contrastato. Zingari, servizi, città: Un incontro possibile*, edited by Alfonso Corradini and Annalisa Cella. Proceedings of the conference held in Reggio Emilia, 28–29 October 1999. Accessed 21 June 2006. http://www.click.vi.it/sistemieculture/ReggioE3.html.

Bhabha, Homi, ed. *Nation and Narration*. London: Routledge, 1990a.

Bhabha, Homi. "The Third Space: Interview with Homi Bhabha". In *Identity: Community, Culture, Difference*, edited by J. Rutherford, 207–221. London: Lawrence and Wishart, 1990b.

Bhabha, Homi. *The Location of Culture*. London: Routledge, 1994.

Bhabha, Homi. "Culture's in-Between". In *Multicultural States: Rethinking Difference and Identity*. Edited by D. Bennett, 29–36. London: Routledge, 1998.

Bhopal, Kalwant. "Gypsy Travellers and Education: Changing Needs and Changing Perceptions". *British Journal of Educational Studies* 52, no. 1 (2004): 47–64.

Bhopal, Kalwant. "'What About Us? Gypsies, Travellers and 'White Racism' in Secondary Schools in England". *International Studies in Sociology of Education* 21, no. 4 (2011): 315–329.

Bhopal, Kalwant, and Martin Myers. "Gypsy, Roma and Traveller Pupils in Schools in the UK: Inclusion and 'Good Practice'". *International Journal of Inclusive Education* 13, no. 3 (2009): 299–314.

Bhopal, Kalwant, with J. Gundara, C. Jones and C. Owen. *Working Towards Inclusive Education for Gypsy Traveller Pupils* (RR 238). London: DfEE, 2000.

Boas, George. *Primitivism and Related Ideas in the Middle Ages*. Baltimore: Johns Hopkins University Press, 1997.

Borrow, George. *The Zincali. An Account of the Gypsies of Spain*. London: Murray, 1841.

Borrow, George. *Lavengro*. London: Murray, 1851.

Borrow, George. *The Romany Rye*. London: Murray, 1858.

Borrow, George. *Romano Lavo-Lil*. London: Murray, 1908.

Bourdieu, Pierre. *The Field of Cultural Production: Essays on Art and Literature*. Edited and introduced by Randal Johnson. Cambridge: Polity Press, 1993.

Bourdieu, Pierre, and Jean Claude Passeron. *Reproduction in Education, Society, and Culture*. London: Sage, 1977.

Bowen, Paul. "The Schooling of Gypsy Children in Surrey 1906–1933". *Journal of Educational Administration and History* 36, no. 1 (2004): 57–67.

Brah, Avtar. *Cartographies of Diaspora: Contesting Identities*. London: Routledge, 1996.

Brunello, Piero. "Cartelli per chiedere la carità (Mestre e Venezia, 1993–1995)". In *Italia Romaní*, vol. 1, edited by L. Piasere, 263–276. Rome: CISU, 1996.

Bruner, Jerome. "On Cognitive Growth II". In *Studies in Cognitive Growth*, edited by Jerome S. Bruner et al., 30–67. New York: Wiley, 1966.

Bruner, Jerome, et al. *Studies in Cognitive Growth*. New York: Wiley, 1966.

Callari Galli, Matilde. *Antropologia sociale e processi educativi*. Florence: Nuova Italia, 1993.

Cardona, Giorgio R. *I linguaggi del sapere*. Bari: Laterza, 1990.

Cari, Olimpio. *Appunti di viaggio. Tracce di un'infanzia zingara*. Trento: Nuove Arti Grafiche, 2003.

Carter, Erica, James Donald and Judith Squires. *Space and Place: Theories of Identity and Location*. London: Lawrence and Wishart, 1993.

Casanova, Pascale. *The World Republic of Letters*. Translated by M. B. DeBevoise. Cambridge, MA: Harvard University Press, 2004.

Cemlyn Sarah, et al. *Inequalities Experienced by Gypsy and Traveller Communities: A Review*. Research report 12. London: Equality and Human Rights Commission, 2009.

Central Advisory Council for Education (England). *Children and their primary schools* (Plowden Report). London: HMSO, 1967.

Cervantes, Miguel de. *Exemplary Stories*. Translated by C.A. Jones. London: Penguin, 1972.

Césaire, Aimé. *Cahier d'un retour au pays natal*. Edited and translated by Abiola Irele. Ibadan: New Horn, 1994.

Chatwin, Bruce. *In Patagonia*. London: Jonathan Cape, 1977.

Chevalier, M. L. *Labouring Classes and Dangerous Classes in Paris during the First Half of the Nineteenth Century*. Translated by Frank Jellinek. London: Routledge and Kegan Paul, 1973.

Cioabă, Luminiţa Mihai. *O Angluno la Phuveako*. Sibiu: Editura Neo Drom, 1994.

Cioabă, Luminiţa Mihai. *Negustorul de Ploaie / O Manuši kai Bitinel Brîšind*. Sibiu: Editura Neo Drom, 1997.

Cirelli, Luigi. *Senza meta*. Milan: Opera Nomadi, 1994.

Clébert, Jean-Paul. *The Gypsies*. Translated by Charles Duff. London: Vista Books, 1963.

Clifford, James. "Diasporas". *Cultural Anthropology* 9, no. 3 (1994): 302–338.

Cohen, Anthony P. "Boundaries and Boundary-Consciousness: Politicizing Cultural Identity". In *The Frontiers of Europe*, edited by M. Anderson and E. Bort, 22–35. London: Continuum, 1998.

Cohen, Robin. *Global Diasporas: An Introduction*. London: UCL Press, 1997.

Cohen, Stanley. *Visions of Social Control*. Cambridge: Polity, 1985.

Cole, Michael, J. Gay, J. A. Glick and D. W. Sharp. *The Cultural Context of Learning and Thinking*. New York: Basic Books, 1971.

Collins, James, and Richard K. Blot, eds. *Literacy and Literacies: Texts Power and Identity*. Cambridge: Cambridge University Press, 2003.

Colocci, Adriano. *Gli Zingari. Storia di un popolo errante*. Turin: Loescher, 1889.

Common European Framework of Reference for Languages: Learning, Teaching, Assessment (CEFR). Cambridge: Cambridge University Press, 2001.

Connerton, Paul. *How Societies Remember*. Cambridge: Cambridge University Press, 1989.

Cook-Gumperz, Jenny. "Literacy and Schooling: An Unchanging Equation?". In *The Social Construction of Literacy*, edited by J. Cook-Gumperz, 19–49. Cambridge: Cambridge University Press, 2006a.

Cook-Gumperz, Jenny, ed. *The Social Construction of Literacy*. 2nd ed. Cambridge: Cambridge University Press, 2006b.
Cooperazione per lo Sviluppo dei Paesi Emergenti (COSPE), National Focal Point Italy. *Roma, Sinti, Gypsies and Travellers in Public Education*. 2006. Accessed 15 August 2013. http://www.cirdi.org/wp/wp-content/uploads/2011/01/ITRoma-Sinti-Travellers-in-public-eduction1.pdf.
Cornerus, Hermann. *Chronica Novella usque ad annum 1435*. In *Corpus historicum medii ævi*, edited by Johannes G. Eccard, vol. 2, 1225. Leipzig, 1723.
Corradini, Alfonso, and Annalisa Cella, eds. "Il cambiamento contrastato. Zingari, servizi, città: Un incontro possibile". Proceedings of the conference held in Reggio Emilia, 28–29 October 1999. Accessed 21 June 2006. http://www.click.vi.it/sistemieculture/ReggioE.html.
Cotten, Rena. "Gypsy Folktales". *Journal of American Folklore* 67, no. 265 (1954): 261–266.
Council of Europe—Committee of Ministers. *Resolution (75) 13 on the Social Situation of Nomads in Europe*. 22 May 1975.
Council of Europe—Standing Conference of Local and Regional Authorities of Europe. *Resolution 125 (1981) on the Role and Responsibility of Local and Regional Authorities in Regard to the Cultural and Social Problems of Populations of Nomadic Origin*. 29 October 1981.
Council of Europe. *Resolution on School Provision for Gypsy and Traveller Children*. (89/C 153/02 No C 153/3), 22 May 1989.
Council of Europe. "European Charter for Regional or Minority Languages". Strasbourg: Council of Europe, 1992. Accessed 9 August 2013. http://conventions.coe.int/Treaty/en/Treaties/Html/148.htm.
Council of Europe—Standing Conference of Local and Regional Authorities of Europe. *Resolution 249 (1993) on Gypsies in Europe: The Role and Responsibility of Local and Regional Authorities*. 16–18 March 1993.
Council of Europe—Standing Conference of Local and Regional Authorities of Europe. *Resolution 16 (1995) on "Towards a Tolerant Europe: The Contribution of Rroma (Gypsies)"*. 31 May 1995.
Council of Europe. "Framework Convention for the Protection of National Minorities and Explanatory Report". Strasbourg: Council of Europe, 1995. Accessed 9 August 2013. http://www.coe.int/t/dghl/monitoring/minorities/1_AtGlance/PDF_H%2895%2910_FCNM_ExplanReport_en.pdf.
Council of Europe. *Roma Children Education Policy Paper: Strategic Elements of Education Policy for Roma Children in Europe*. MG-S-ROM (97) 11. Strasbourg: Council of Europe, 1997.
Council of Europe—Committee of Ministers. *Recommendation 4 (2000) on the Education of Roma/Gypsy Children in Europe*. 3 February 2000.
Council of Europe—Commissioner for Human Rights. *Human Rights of Roma and Travellers in Europe*. Strasbourg: Council of Europe, 2012. Accessed 9 August 2013. http://www.coe.int/t/commissioner/source/prems/prems79611_GBR_CouvHumanRightsOfRoma_WEB.pdf.
Council of Ministers of the European Community. "Resolution of the Council and the Ministers of Education meeting within the Council of 22 May 1989 on School Provision for Gypsy and Traveller Children (89/C 153/02)". *Official Journal of the European Communities* 153 (21 June 1989): 3–4.
Courthiade, Marcel. "Between Oral and Written Textuality: The Lila of the Young Romani Poets in Kosovia". *Lacio Drom* 6 (1985): 2–20.
Courthiade, Marcel. "Les voies de l'émergence du romaní commun". *Études Tsiganes* 3 (1990): 26–51.
Courthiade, Marcel. "La langue romani". *Études Tsiganes* 5 (1993): 94–109.
Courthiade, Marcel. "'Papuśa' des mots, un destin". *Études Tsiganes* 9 (1997): 35–52.

Crabb, James. *The Gipsies' Advocate: or, Observations on the Origin, Character, Manners, and Habits of the English Gipsies.* London: Nisbet, 1832.

Crowe, David. "The Gypsies in Hungary". In *The Gypsies of Eastern Europe*, edited by David Crowe and John Kolsti, 117–131. Armonk, NY: Sharpe, 1991.

Crowe, David. *A History of the Gypsies of Eastern Europe and Russia.* New York: Saint Martin's Press, 1996.

Crowe, David. "The Roma in Post-Communist Eastern Europe: Questions of Ethnic Conflict and Ethnic Peace". *Nationalities Papers* 36, no. 3 (2008): 521–552.

Crowe, David, and John Kolsti, eds. *The Gypsies of Eastern Europe.* Armonk, NY: Sharpe, 1991.

Čvorović, Jelena. "What Makes Them Tick: The Social Significance of Serbian Gypsy Oral Tradition". *Fabula* 50, nos. 1–2 (2009): 37–53.

Cybulski, Mariusz. "Papusza and her poems". *Lacio Drom* 6 (1985): 21–31.

Cypess, Sandra M. *La Malinche in Mexican Literature: From History to Myth.* Austin: University of Texas Press, 1991.

D'haen, Theo, David Damrosch and Djelal Kadir, eds. *The Routledge Companion to World Literature.* London: Routledge, 2011.

D'haen, Theo. *The Routledge Concise History of World Literature.* London: Routledge, 2011.

Dalzell, Tom, and Terry Victor. *The New Partridge Dictionary of Slang and Unconventional English.* London: Routledge, 2006.

Damrosch, David. *What is World Literature?* Princeton and Oxford: Princeton University Press, 2003.

Danaher, Patrick Alan, Phyllida Coombes and Cathy Kiddle. *Teaching Traveller Children: Maximising Learning Outcomes.* Stoke on Trent: Trentham Books, 2007.

De Bar, Gnugo. *Strada, patria sinta. Cento anni di storia nel racconto di un saltimbanco sinto.* Florence: Fatatrac, 1998.

de Certeau, Michel. *The Practice of Everyday Life.* Berkeley and Los Angeles, CA; London: University of California Press, 1988.

De Schutter, Olivier. "La contribution de la charte sociale européenne à l'intégration des roms d'Europe". *L'Europe des Libertés* 23 (2007): 2–16. Accessed 8 August 2012. http://leuropedeslibertes.u-strasbg.fr.

Debar, Floriano. *Vita di Zingaro.* Bologna, 1989. Photocopy.

Dégh, Linda. "Folk Narrative". In *Folklore and Folklife: An Introduction*, edited by Richard M. Dorson, 53–83. Chicago: University of Chicago Press, 1972.

Dekker, Thomas. "Lanthorn and Candle-light". In *The Elizabethan Underworld*, edited by A. V. Judges, 312–365. London: Routledge, 1930.

Deleuze, Gilles, and Félix Guattari. *Kafka: Toward a Minor Literature.* Translated by Dana Polan. Minneapolis: University of Minnesota Press, 1986.

Deleuze, Gilles, and Félix Guattari. *A Thousand Plateaus: Capitalism and Schizophrenia.* Translated by Brian Massumi. London: The Athlone Press, 1988.

Department of Education and Science. *Education for All, Report of the Committee of Enquiry into the Education of Children from Ethnic Minority Groups* (The Swann Report). London: HMSO, 1985.

Derrington, Chris. "Fight, Flight and Playing White: An Examination of Coping Strategies Adopted by Gypsy Traveller Adolescents in English Secondary Schools". *International Journal of Educational Research* 46, no. 6 (2007): 357–367.

Dick-Zatta, Jane. "I Rom Sloveni di Piove di Sacco". *Lacio Drom* 21, nos. 1–2 (1985a): 2–79.

Dick-Zatta, Jane. "The Metonymic Pole of Language and the Referential Function in Rom Sloveni Narration". *Lacio Drom*, supplement to 21, no. 6 (1985b): 32–41.

Dick-Zatta, Jane. "La tradizione orale dei Rom Sloveni". *Lacio Drom* 22, nos. 3–4 (1986): 2–55.

Dick-Zatta, Jane. "Oral Tradition and Social Context: Language and Cognitive Structure among the Roma". In *100 Years of Gypsy Studies*, edited by M. Salo, 51–76. Cheverly: Gypsy Lore Society, 1990.

Dick-Zatta, Jane. "Gli Zingari: Educare al diverso con l'educazione linguistica". In *La questione zingara*, edited by P. Zatta, 184–203. Padua: Francisci, 1992.

Dick-Zatta, Jane. "The Use of Romanes in an Italian School". In *Language, Blacks and Gypsies: Languages without a Written Tradition and Their Role in Education*, edited by Thomas Acton and M. Dalphinis, 187–211. London: Withing and Birch, 2000.

Djurić, Rajko. *Bi kheresqo bi limoresqo/Sans maison sans tombe*. Translated by Marcel Courthiade. Paris: Études Tsiganes/L'Harmattan, 1990.

Djurić, Rajko. "Rom e Sinti nella letteratura". *Lacio Drom* 1 (1993a): 18–32.

Djurić, Rajko. "Gli inizi di una nuova letteratura". In *Zingari ieri e oggi*, edited by M. Karpati, 175–179. Rome: Lacio Drom, 1993b.

Djurić, Rajko. *Romanies and Europe*. Strasbourg: Council of Europe, 1996.

Djurić, Rajko. *Die Literatur der Roma und Sinti*. Berlin: Parabolis, 2002.

Djurić, Rajko, J. Becken and A. B. Bengsch. *Ohne Heim—Ohne Grab: The Geschichte der Roma und Sinti*. Berlin: Verlag, 2002.

Djurić, Rajko, and M. Courthiade. *Les Rroms dans les belles-lettres européennes*. Paris: L'Harmattan, 2004.

Douglas, Mary. *Purity and Danger*. London: Routledge and Kegan Paul, 1978.

Eagleton, Terry. "Maybe He Made It Up". Review of *The Forger's Shadow: How Forgery Changed the Course of Literature*, by Nick Groom. *London Review of Books*, 6 June 2002.

Eccard, J.G. *Corpus historicum medii ævi*. 2 vols. Leipzig, 1723.

Eder-Jordan, Beate. *Geboren bin ich vor Jahrtausenden . . . Bilderwelten in der Literatur der Roma und Sinti*. Klagenfurt: Drava, 1993.

Eder-Jordan, Beate. "'Die Urmusik der Roma lebt in mir und in meinem Buch.' Gespräche mit József Holdosi". *Stimme von und für Minderheiten* 11 (1994): 8.

Eder-Jordan, Beate. "Les Rom écrivent. Remarques sur la literature d'une minorité ethnique". *Études Tsiganes* 9 (1997): 12–25.

Eder-Jordan, Beate. "La littérature romani: une aubaine pour la littérature comparée". *Études Tsiganes* 36 (2009): 146–179.

Eliot, George. *The Spanish Gypsy Edinburgh*. London: Blackwood, 1868.

Ette, Ottmar. *Literature on the Move: Space and Dynamics of Bordercrossing Writings in Europe and America*. Translated by Katharina Vester. Amsterdam; New York: Rodopi, 2003.

Ette, Ottmar. *ZwischenWeltenSchreiben. Literaturen ohne festen Wohnsitz*. Berlin: Kulturverlag Kadmos, 2005.

Ette, Ottmar. "Literatures without a Fixed Abode". In *ArabAmericas: Literary Entanglements of the American Hemisphere and the Arab World*, edited by O. Ette and F. Pannewick, 19–68. Madrid: Iberoamericana, 2006.

European Commission. *School Provision for Gypsy and Traveller Children*. Report on the implementation of measures envisaged in the Resolution of the Council and of the Ministers of Education meeting within the Council of 22 May 1989 (89/C 153/02). Brussels: European Commission, 1996.

European Commission. *Communication from the Commission to the European Parliament, the Council, the European Economic and Social Committee and the Committee of the Regions on "An EU Framework for National Roma Integration Strategies up to 2020"* (COM(2011) 173 final). Brussels: European Commission, 2011.

European Commission against Racism and Intolerance (ECRI). *Third Report on Italy*. Strasbourg: Council of Europe, 2006. Accessed 9 August 2013. http://www.coe.int/t/dghl/monitoring/ecri/country-by-country/italy/ITA-CbC-IV-2012-002-ENG.pdf.

European Commission against Racism and Intolerance (ECRI). *ECRI Report on Italy (Fourth Monitoring Cycle)*. Strasbourg: Council of Europe, 2012. Accessed 9 August 2013. http://www.coe.int/t/dghl/monitoring/ecri/country-by-country/italy/ITA-CbC-IV-2012-002-ENG.pdf.

European Court of Human Rights (ECHR). *D.H. and Others/The Czech Republic*. Case no. 57325/00. Strasbourg, 13 November 2007.

European Monitoring Centre on Racism and Xenophobia (EUMC). *Roma and Travellers in Public Education. An Overview of the Situation in the EU Member States*. Vienna: EUMC, 2006.

European Parliament. *Resolution on the Education of Children of Occupational Travellers*. (89/C 153/01 No C 153/3), 22 May 1989.

European Parliament. *Resolution on the Situation of the Roma in the European Union*. (RC-B6–0272/2005), 28 April 2005.

European Roma Rights Center (ERRC). *A Special Remedy: Roma and Schools for the Mentally Handicapped in the Czech Republic*. Budapest: European Roma Rights Center, 1998.

European Roma Rights Center (ERRC). *Stigmata: Segregated Schooling of Roma in Central and Eastern Europe*. Budapest: European Roma Rights Center, 2004.

European Roma Rights Center (ERRC). *The Impact of Legislation and Policies on School Segregation of Romani Children: A Study of Anti-Discrimination Law and Government Measures to Eliminate Segregation in Education in Bulgaria, Czech Republic, Hungary, Romania and Slovakia*. Budapest: European Roma Rights Center, 2007.

European Union Agency for Fundamental Rights (FRA). "Data in Focus Report 1: The Roma". EU MIDIS: European Union Minorities and Discrimination Survey, 2009. Accessed 13 August 2012. http://fra.europa.eu/fraWebsite/attachments/EU-MIDIS_ROMA_EN.pdf.

Evans, Simon. *Stopping Places. A Gypsy History of South London and Kent*. Hatfield: University of Hertfordshire Press, 2005.

Ferdman, Bernardo M., Rose-Marie Weber and Arnulfo G. Ramírez, eds. *Literacy across Languages and Cultures*. Albany: State University of New York Press, 1994.

Fielding, Henry. *The History of Tom Jones: A Foundling*. 2 vols. Oxford: Clarendon Press, 1974.

Finnegan, Ruth. *Oral Poetry: Its Nature, Significance and Social Context*. Cambridge: Cambridge University Press, 1977.

Finnegan, Ruth. *Literacy and Orality: Studies in the Social Organization of Society*. Cambridge: Cambridge University Press, 1988.

Folengo, Teofilo. *Le Maccheronee*. Edited by A. Luzio. 2 vols. Bari: Laterza, 1911.

Fonseca, Isabel. *Bury Me Standing: The Gypsies and Their Journey*. London: Vintage, 1996.

Forgaçs, David, ed. *A Gramsci Reader: Selected Writings 1916–1935*. London: Lawrence and Wishart, 1988.

Foucault, Michel. *Discipline and Punish*. Translated by A.M. Sheridan. London: Penguin, 1977.

Foucault, Michel. *Power/Knowledge*. Brighton: Harverster, 1980.

Franz, Philomena. *Zwischen Liebe und Hass. Ein Zigeunerleben*. Norderstedt: BoD GmbH., 2001.

Franzese, Sergio. "Un giovane Sinto piemontese e la sua poesia". *Lacio Drom* 1 (1991): 34–37.

Fraser, Angus. "Tramps' Sign Language". *Notes and Queries* 14, no. 10 (1967): 387–388.

Fraser, Angus. *The Gypsies*. 2nd ed. Oxford: Blackwell, 1995.

Fraser, Angus. "Juridical Autonomy among Fifteenth and Sixteenth Century Gypsies". *The American Journal of Comparative Law* 45, no. 1 (1997): 291–304.

Freire, Paulo. *The Politics of Education: Culture, Power, and Liberation*. London: Macmillan, 1985.

Freire, Paulo. *Pedagogy of the Oppressed*. Translated by Myra Bergman Ramos. New York: Continuum, 1986.

Freire, Paulo, and Donaldo Macedo. *Literacy: Reading the Word and the World*. London: Routledge and Kegan Paul, 1987.

Friedman, Victor A. "The Romani Language in the Republic of Macedonia: Status, Usage, and Sociolinguistic Perspectives". *Acta Linguistica Hungarica* 46 (1999): 317–339.

Garreta Bochaca, Jordi. "Ethnic Minorities and the Spanish and Catalan Educational Systems: From Exclusion to Intercultural Education". *International Journal of Intercultural Relations* 30, no. 2 (2006): 261–279.

Gebauer, Mirjam, and Pia Schwarz Lausten, eds. *Migration and Literature in Contemporary Europe*. Munich: Martin Meidenbauer, 2010.

Gee, James. *Social Linguistics and Literacies*. Basingstoke: Falmer Press, 1990.

Geertz, Clifford. "The Javanese Kijaji: The Changing Role of a Cultural Broker". *Comparative Studies in Society and History* 2 (1960): 228–249.

Gentemann, Karen M., and Tony L. Whitehead. "The Javanese Kijaji: The Changing Role of a Cultural Broker". *The Journal of Negro Education* 52, no. 2 (1983): 118–129.

Geremek, Bronislaw. *Inutiles au monde: truands et misérables dans l'Europe moderne (1350–1600)*. Paris: Gallimard/Julliard, 1980.

Geremek, Bronislaw. "The Marginal Man". In *The Medieval World*. Translated by Lydia G. Cochrane; edited by J. Le Goff, 346–373. London: Collins and Brown, 1990.

Gheorghe, Nicolae. "Roma-Gypsy Ethnicity in Eastern Europe". *Social Research* 58, no. 4 (1991): 829–844.

Gheorghe, Nicolae. "The Social Construction of Romani Identity". In *Gypsy Politics and Traveller Identity*, edited by Thomas Acton, 153–163. Hatfield: University of Hertfordshire Press, 1997.

Gheorghe, Nicolae, and Thomas Acton. "Citizens of the World and Nowhere". In *Between Past and Future: The Roma of Central and Eastern Europe*, edited by W. Guy, 54–70. Hatfield: University of Hertfordshire Press, 2001.

Gheorghe, Nicolae, and Andrzej Mirga. *The Roma in the Twenty-First Century: A Policy Paper*. Princeton: PER, 1998.

Gilroy, Paul. *The Black Atlantic: Modernity and Double Consciousness*. Cambridge: Harvard University Press; London and New York: Verso, 1993.

Glajar, Valentina, and D. Radulescu, eds. *"Gypsies" in European Literature and Culture*. New York: Palgrave Macmillan, 2008.

Glissant, Édouard. *Traité du tout-monde*. Paris: Gallimard, 1997.

Gmelch, George. *The Irish Tinkers: The Urbanization of an Itinerant People*. Menlo Park, CA: Cummings, 1977.

Gmelch, Sharon. "Groups That Don't Want In: Gypsies and Other Artisan, Trader, and Entertainer Minorities". *Annual Review of Anthropology* 15 (1986a): 307–330.

Gmelch, Sharon. *Nan: The Life of an Irish Travelling Woman*. Long Grove, IL: Waveland, 1986b.

Gomes, Ana Maria. *"Vegna che ta fago scriver": Etnografia della scolarizzazione in una comunità di Sinti.* Rome: CISU, 1998.

Gomes, Ana Maria. "Gypsy Children and the Italian School System: A Closer Look". *European Journal of Intercultural Studies* 10, no. 2 (1999): 163–172.

Goody, Jack. *The Domestication of the Savage Mind.* Cambridge: Cambridge University Press, 1977.

Goody, Jack, and Ian Watt. "The Consequences of Literacy". In *Literacy in Traditional Societies,* edited by J. Goody, 27–68. Cambridge: Cambridge University Press, 1968.

Graff, Harvey J. *The Literacy Myth: Literacy and Social Structure in the 19th Century City.* New York: Academic Press, 1979.

Graff, Harvey J. *The Legacies of Literacy.* Bloomington: Indiana University Press, 1991.

Gramsci, Antonio. *Quaderni del carcere.* 4 vols. Turin: Einaudi, 1997.

Green, Rose Basile. *The Italian-American Novel: A Document of the Interaction of Two Cultures.* Rutherford: Fairleigh Dickinson University Press, 1974.

Grellmann, Heinrich. *Die Zigeuner.* Dessau and Leipzig, 1783.

Grellmann, Heinrich. *Dissertation on the Gipseys.* London: Ballantine, 1807.

Gresham, David, et al. "Origins and Divergence of the Roma (Gypsies)". *American Journal of Human Genetics* 96, no. 6 (2001): 1314–1331.

Grice, Helena, et al. *Beginning Ethnic American Literatures.* Manchester: Manchester University Press, 2001.

Groome, Francis Hindes. "Gipsies". *Encyclopaedia Britannica,* vol. 10 (1879): 611–618.

Groome, Francis Hindes. *Gypsy Folk Tales.* London: Hurst and Blackett, 1899.

Gross, H. *Manuel pratique d'instruction judiciare.* Paris: Marchal and Billard, 1899.

Guillory, John. "Canonical and Non-canonical: A Critique of the Current Debate". *ELH* 54 (1987): 483–527.

Gutiérrez, Kris D., Patricia Baquedano-López and Héctor H. Alvarez. "Literacy as Hybridity: Moving Beyond Bilingualism in Urban Classrooms". In *The Best for Our Children: Latina/Latino Voices in Literacy,* edited by M. Reyes and J. Halcon, 122–141. New York: Teachers College Press, 2001.

Gutiérrez, Kris D., Patricia Baquedano-López, Héctor H. Alvarez and Ming Ming Chiu. "Building a Culture of Collaboration through Hybrid Language Practices". *Theory into Practice* 38, no. 2 (1999): 87–93.

Gutiérrez, Kris D., Patricia Baquedano-López and Carlos Tejeda. "Rethinking Diversity: Hybridity and Hybrid Language Practices in the Third Space". *Mind, Culture, and Activity* 6, no. 4 (1999): 286–303.

Guy, Will, ed. *Between Past and Future: The Roma of Central and Eastern Europe.* Hatfield: University of Hertfordshire Press, 2001.

Halbwachs, Maurice. *On Collective Memory.* Edited by Lewis A. Coser. Chicago: University of Chicago Press, 1992.

Hall, Stuart. "Cultural Identity and Cinematic Representation". *Framework* 36 (1989): 68–81.

Hall, Stuart. "Cultural Diversity and Diaspora". In *Identity: Community, Culture, Difference,* edited by J. Rutherford, 222–237. Lawrence and Wishart: London, 1990.

Hall, Stuart. "Old and New Identities, Old and New Ethnicities". In *Culture, Globalization and the World-System: Contemporary Conditions for the Representation of Identity,* edited by Anthony D. King, 41–68. Basingstoke: Macmillan, 1991.

Hall, Stuart. "New Ethnicities". In *Critical Dialogues in Cultural Studies,* edited by David Morley and Kuan-Hsing Chen, 441–449. London: Routledge, 1996.

Hall, Stuart, David Held and Tony McGrew, eds. *Modernity and Its Futures.* Cambridge: Polity Press and Open University, 1992.

Hallpike, Christopher R. *The Foundations of Primitive Thought.* Oxford: Clarendon Press, 1979.

Halwachs, D.W. "Roma and Romani in Austria". *Romani Studies* 15, no. 2 (2005): 145–196.

Hancock, Ian. "Na Achel Amari Cungar". *Roma* 7, no. 2 (1983): 11–14.

Hancock, Ian. "Non-Gypsy Attitudes towards Rom: The Gypsy Stereotype". *Roma* 9, no. 1 (1985): 50–65.

Hancock, Ian. *The Pariah Syndrome: An Account of Gypsy Persecution and Slavery.* Ann Arbor: Karoma, 1987.

Hancock, Ian. "The East European Roots of Romani Nationalism". In *The Gypsies of Eastern Europe*, edited by D. Crowe and J. Kolsti, 133–150. Armonk, NY: M.E. Sharpe, 1991.

Hancock, Ian. "Roots of Inequity: Romani Cultural Rights in Their Historical and Social Context". *Immigrants and Minorities* 2, no. 1 (1992): 3–20.

Hancock, Ian. "Anti-Gypsyism in the New Europe". *Roma* 17, no. 1 (1993): 5–29.

Hancock, Ian. *A Handbook of Vlax Romani.* Columbus: Slavica Publishers, 1995.

Hancock, Ian. "Responses to the Porrajmos: The Romani Holocaust". In *Is the Holocaust Unique? Perspectives on Comparative Genocide*, edited by A. Rosenbaum, 39–64. Oxford: Westview Press, 1996.

Hancock, Ian. "The Struggle for the Control of Identity". *The Patrin Web Journal.* 1997a. Accessed 12 February 2011. http://reocities.com/Paris/5121/identity. htm.

Hancock, Ian. "A Glossary of Romani Terms". *The American Journal of Comparative Law* 45, no. 2, (1997b): 329–344.

Hancock, Ian. "Introduction". In *The Roads of the Roma*, edited by Ian Hancock, Siobhan Dowd and Rajko Djurić, 9–21. Hatfield: University of Hertfordshire Press, 1998.

Hancock, Ian. "The Roma: Myth and Reality". *The Patrin Web Journal.* 1999. Accessed 12 February 2011. http://www.reocities.com/~patrin/mythandreality. htm.

Hancock, Ian. "Standardisation and Ethnic Defence in Emergent Non-Literate Societies: The Gypsy and Caribbean Cases". In *Language, Blacks and Gypsies: Languages without a Written Tradition and their Role in Education*, edited by Acton Thomas and M. Dalphinis, 9–23. London: Whiting and Birch, 2000a.

Hancock, Ian. "The Consequences of Anti-Gypsy Racism in Europe". *Other Voices* 2, no. 1 (2000b). Accessed 13 August 2012. http://www.othervoices. org/2.1/hancock/roma.html.

Hancock, Ian. *We are the Romany People: Ame Sam e Rromane Džene.* Hatfield: University of Hertfordshire Press, 2002.

Hancock, Ian. "On Romani Origins and Identity: Questions for Discussion". In *Gypsies and the Problem of Identities: Contextual, Constructed and Contested*, edited by Adrian Marsh and Elin Strand, 68–92. Istanbul: Swedish Research Institute, 2006a.

Hancock, Ian. "On the Interpretation of a Word: Porrajmos as Holocaust". In *Travellers, Gypsies, Roma: The Demonisation of Difference*, edited by Thomas Acton and Michael Hayes, 53–57. Newcastle: Cambridge Scholars Publishing, 2006b.

Hancock, Ian. "Issues in the Standardization of the Romani Language: An Overview and Some Recommendations". *RADOC* 2007. Accessed 30 July 2012. http:// www.radoc.net/radoc.php?doc=art_c_language_recommendations&lang= fr&articles=true.

Hancock, Ian. *Danger! Educated Gypsy: Selected Essays.* Edited by Dileep Karanth. Hatfield: University of Hertfordshire Press, 2010.

Hancock, Ian, Siobhan Dowd and Rajko Djurić, eds. *The Roads of the Roma.* Hatfield: University of Hertfordshire Press, 1998.

Harman, Thomas. *A Caveat or Warning for Common Cursetors, Vulgarly Called Vagabonds.* London: T. Bensley, 1814.

Hava-Robbins, Nadia. "Spirit and Sound of the Gypsies". Letter to "Sound and Spirit". 17 February 1997. Accessed 29 March 2009. http://www.Romani.org/local/rwgbhltr.txt.

Hawes, Derek, and Barbara Perez. *The Gypsy and the State: The Ethnic Cleansing of British Society.* 2nd ed. Bristol: Policy Press, 1996.

Heath, Shirley Brice. "The Functions and Uses of Literacy". *Journal of Communication* 30 (1980): 123–133.

Heath, Shirley Brice. *Ways with Words.* Cambridge: Cambridge University Press, 1983.

Henderson, Mae Gwendolyn. "Speaking in Tongues: Dialogics, Dialectics, and the Black Woman Writer's Literary Tradition". In *Women, Autobiography, Theory: A Reader,* edited by Sidonie Smith and Julia Watson, 343–351. Madison: University of Wisconsin Press, 1998.

Hicks, Emily. *Border Writing: The Multidimensional Text.* Minneapolis: University of Minnesota Press, 1991.

Hodgen, Margaret T. *Early Anthropology in the Sixteenth and Seventeenth Centuries.* Philadelphia: University of Philadelphia Press, 1964.

Horton, Robin, and Ruth Finnegan, eds. *Modes of Thought: Essays on Thinking in Western and non-Western Societies.* London: Faber and Faber, 1973.

Hoyland, John. *A Historical Survey of the Customs, Habits and Present State of the Gypsies.* York: The author, 1816.

Hübschmannová, Milena. "Oral Folklore of Slovak Roms". *Lacio Drom,* Supplement to vol. 21, no. 6 (1985): 61–70.

Hübschmannová, Milena. "La credenza nel 'mulo' fra i Rom Slovacchi". *Lacio Drom* 23, nos. 2–3 (1987): 2–74.

Hübschmannová, Milena. "The Treasure of Romani Folk Tales". *Roma* 44–45 (1996): 68–79.

Hübschmannová, Milena. "Czech School and 'Romipen'—the Core-Identities of a Roma Child". In *New Aspects of Roma Children Education,* edited by Hristo Kyuchukov, 59–72. Sofia: Diversity Publications, 2002.

Hübschmannová, Milena. "My Encounters with Romano šukar laviben". *Études Tsiganes* 36, vol. 1 (2009): 98–135.

Igarashi, Kazuyo. "Support Programmes for Roma Children: Do They Help or Promote Exclusion?". *Intercultural Education* 16, no. 5 (2005): 443–452.

Ignazi, Sabrina, and Monica Napoli, eds. *L'inserimento scolastico dei bambini rom e sinti.* Milan: Franco Angeli, 2004.

"Index vocabulorum linguae Nubianorum erronum". In *De literis & lingua getarum, siue Gothorum,* edited by Bonaventura Vulcanius 102–105. Ludguni Batavorum, apud Franciscum Raphelengium, 1597.

Ingold, Tim, ed. *Companion Encyclopaedia of Anthropology.* London: Routledge, 1994.

Irishkanova, K., Christoph Röcklinsberg, O. Ozolina and Ioana Anamaria Zaharia. "Empathy as Part of Cultural Mediation". In *Cultural Mediation in Language Learning and Teaching,* edited by G. Zarate, A. Gohard-Radenkovic, D. Lussier and H. Penz, 101–131. Strasbourg: Council of Europe, 2004.

Isidore of Seville, Saint. *The Etymologies.* Edited and translated by Stephen A. Barney et al. Cambridge: Cambridge University Press, 2006.

Jameson Fredric. "Third-World Literature in the Era of Multinational Capitalism". *Social Text* 15 (1986): 65–88.

JanMohamed, A.R. "Worldliness-without-World, Homelessness-as-Home: Toward a Definition of the Specular Border Intellectual". In *Edward Said: A Critical Reader*, edited by M. Sprinker, 96–120. Oxford: Blackwell, 1992.

JanMohammed, A.R., and D. Lloyd. *The Nature and Content of Minority Discourse*. New York: Oxford University Press, 1990.

Journal d'un bourgeois de Paris (1405–1449). Edited by A. Tuetey. Edited and annotated by Colette Beaune. Translated by Janet Shirley. Paris: Librairie générale française, 1990.

Kafanova, Ludmilla. "Gypsy Theatre Romen". *Sputnik* 9 (1972): 91–99.

Kalaydjieva, Luba, D. Gresham and F. Calafell. "Genetic Studies of the Roma (Gypsies): A Review". *BMC Medical Genetics* 2 (2001). Accessed 12 August 2012. http://www.biomedcentral.com/1471–2350/2/5.

Kalinin, Valdemar. *Romany Dreams*. London: Stepping Stones School, 2005.

Kaminski, Ignacy-Marek. *The State of Ambiguity: Studies of Gypsy Refugees*. Gothenburg: Gothenburg University Press, 1980.

Kandiyoti, Dalia. *Migrant Sites: America, Place, and Diaspora Literatures*. Hanover, NH: Dartmouth College Press, 2009.

Kann, Emma. "Wir lebten einst auf einer Erde". *Exil* 6, no.1 (1986): 70.

Kann, Emma. "Der Vagabund". *Mnemosyne* 24 (1998): 15.

Kapchan, D.A., and P. Turner Strong. "Theorizing the Hybrid". *The Journal of American Folklore* 112, no. 445 (1999): 239–253.

Kappen, O. van. *Geschiedenis der Zigeuners in Nederland*. Assen: Van Gorcum, 1965.

Kaprow, Miriam Lee. "L'addomesticamento dei Gitanos e delle altre classi pericolose". *La Ricerca Folklorica* 22 (1991): 17–35.

Karpati, Mirella. *Romano Them*. Rome: Missione cattolica degli Zingari, 1962.

Karpati, Mirella. "La scolarizzazione dei ragazzi zingari: L'esperienza italiana". *Lacio Drom* 3 (1979): 40–50.

Karpati, Mirella. "Ricerca sulla scolarizzazione dei bambini zingari in età dell'obbligo". *Lacio Drom* 6, no. 2 (1982): 47–55.

Karpati, Mirella. "La tradizione romani fra oralità e scrittura". *Lacio Drom* 1 (1989): 30–34.

Karpati, Mirella, ed. *Zingari ieri e oggi*. Rome: Lacio Drom, 1993.

Karpati, Mirella. "La funzione della fiaba nella tradizione culturale zingara". *Lacio Drom* 1 (1994): 7–14.

Kenrick, Donald. *Historical Dictionary of the Gypsies (Romanies)*. Lanham, MD: Scarecrow Press, 1998.

Kenrick, Donald. "Former Yugoslavia: A Patchwork of Destinies". In *Between Past and Future: The Roma of Central and Eastern Europe*, edited by W. Guy, 405–425. Hatfield: University of Hertfordshire Press, 2001.

Kenrick, Donald, and Grattan Puxon. *The Destiny of Europe's Gypsies*. London: Chatto; Heinemann Educational for Sussex University Press, 1972.

Kenrick, Donald, and Grattan Puxon. *Gypsies under the Swastika*. Hatfield: University of Hertfordshire Press, 1995.

Kiddle, Cathy. *Traveller Children: A Voice for Themselves*. London; Philadelphia: J. Kingsley, 1999.

Kidwell, Clara S. "Indian Women as Cultural Mediators". *Ethnohistory* 39, no. 2 (1992): 97–107.

King, Russell, John Connell and Paul White, eds. *Writing Across Worlds: Literature and Migration*. London: Routledge, 1995.

Kochanowski, Jan. "The Origins of the Gypsies". *Roma*, UNESCO Features no. 477 (1980): 25–28.

Kochanowski, Vania de Gila. "Black Gypsies, White Gypsies". *Diogenes* 63 (1968): 27–47.

Kochanowski, Vania de Gila. "Roma. History of their Indian Origin". *Roma* 4, no. 1 (1979): 16–32.

Kochanowski, Vania de Gila. "Causes and Consequences of Nomadism among the Gypsies of Europe". Meeting of experts on the study of ethno-development and ethnocide in Europe, Karasjok (Norway): United Nations Educational, Scientific and Cultural Organization, 29 May–2 June 1983.

Kovacshazy, Cécile. "Littératures Romani: cas exemplaire de la littérature-monde?". *Études Tsiganes* 36, no. 1 (2009): 136–145.

Kovalcsik, Katalin. "Chansons tsiganes lentes sur des expériences personnelles". *Cahiers de littérature orale* 30 (1991): 45–64.

Kovats, Martin. "The Politics of Roma Identity: Between Nationalism and Destitution". *Open Democracy*. 30 July 2003. Accessed 10 August 2012. www.opendemocracy.net/content/articles/PDF/1399.pdf.

Krashen, Stephen D. *Under Attack: The Case against Bilingual Education.* Culver City, CA: Language Education Associates, 1996.

Krashen, Stephen D. "Bilingual Education: Arguments For and (Bogus) Arguments Against". In *Language in Our Time: Bilingual Education and Official English, Ebonics and Standard English, Immigration and the Unz Initiative*, Georgetown University Round Table on Languages and Linguistics (GURT), edited by James E. Alatis and Ai-Hui Tan, 111–127. Washington, DC: Georgetown University Press, 2001.

Kristeva, Julia. *Desire in Language: A Semiotic Approach to Literature and Art.* Edited by Leon S. Roudiez; translated by Thomas Gora, Alice Jardine and Leon S. Roudiez. Oxford: Blackwell, 1981.

Krupat, Arnold. *Ethnocriticism: Ethnography, History, Literature.* Berkeley: Oxford University Press, 1992.

Krupat, Arnold, ed. *New Voices in Native American Literary Criticism.* Washington: Smithsonian Institution Press, 1993.

Jayat, Sandra. *La longue route d'une Zingarina.* Paris: Bordas, 1978.

Jayat, Sandra. *Nomad Moons.* Translated by Ruth Partington. St Albans: Brentham Press, 1995.

Jayat, Sandra. *La Zingarina ou l'herbe sauvage.* Paris: Max Milo, 2010.

Lacková, Ilona. *A False Dawn: My Life as a Gypsy Woman in Slovakia.* Edited by Milena Hübschmannová; translated by Carleton Bulkin. Hatfield: Centre de Recherches Tsiganes and University of Herfordshire Press, 2000.

Ladner, Gerhart B. "*Homo Viator*: Mediaeval Ideas on Alienation and Order". *Speculum* 42 (1967): 233–259.

Lapage, Ginny. "The English Folktale Corpus and Gypsy Oral Tradition". In *Romani Culture and Gypsy Identity*, edited by Thomas Acton and Gary Mundy, 18–30. Hatfield: University of Hertfordshire Press, 1997.

Latham, Judith. "Roma of the Former Yugoslavia". *Nationalities Papers* 27, no. 2 (1999): 205–226.

Lauret, Maria. "Introduction". In *Beginning Ethnic American Literatures*, edited by Helena Grice et al., 1–9. Manchester: Manchester University Press, 2001.

Lee, Ken. "Belated Travelling Theory, Contemporary Wild Praxis: A Romani Perspective on the Practical Politics of the Open End". In *The Role of the Romanies. Images and Counter-Images of "Gypsies"/Romanies in European Cultures*, edited by Nicholas Saul and Susan Tebbutt, 31–49. Liverpool: Liverpool University Press, 2004.

Lee, K., and W.G. Warren. "Alternative Education: Lessons from Gypsy Thought and Practice". *British Journal of Educational Studies* 39, no. 3 (1991): 311–324.

Lee, Ronald. *Goddam Gypsy: An Autobiographical Novel.* Montreal: Tundra, 1971.
Lee, Ronald. "The Roma: Origins and Diaspora". 1998. Accessed 12 February 2012. http://home.cogeco.ca/~rcctoronto/diaspora.html.
Lee, Ronald. *Learn Romani: Das-duma Rromanes.* Hatfield: University of Hertfordshire Press, 2005.
Lee, Ronald. "Roma and Education". 2009. Accessed 11 June 2012. http://kopachi.com/articles/roma-and-education-by-ronald-lee/.
Lefevere, André. *Translation, Rewriting and the Manipulation of Literary Fame.* London: Routledge, 1992.
Le Goff, Jacques. *Time, Work, and Culture in the Middle Ages.* Translated by Arthur Goldhammer. Chicago: University of Chicago Press, 1980.
Le Goff, Jacques. *History and Memory.* Translated by Steven Rendall and Elizabeth Claman. New York: Columbia University Press, 1992.
Leland, Charles Godfrey. *The English Gipsies and Their Language.* London: Trubner, 1873.
Lemon, Alaina. "Roma (Gypsies) in the USSR: The Moscow Romani Theater", *Nationalities Papers* 19, no. 3 (1991): 359–372.
Lemon, Alaina. *Between Two Fires: Gypsy Performance and Romani Memory from Pushkin to Postsocialism.* Durham, NC: Duke University Press, 2000.
Leopardi, Giacomo. *Canti.* Edited by Mario Fubini in collaboration with Emilio Bigi. Turin: Loescher, 1964.
Lesovitch, Louise. *Roma Educational Needs in Ireland: Context and Challenges.* Dublin: City of Dublin VEC in association with Pavee Point Travellers Centre and the Roma Support Group, 2005.
Lessing, Alfred. *Mein Leben im Versteck: Wie ein deutscher Sinti den Holocaust überlebte.* Dusseldorf: Zebulon, 1993.
Levacovich, Giuseppe, and G. Ausenda. *Tzigari: Vita di un nomade.* Milan: Bompiani, 1975.
Levacovich, Mansueto. *Popolo mio dei Rom.* Edited by Paolo Zatta. Abano Terme: Francisci, 1991.
Levak, Bruno, and Mirella Karpati. *Rom sim. La tradizione dei Rom Kalderaša.* Rome: Lacio Drom, 1984.
Levi, Primo. *Se questo è un uomo.* Turin: Einaudi, 1958.
Levi, Primo. *I sommersi e i salvati.* Turin: Einaudi, 1986.
Lévi-Strauss, Claude. *Tristes Tropiques.* Paris: Plon, 1955.
Lévi-Strauss, Claude. *La pensée sauvage.* Paris: Plon, 1962.
Lévi-Strauss, Claude. "The Story of Asdiwal". In *The Structural Study of Myth and Totemism,* edited by Edmund Leach, 1–48. London: Routledge, 1967.
Lévi-Strauss, Claude. *Myth and Meaning.* London: Routledge and Kegan Paul, 1978.
Levinson, Martin P. "Literacy in English Gypsy Communities: Cultural Capital Manifested as Negative Assets". *American Educational Research Journal* 44, no. 1 (2007): 5–39.
Levinson, Martin P., and Andrew C. Sparkes. "Gypsy Children, Space, and the School Environment". *International Journal of Qualitative Studies in Education* (QSE) 18, no. 6 (2005): 751–772.
Lévy-Bruhl, Lucien. *La mentalité primitive.* Paris: Alcan, 1922.
Lewy, Guenter. *The Nazi Persecution of the Gypsies.* Oxford: Oxford University Press, 2000.
Liégeois, Jean-Pierre. *Gypsies and Travellers: Dossiers for the Intercultural Training of Teachers.* Strasbourg: Council of Europe, 1987a.
Liégeois, Jean-Pierre. *School Provision for Gypsy and Traveller Children: A Synthesis Report.* Luxembourg: Office for Official Publications of the European Communities, 1987b.

Liégeois, Jean-Pierre. *Roma, Gypsies, Travellers*. Strasbourg: Council of Europe, 1994.

Liégeois, Jean-Pierre. *School Provision for Gypsy and Traveller Children: The Gypsy Paradigm*, Interface Collection 11. Hatfield: University of Hertfordshire Press, 1998.

Liégeois, Jean-Pierre. "Statement Related to the Proposal on an 'Encyclopaedia' on Roma/Gypsy Culture and History". In *Report on "Cultural Identities of Roma, Gypsies, Travellers and Related Groups in Europe"*, edited by Alexandra Rayková. Strasbourg, 15–16 September 2003. Accessed 13 June 2012. http://www.coe.int/t/dg3/romatravellers/archive/documentation/culture/repseminaronCulturalIdentities_en.asp.

Liégeois, Jean-Pierre. *Roma in Europe*. Strasbourg: Council of Europe Publishing, 2007.

Liégeois, Jean-Pierre. *Developments in Mediation, Current Challenges and the Role of ROMED. Training Programme for Roma Mediators*. Strasbourg: Council of Europe, 2013.

Little, David, and Barbara Lazenby Simpson. *A Curriculum Framework for Romani*. Strasbourg: Council of Europe, 2008.

Lloyd, D. "Ethnic Cultures, Minority Discourse and the State". In *Colonial Discourse/Postcolonial Theory*, edited by F. Barker, P. Hulme and M. Iversen, 221–238. Manchester: Manchester University Press, 1994.

Lloyd, G., and C. Norris. "From Difference to Deviance: The Exclusion of Gypsy Traveller Pupils from School". *International Journal of Inclusive Education* 2, no. 4 (1998): 359–369.

Lloyd, Gwynedd, Joan Stead and Betty Jordan. *Travellers at School: The Experience of Parents, Pupils and Teachers*. Edinburgh: Moray House Institute of Education, Department of Equity Studies and Special Education, University of Edinburgh, 1999.

Lombroso, Cesare. *L'uomo delinquente*. Turin: Bocca, 1897.

Lucassen, Jan, and Leo Lucassen, eds. *Migration, Migration History, History: Old Paradigms and New Perspectives*. Bern: Peter Lang, 1997.

Lucassen, Leo. "A Blind Spot: Migratory and Travelling Groups in Western European Historiography". *International Review of Social History* 38, no. 2 (1993): 209–235.

Lucassen, Leo. "Eternal Vagrants? State Formation, Migration and Travelling Groups in Western Europe, 1350–1914". In *Gypsies and Other Itinerant Groups: A Socio-historical Approach*, edited by L. Lucassen, W. Willems and A. Cottaar, 55–73. Basingstoke: Macmillan, 1998.

Lucassen, Leo, Wim Willems and Annemarie Cottaar, eds. *Gypsies and Other Itinerant Groups: A Socio-Historical Approach*. Basingstoke: Macmillan, 1998.

Lundquist, Suzanne. *Native American Literatures: An Introduction*. New York: Continuum, 2004.

Luria, A.R. *Cognitive Development: Its Cultural and Social Foundations*. Translated by Martin Lopez-Morillas and Lynn Solotaroff; edited by Michael Cole. Cambridge: Harvard University Press, 1976.

Luther, Martin, ed. *The Book of Vagabonds and Beggars*. Translated by J.C. Hotten. London, 1860.

Mabardi, Sabine. "Encounters of an Heterogeneous Kind: Hybridity in Cultural Theory". *Critical Studies* 13, no. 1 (2000): 1–20.

Macfie, Robert Andrew Scott. "The Gypsy Visit to Rome in 1422". *Journal of the Gypsy Lore Society* (3), 11 (1932): 111–115.

Macfie, Robert Andrew Scott. "Gypsy Persecutions: A Survey of a Black Chapter in European History". *Journal of the Gypsy Lore Society* (3), 22 (1943): 65–78.

MacLaughlin, Jim. "The Political Geography of Anti-Traveller Racism in Ireland: The Politics of Exclusion and the Geography of Closure". *Political Geography* 17 (1998): 417–435.

MacLaughlin, Jim. "The Gypsy as 'Other' in European Society: Towards a Political Geography of Hate". *The European Legacy* 4, no. 3 (1999): 35–49.

Magris, Claudio. "Narrativa". *Enciclopedia del Novecento*. 1979. Accessed 12 February 2012. http://www.treccani.it/enciclopedia/narrativa_%28Enciclopedia-del-Novecento%29/.

Mair, Lucy P. *Primitive Government*. Baltimore: Penguin, 1962.

Mardorossian, Carine M. "From Literature of Exile to Migrant Literature". *Modern Language Studies* 32, no. 2 (2002): 15–33.

Marta, Claudio. *A Group of Lovara Gypsies Settle down in Sweden*. Stockholm: IMFO Gruppen Stockholms Universitet, 1979.

Martin-Jones, Marylin, and Kathryn Jones, eds. *Multilingual Literacies: Reading and Writing Different Worlds*. Amsterdam: John Benjamins, 2000.

Marushiakova, Elena, and Vesselin Popov. "The Bulgarian Gypsies: Searching their Place in the Society". *Balkanologie* 4, no. 2 (2000): 33–54.

Matras, Yaron. "Writing Romani: The Pragmatics of Codification in a Stateless Language". *Applied Linguistics* 20, no. 4 (1999): 481–502.

Matras, Yaron. *Romani: A Linguistic Introduction*. Cambridge: Cambridge University Press, 2002.

Matras, Yaron. "The Role of Language in Mystifying and Demystifying Gypsy Identity". In *The Role of the Romanies: Images and Counterimages of 'Gypsies'/Romanies in European Cultures*, edited by Nicholas Saul and Susan Tebbutt, 53–78. Liverpool: Liverpool University Press, 2004.

Matras, Yaron. "The Status of Romani in Europe". Report submitted to the Council of Europe's Language Policy Division, October 2005a. Accessed 22 June 2012. http://academos.ro/sites/default/files/biblio-docs/341/plugin-statusofromani.pdf.

Matras, Yaron. "The Future of Romani: Toward a Policy of Linguistic Pluralism". *Roma Rights Quarterly* 1 (2005b): 31–44.

Matras, Yaron, and Gertrud Reershemius. "Standardization beyond the State: The Case of Yiddish, Kurdish and Romani". In *Standardization of National Languages*, edited by U. von Gleich and E. Wolff, 103–123. Hamburg: UNESCO and Institut für Pädagogik, 1991.

Maximoff, Matéo. *Le prix de la liberté*. Romainville, Paris: The author, 1981.

Maximoff, Matéo. *La septième fille*. Romainville, Paris: The author, 1982.

Maximoff, Matéo. *Condamné à survivre*. Concordia: Champigny/Marne, 1984a.

Maximoff, Matéo. *Vinguerka*. Romainville, Paris: The author, 1984b.

Maximoff, Matéo. *La poupée de Maméliga*. Romainville, Paris: The author, 1986.

Maximoff, Matéo. *Les Ursitory*. Romainville, Paris: The author, 1988.

Maximoff, Matéo. *Dites-le avec des pleurs*. Romainville, Paris: The author, 1990.

Maximoff, Matéo. *Routes sans roulottes*. Romainville, Paris: The author, 1993.

Maximoff, Matéo. *Les gens du voyage*. Romainville, Paris: The author, 1995.

Mayall, David. *Gypsy-Travellers in the Nineteenth Century*. Cambridge: Cambridge University Press, 1988.

Mayall, David. *Gypsy Identities 1500–2000: From Egipcyans and Moon-men to the Ethnic Romany*. Abingdon: Routledge, 2004.

McVeigh, R. "Theorizing Sedentarism: The Roots of Anti-Nomadism". In *Gypsy Politics and Traveller Identity*, edited by Thomas Acton, 7–25. Hatfield: University of Hertfordshire Press, 1997.

Mehr, Mariella. *steinzeit*. Bern: Zytglogge-Verlag, 1981.

Mehr, Mariella. *steinzeit*. Rimini: Guaraldi; San Marino: AIEP, 1995.

Mehr, Mariella. *Brandzauber*. Zürich: Nagel and Kimche, 1998.

Melis, Alberto. *Fiabe Zingare*. Cagliari: Condaghes, 2000.

Meltzl, de Lomnitz, Hugo. "Present Tasks of Comparative Literature, Parts I and II". In *Comparative Literature: The Early Years*, edited by Hans-Joachim Schulz and Philip H. Rhein, 56–62. Chapel Hill: University of North Carolina Press, 1973.

Merolla, D., and S. Ponzanesi, eds. *Migrant Cartographies. New Cultural and Literary Spaces in Post-Colonial Europe.* Lexington Books: London, 2005.

Mode, Heinz, and Hübschmannová, Milena, eds. *Zigeunermärchen aus aller Welt. Erste Sammlung.* Leipzig: Insel-Verlag, 1983.

Moretti, Franco. "Conjectures on World Literature". *New Left Review* 1 (2000): 54–68.

Moretti, Franco. *Graphs, Maps, Trees: Abstract Models for a Literary Theory.* London: Verso, 2005.

Morley, David. *Clearing a Name.* Todmorden, Lancs: Arc Publications, 2000.

Mossa, and Bernard Leblon. *Mossa: La gitane et son destin.* Paris: L'Harmattan, 1992.

Muratori, Ludovico Antonio, ed. *Rerum Italicarum Scriptores.* Milan, 1723–1751.

Muyart de Vouglands, Pierre François. *Les loix criminelles de France, dans leur ordre naturel.* Paris: 1780.

Münster, Sebastian. *Cosmographia universalis.* Basel: 1550.

Myers, Martin, Derek McGhee and Kalwant Bhopal. "At the Crossroads: Gypsy and Traveller Parents' Perceptions of Education, Protection and Social Change". *Race, Ethnicity and Education* 13, no.4 (2010): 533–548.

Naficy, Hamid. *The Making of Exile Cultures: Iranian Television in Los Angeles.* Minneapolis: University of Minnesota Press, 1993.

Nederveen Pieterse, Jan. "Hybridity, So What? The Anti-Hybridity Backlash and the Riddles of Recognition". *Theory, Culture and Society* 18, nos. 2–3 (2001): 219–245.

Nicolae, Valeriu. "Who Now Remembers the Roma?". *Index on Censorship* 34, no. 2 (2005): 65–69.

Nicolini, Bruno. "La chiesa cattolica e gli zingari". *Lacio Drom* 23, no. 6 (1987): 21–22.

Nigris, Elisabetta. *Educazione interculturale.* Milan: Mondadori, 1996.

Nigris, Elisabetta, and Anna Ricci. *Bambini zingari a scuola. Una ricerca qualitativa sull'inserimento dei Rom in Lombardia. Analisi e proposte.* Bergamo: Edizioni Junior, 1997.

Nikolić, Jovan. *Zimmer mit Rad.* Klagenfurt: Drava-Verlag, 2004.

Nikolić, Jovan. *Weisser Rabe, Schwarzes Lamm.* Klagenfurt: Drava-Verlag, 2006.

Nikolić, Jovan. *Seelenfänger, lautlos lärmend.* Klagenfurt: Drava, 2011.

Nikolić, Jovan, and Ruždija Russo Sejdović. *Kosovo mon amour: Tragi-comédie ou drame tsigane.* Translated by Marcel Courthiade. Paris: L'Espace d'un instant, 2002.

Nirañjana, Tējasvini. *Siting Translation: History, Post-Structuralism, and The Colonial Context.* Berkeley; Oxford: University of California Press, 1992.

Nord, Deborah Epstein. *Gypsies and the British Imagination, 1807–1930.* New York: Columbia University Press, 2006.

Nurse, Keith. "Globalization and Trinidad Carnival: Diaspora, Hybridity and Identity in Global Culture". *Cultural Studies* 13, no. 4 (1999): 661–690.

O'Hanlon, Christine, and Pat Holmes. *The Education of Gypsy and Traveller Children: Towards Inclusion and Educational Achievement.* Stoke on Trent: Trentham Books, 2004.

O'Nions, Helen. *Minority Rights Protection in International Law: The Roma of Europe.* Aldershot; Burlington: Ashgate, 2007.

O'Nions, Helen. "Different and Unequal: The Educational Segregation of Roma Pupils in Europe". *Intercultural Education* 21, no. 1 (2010): 1–13.

Oefelius, A.F. *Rerum boicarum scriptores*, vol. no. 1. Augsburg, 1763.

Ofsted. *A Survey of Educational Provision for Travelling Children*. London: OFSTED, 1996.

Ofsted. *Raising the Attainment of Minority Ethnic Pupils: School and LEA Responses*. London: OFSTED, 1999.

Ofsted. *Managing Support for the Attainment of Pupils from Minority Ethnic Groups*. London: OFSTED, 2001.

Ofsted. *Provision and Support for Traveller Pupils*. 2003. Accessed 12 August 2012. www.ofsted.gov.uk.

Ogbu, John U. "Cultural Discontinuities and Schooling". *Anthropology and Education Quarterly* 13, no. 4 (1982): 290–307.

Ogbu, John U. "Variability in Minority School Performance: A Problem in Search of an Explanation". *Anthropology and Education Quarterly* 18, no. 4 (1987): 312–334.

Ogbu, John U. "Minority Status and Literacy in Perspective". *Daedalus* 119, no. 2 (1990): 141–168.

Ogbu, John U., and H.D. Simons. "Voluntary and Involuntary Minorities: A Cultural-Ecological Theory of School Performance with Some Implications for Education". *Anthropology and Education Quarterly* 29, no. 2 (1998): 155–188.

Okely, Judith. "Gypsy Women: Models in Conflict". In *Perceiving Women*, edited by S. Arden, 55–86. London: Malaby, 1975.

Okely, Judith. *The Traveller-Gypsies*. Cambridge: Cambridge University Press, 1983.

Okely, Judith. "Non-Territorial Culture as the Rationale for the Assimilation of Gypsy Children". *Childhood* 4, no. 1 (1997): 63–80.

Okely, Judith. "Cultural Ingenuity and Travelling Autonomy: Not Copying, Just Choosing". In *Romani Culture and Gypsy Identity*, edited by Thomas Acton and Gary Mundy, 190–205. Hatfield: University of Hertfordshire Press, 1999.

Olson, David R. *The World on Paper: The Conceptual and Cognitive Implications of Writing and Reading*. Cambridge: Cambridge University Press, 1994.

Olson, David R., and Nancy Torrance, eds. *The Making of Literate Societies*. Malden, Mass.; Oxford: Blackwell, 2001.

Olson, David R., Nancy Torrance and Angela Hildyard. *Literacy, Language and Learning: The Nature and Consequences of Reading and Writing*. Cambridge: Cambridge University Press, 1985.

Ong, Walther J. *Orality and Literacy: The Technologizing of the Word*. London: Methuen, 1982.

Open Society Institute (OSI). *Transition of Students: Roma Special Schools Initiative*, Year 4 Evaluation, Final Report. Budapest: Open Society Institute, 2004.

Opfermann, U.F. *"Seye kein Zigeuner, sondern Kayserlicher Cornet". Sinti im 17. und 18. Jahrhundert*. Berlin: Metropol Verlag, 2007.

Opre Roma Report. *The Education of Gypsy Childhood in Europe*. 2002. Accessed 15 August 2013. http://cordis.europa.eu/documents/documentlibrary/82608111EN6.pdf.

Pahor, Boris. "La cella dalle piastrelle bianche. La camera a gas per gli Zingari a Struthof". *Lacio Drom* 5 (1980): 30–32.

Palumbo-Liu, David, ed. *The Ethnic Canon: Histories, Institutions, and Interventions*. Minneapolis and London: University of Minnesota Press, 1995.

Papastergiadis, Nikos. "Tracing Hybridity in Theory". In *Debating Cultural Hybridity: Multi-Cultural Identities and the Politics of Anti-Racism*, edited by P. Werbner and T. Modood, 257–281. London: Zed Books, 1997.

Papastergiadis, Nikos. *The Turbulence of Migration: Globalization, Deterritorialization, and Hybridity*. Cambridge: Polity Press, 2000.

Payne, Pierre S.R. "Trail-Signs". *Journal of the Gypsy Lore Society* (3), 14, no. 4 (1935): 169–174.

Project on Ethnic Relations Report. "The Romanies in Central and Eastern Europe: Illusions and Reality". Princeton: PER, 1992.

Petrova, Dimitrina. "The Romani Movement: What Shape, What Direction?". ERRC, 7 November 2001. Accessed 18 June 2012. http://www.errc.org/article/the-romani-movement-what-shape-what-direction/1292.

Piasere, Leonardo. "Māre Roma: catégories humaines et structure sociale: une contribution à l'ethnologie tsigane". Ph.D. diss., Paris: École des Hautes Études en Sciences Sociales, 1984.

Piasere, Leonardo. "A scuola dai Gage: ovvero quando l'educatore diventa disadattato". In *Scuola di Stato e nomadi*, edited by P. Zatta, 33–59. Abano Terme: Francisci e Università verde, 1986.

Piasere, Leonardo. "In Search of New Niches: The productive organization of the peripatetic Xoraxané in Italy". In *The Other Nomads: Peripatetic Minorities in Cross-Cultural Perspective*, edited by Aparna Rao, 111–132. Cologne: Böhlau, 1987.

Piasere, Leonardo. "De origine Cinganorum". *Études et documents balkaniques et méditerranéens* 14 (1989): 105–126.

Piasere, Leonardo. *Popoli delle discariche: Saggi di Antropologia Zingara*. Rome: CISU, 1991.

Piasere, Leonardo. "'Etnoantropologie' a confronto: a proposito di due opere recenti di M. Levakovich e C. Sgorlon". In *La cultura popolare in Friuli: "lo sguardo da fuori"*, edited by Giuseppe Fornasari and Gian Paolo Gri, 105–131. Udine: Accademia di Scienze, Lettere e Arti, 1993.

Piasere, Leonardo. *Il più antico testo italiano in romanes (1646): una riscoperta e una lettura etnostorica*. Verona: Libreria Universitaria, 1994.

Piasere, Leonardo. "I segni 'segreti' degli Zingari". *Ricerca Folklorica* 31 (1995): 83–105.

Pizer, John. *The Idea of World Literature: History and Pedagogical Practice*. Baton Rouge: Louisiana State University Press, 2006.

Polányi, Karl. *The Great Transformation*. Boston: Beacon Press, 1957.

Poueyto, Jean-Luc, ed. *Illettrismes et Cultures*. Paris: L'Harmattan, 2001.

Pratt, Mary Louise. *Imperial Eyes: Travel Writing and Transculturation*. London: Routledge, 1992.

Pratt, Mary Louise. "'Yo Soy La Malinche': Chicana Writers and the Poetics of Ethnonationalism". *Callaloo* 16, no. 4 (1993): 859–873.

Pratt, Mary Louise. "Transculturation and Autoethnography: Peru, 1615/1980". In *Colonial Discourse/Postcolonial Theory*, edited by Francis Barker, Peter Hulme and Margaret Iversen, 24–46. Manchester: Manchester University Press, 1994.

Predari, Francesco. *Origini e vicende degli Zingari*. Milan: Lampato, 1841.

Prendergast, Christopher, ed. *Debating World Literature*. London: Verso, 2004.

Pushkin, Alexander. *Tsygany*. Translated by Nikolai Pankov as *Roma*. Gosudarstvennoe Izdatel'stvo: Moscow, 1937.

Pushkin, Alexander. *The Bronze Horseman: Selected Poems of Alexander Pushkin*. Translated by D.M. Thomas. London: Secker and Warburg, 1982.

Rao, Aparna. "Les Tsiganes Sinte du Polygone". *Revue des Sciences Sociales de la France de l'Est* 5 (1976): 182–201.

Rao, Aparna, ed. *The Other Nomads: Peripatetic Minorities in Cross-Cultural Perspective*. Cologne: Böhlau, 1987.

Records of the Parliaments of Scotland to 1707 (University of St Andrews: 2007–2009). Accessed: 26 June 2012. http://www.rps.ac.uk/.

Reilly, John. "Criticism of Ethnic Literature: Seeing the Whole Story". *MELUS* 5, no. 1 (1978): 2–13.

Reyniers, A., and J. Valet. "Les Jeniš". *Études Tsiganes* 2 (1991): 11–35.

Ribton-Turner, C.J. *A History of Vagrants and Vagrancy and Beggars and Begging*. London, 1887.

Ringold, Dena, Mitchell A. Orenstein and Erika Wilkens. "Roma in an Expanding Europe: Breaking the Poverty Cycle". Washington, DC: The World Bank, 2005. Accessed 12 August 2012. http://siteresources.worldbank.org/EXTROMA/Resources/roma_in_expanding_europe.pdf.

Roek, Bernd. "The Enchantment of the Alien: Metaphysics and Marginality in Late Medieval and Early Modern Europe". *The Medieval History Journal* 7, no. 1 (2004), 39–57.

Romane krle/Voci zingare. Rome: Sensibili alle Foglie, 1992.

Romanès, Alexandre. *Paroles perdues*. Paris: Gallimard, 2004.

Romanès, Alexandre. *Sur l'épaule de l'ange*. Paris: Gallimard, 2010.

Rose, Romani. *The Nazi Genocide of the Sinti and Roma*. Heidelberg: Documentary and Cultural Centre of German Sinti and Roma, 1995.

Rose, Romani. "The Roma and Sinti during the Holocaust and Today". *UN Chronicle* 43 (2006): 66.

Rose, Romani, and W. Weiss. *Sinti und Roma im "Dritten Reich"*. Göttingen: Lamuv Taschenbuch, 1995.

Rosenberg, Karen, and Ceija Stojka. "They Couldn't Take Our Thoughts: A Conversation with Ceija Stojka". *The Women's Review of Books* 12, no. 6 (1995): 18–20.

Ruoff, A. LaVonne Brown. *American Indian Literatures: An Introduction, Bibliographic Review, and Selected Bibliography*. New York: Modern Language Association of America, 1990.

Rushdie, Salman. *Imaginary Homelands: Essays and Criticism 1981–1991*. London: Granta Books in association with Penguin, 1991.

Safran, William. "Diaspora in Modern Societies: Myths of Homeland and Return". *Diaspora* 1, no. 1 (1991): 83–99.

Sahlins, Marshall. *Stone Age Economics*. Chicago: Aldine-Atherton, 1972.

Said, Edward. *Orientalism*. London: Routledge and Kegan Paul, 1978.

Salijesor, Seljajdin. *Dzivdipe maškaro Roma*. Preševa: Grafolex, 1988.

Salo, Matt T. "Gypsy Ethnicity: Implications of Native Categories and Interaction for Ethnic Classification". *Ethnicity* 6 (1979): 73–96.

Salo, Matt T., and Sheila Salo. "Romnichel Economic and Social Organization in Urban New England, 1850–1930". *Urban Anthropology* 11, nos. 3–4 (1982): 273–313.

Sampson, John. "Dekker on the Gypsies". *Journal of the Gypsy Lore Society* 3 (1891–1892): 248–250.

Sampson, John. "On the Origin and Early Migrations of the Gypsies". *Journal of the Gypsy Lore Society* (3), 2, no. 4 (1923): 156–169.

Sampson, John, ed. *The Wind on the Heath: A Gypsy Anthology*. London: Chatto and Windus, 1930.

Saul, Nicholas, and Susan Tebbutt, eds. *The Role of the Romanies: Images and Counterimages of "Gypsies"/Romanies in European Cultures*. Liverpool: Liverpool University Press, 2004.

Save the Children. *Denied a Future?: The Right to Education of Roma/Gypsy & Traveller Children in Europe*. London: Save the Children, 2001.

Schöpf, Paula. *La mendicante dei sogni*. Bolzano: Atelier grafico, 1997.

Schreiber, Heinrich, ed. *Taschenbuch für Geschichte und Alterthum in Süddeutschland*. Freiburg, 1839.

Scribner, Sylvia, and Michael Cole. "Cognitive Consequences of Formal and Informal Education". *Science* 182 (1973): 553–559.

Scribner, Sylvia, and Michael Cole. *Culture and Thought: A Psychological Introduction*. New York: Wiley, 1974.

Scribner, Sylvia, and Michael Cole. *The Psychology of Literacy*. Cambridge, MA: Harvard University Press, 1981.

Sebald, Winfried G. *The Emigrants*. London: Harvill Press, 1997.

Sebald, Winfried G. *Austerlitz*. London: Penguin, 2001.

Sejdić, Aladin. *Me aváv durál / Io vengo da lontano*. Milan: ISU, 2000.

Sejdić, Rasim. *Rasim poeta zingaro*. Edited and translated by Giulio Soravia. Rho: Publi and Press, 1987.

Sejdić, Rasim, and Giulio Soravia. "Lo zingaro e il Gagio". *Lacio Drom* 5 (1978): 4–24.

Sejdić, Rasim, and Giulio Soravia. "Due testi di R. Sejdić: Sar o Rom postanisarda Hoga, O Rom taj e ciréš. Note linguistiche". *Lacio Drom* 5 (1980): 2–8.

Sejdić, Rasim, and Giulio Soravia. "I tre doni. Note su I tre doni, con un cenno sul sistema di parentela xoraxano". *Lacio Drom* 2 (1981): 2–7.

Seyhan, Azade. *Writing Outside the Nation*. Princeton: Princeton University Press, 2001.

Seymour-Smith, Charlotte. *Macmillan Dictionary of Anthropology*. London and Basingstoke: Macmillan, 1986.

Sheffer, Gabriel. *Diaspora Politics: At Home Abroad*. Cambridge: Cambridge University Press, 2003.

Shor, Ira. "Education is Politics: Paulo Freire's Critical Pedagogy". In *Paulo Freire: A Critical Encounter*, edited by Peter Mclaren and Peter Leonard, 25–35. London: Routledge, 1993.

Sibley, David. *Outsiders in Urban Societies*. Oxford: Blackwell, 1982.

Sibley, David. *Geographies of Exclusion*. London and New York: Routledge, 1995.

Sigona, Nando. "Locating 'The Gypsy Problem'. The Roma in Italy: Stereotyping, Labelling and 'Nomad Camps'". *Journal of Ethnic and Migration Studies* 31, no. 4 (2005): 741–756.

Simson, Walter. *A History of the Gipsies: With Specimens of the Gipsy Language*. Edited by James Simson. New York: Sampson Low, Son & Marston, 1866.

Smith, Anthony D. *Nationalism: Theory, Ideology, History*. Cambridge: Polity Press, 2001.

Smith, Charlie. *The Spirit and the Flame*. Manchester: Traveller Education Service, 1990.

Smith, David M. "The Anthropology of Literacy Acquisition". In *The Acquisition of Literacy: Ethnographic Perspectives*, edited by B. Schieffelin and P. Gilmore, 261–275. Norwood, NJ: Ablex, 1986.

Smith, Tracy. "Recognising Difference: The Romani 'Gypsy' Child Socialisation and Education Process". *British Journal of Sociology of Education* 18, no. 2 (1997): 243–256.

Sollors, Werner. *Beyond Ethnicity*. New York: Oxford University Press, 1986.

Sollors, Werner, ed. *The Invention of Ethnicity*. New York: Oxford University Press, 1989.

Sonneman, Toby. "Dark Mysterious Wanderers: The Migrating Metaphor of the Gypsy". *Journal of Popular Culture* 32, no. 4 (1999): 119–139.

Sonneman, Toby. *Shared Sorrows: A Gypsy Family Remembers the Holocaust*. Hatfield: University of Hertfordshire Press, 2002.

Soravia, Giulio. *Dialetti degli Zingari italiani*. Pisa: Pacini, 1977.

Soravia, Giulio. "A Wandering Voice". *Unesco Courier* 37, no. 10 (1984): 21–23.

Soravia, Giulio. "La lingua zingara in Italia". In *Rom, Sinti, Kalé ... Zingari e Viaggianti in Europa*, edited by Jean-Pierre Liégeois, 283–285. Rome: Lacio Drom, 1994.

Spelman, Henry. *Archeologus: In Modum Glossarii ad Rem Antiquam Posteriorem: continentis Latino-Barbara Peregrina, Obsoleta, et Novatae Significationis Vocabula.* London: John Beale, 1626.

Spinelli, Alessandro G. "Gli Zingari nel Modenese". *Lacio Drom* 5 (1978): 25–55.

Spinelli, Santino. *Gilí Romaní/Canto Zingaro.* Rome: Lacio Drom, 1988.

Spinelli, Santino. *Romanipè/Ziganità.* Chieti: Solfanelli, 1993.

Spinelli, Santino, ed. *Šunge luluda/Fiori profumati.* Pescara: Italica, 1994a.

Spinelli, Santino. *Princkaràng/Conosciamoci.* Pescara: Italica. 1994b.

Spinelli, Santino, ed. *Baxtalo Drom/Felice Cammino.* 3 vols. Pescara: Tracce, 1995–1997.

Spinelli, Santino. "Introduction". In *Baxtaló Drom/Felice Cammino vol. III: Antologia delle migliori opere del 4° Concorso Artistico Internazionale "Amico Rom"*, edited by Santino Spinelli, 9–12. Lanciano: Thèm Romanó, 1997.

Spinelli, Santino. "Il mondo, la cultura e la lingua degli zingari di George Borrow e la letteratura zingara in lingua inglese". Undergraduate diss., University of Bologna, 1998.

Spinelli, Santino. *Baro Romano Drom: The Long Road of Rom, Sinti, Kale, Manouches and Romanichals.* Rome: Meltemi, 2003.

Spivak, Gayatri Chakravorty. *In Other Worlds: Essays in Cultural Politics.* New York; London: Methuen, 1987.

Spivak, Gayatri Chakravorty. "Can the Subaltern Speak?". In *Marxism and the Interpretation of Culture*, edited by Larry Grossberg and Cary Nelson, 271–313. Urbana: University of Illinois Press, 1988.

Spivak, Gayatri Chakravorty. *Outside the Teaching Machine.* New York: Routledge, 1993.

Spivak, Gayatri Chakravorty. *A Critique of Postcolonial Reason.* Cambridge: Harvard University Press, 2003a.

Spivak, Gayatri C. *Death of a Discipline.* New York: Columbia, 2003b.

Stewart, Michael. "'True Speech': Song and the Moral Order of a Hungarian Vlach Gypsy Community". *Man* 24 (1989): 79–102.

Stewart, Michael. "The Puzzle of Roma Persistence: Group Identity without a Nation". In *Gypsy Politics and Traveller Identity*, edited by Thomas Acton, 84–98. Hatfield: University of Hertfordshire Press, 1997.

Stewart, Michael. "Remembering without Commemoration: The Mnemonics and Politics of Holocaust Memories among European Roma". *Journal of the Royal Anthropological Institute* 10, no. 4 (2004): 967–976.

Stock, Brian. *The Implications of Literacy.* Princeton: Princeton University Press, 1983.

Stojka, Ceija. *Wir leben im Verborgenen: Erinnerungen einer Rom-Zigeunerin.* Edited by Karin Berger. Vienna: Picus, 1988.

Stojka, Ceija. *Reisende auf dieser Welt: Aus dem Leben einer Rom-Zigeunerin.* Vienna: Picus, 1992.

Stojka, Ceija. *Meine Wahl zu schreiben—ich kann es nicht/O fallo de isgiri—me tschschanaf les: Gedichte und Bilder.* Landeck: Emigan Yayinlari Editions, 2003.

Stojka, Ceija. *Träume ich, dass ich lebe? Mein Leben in Bergen-Belsen.* Vienna: Picus, 2005.

Stojka, Karl. *The Story of Karl Stojka: A Childhood in Birkenau.* Washington, DC: Unites States Holocaust Memorial Council, 1992.

Stojka, Mongo. *Papierene Kinder: Glück, Zerstörung und Neubeginn einer Roma-Familie in Osterreich.* Wien: Molden, 2000.

Street, Brian V. *Literacy in Theory and Practice.* Cambridge: Cambridge University Press, 1984.

Street, Brian V. *Cross-Cultural Approaches to Literacy*. Cambridge: Cambridge University Press, 1993.

Street, Brian V. *Social Literacies: Critical Approaches to Literacy in Development, Ethnography and Education*. London: Longman, 1995.

Štrukelj, Pavla. *Romi na Slovenskem*. Ljubljana: Cankarjeva Založba, 1980.

Sutherland, Anne. *Gypsies: The Hidden Americans*. Long Grove, IL: Waveland Press, 1975.

Symons, Arthur. "In Praise of Gypsies". *Journal of the Gypsy Lore Society* (2), 1, no. 4 (1908): 294–299.

Tamburri, Anthony. *To Hyphenate or not to Hyphenate: The Italian/American Writer: An Other American*. Montréal: Guernica, 1991.

Tauber, Elisabeth. *Men ham sinti—men ham kek gage! About Sinti, Childhood, School and the Others*. Report for the *Opre Roma* Project. University of Florence, 2002.

Tauber, Elisabeth. "Sinti Estraixaria Children at School, or, How to Preserve 'the Sinti Way of Thinking'". *Romani Studies* (5), 4, no. 2 (2003): 1–23.

Thomas, Keith. "The Meaning of Literacy in Early Modern England". In *The Written Word: Literacy in Transition*, edited by Gerd Baumann, 97–131. Oxford: Clarendon, 1986.

Thomsen, Mads Rosendahl. *Mapping World Literature: International Canonization and Transnational Literatures*. London: Continuum, 2008.

Thompson, T. W. "English Gypsy Folktales and Other Traditional Stories". *Journal of the Gypsy Lore Society* (3), 8 (1914–1915).

Thurmair, Johann (Johannes Aventinus). *Annalium Boiorum Libri VII*. Lipsia, 1710.

Tipler, Derek A. "From Nomads to Nation". *Midstream* (August/September) (1968): 61–70.

Tomasi, Piergiorgio. "La vita in un campo sosta regolamentato: il caso di Trento". In *Italia Romanì*, vol. 2, edited by Leonardo Piasere, 71–91. Rome: CISU, 1999.

Tong, Diane. *Gypsy Folktales*. San Diego: Harvest Books, 1989.

Toninato, Paola. "La funzione della scrittura fra i Roma Sloveno-Croati: un utilizzo diversificato". Undergraduate thesis, University of Trieste, 1997.

Toninato, Paola. "L'uso femminile della scrittura fra i Roma sloveno-croati". In *Italia Romanì*, vol. 2, edited by Leonardo Piasere, 147–168. Rome: CISU, 1999.

Toninato, Paola. "The Rise of Written Literature among the Roma: A Study of the Role of Writing in the Current Re-Definition of Romani Identity with Specific Reference to the Italian Case". Ph.D. diss., University of Warwick, 2004.

Toninato, Paola. "Translating Gypsies: Nomadic Writing and the Negotiation of Romani Identity". *The Translator* 12, no. 2 (2006): 233–251.

Toninato, Paola. "Deterritorialization and Subversive Mimicry in Contemporary Romani Writing". Paper presented at the workshop *The "field of literature" in the context of ethno-national conflicts*. University of Exeter, Exeter Centre for Ethno-political Studies, 13 March 2009.

Toninato, Paola. "The Making of Gypsy Diasporas". *Translocations* 5, no. 1, (2009). Accessed 8 August 2012. http://www.translocations.ie/docs/v05i01/Vol_5_Issue_1_c.pdf.

Toninato, Paola. "The Political Use of Romani Writing". In *Grenzerfahrungen: Roma-Literaturen in der Romania*, edited by J. Blandfort and M. Hertrampf, 85–98. Berlin: LIT, 2011.

Tosuner, Hakan, Simona Pagano and Pauline Vermeren. "Debates on Difference and Integration in Education in France, Italy and Germany". Working paper produced within the TOLERACE project. Accessed 5 August 2012. http://www.ces.uc.pt/projectos/tolerace/pages/en/publications/working-papers.php.

Turner, Victor. *The Ritual Process: Structure and Anti-structure*. London: Routledge and Kegan Paul, 1969.

Tymoczko, Maria, and Edwin Gentzler, eds. *Translation and Power*. Amherst: University of Massachusetts Press, 2002.

UNESCO. "The Plurality of Literacy and Its Implications for Policies and Programmes". UNESCO Education Sector Position Paper. Paris: UNESCO, 2004.

UNICEF. *Education for All?* Regional Monitoring Report no. 5. Florence: UNICEF International Child Development Centre, 1998.

UNICEF. "Romani Children in South East Europe. The Challenge of Overcoming Centuries of Distrust and Discrimination". Regional Office for CEE/CIS, Social and Economic Policy for Children. Discussion Paper ISSUE no. 7, March 2007.

Van Gennep, A. *The Rites of Passage*. Translated by Monika B. Vizedom and Gabrielle L. Caffee. Chicago: Chicago University Press, 1960.

Vaux de Foletier, François. *Les Tsiganes dans l'ancienne France*. Paris: Connaissance du Monde, 1961.

Vaux de Foletier, François. "Le pèlerinage romain des Tsiganes en 1422 et les letters du Pape Martin V". *Études Tsiganes* 4 (1965): 13–19.

Vaux de Foletier, François. *Mille ans d'histoire des Tsiganes*. Paris: Fayard, 2003.

Venuti, Lawrence. *The Translator's Invisibility: A History of Translation*. London: Routledge, 1995.

Vermeersch, Peter. "Roma Identity and Ethnic Mobilisation in Central European Politics". Paper presented at the European Consortium for Political Research, Grenoble, 6–11 April 2001.

Vermeersch, Peter. "Ethnic Mobilization and the Political Conditionality of European Union Accession: The Case of the Roma in Slovakia". *Journal of Ethnic and Migration Studies* 28 (2002): 1–21.

Vermeersch, Peter. "Ethnic Minority Identity and Movement Politics: The Case of the Roma in the Czech Republic and Slovakia". *Ethnic and Racial Studies* 26, no. 5 (2003): 879–901.

Vygotsky, Lev S. *Thought and Language*. Edited and translated by E. Hanfmann and G. Vakar. Massachusetts Institute of Technology: M.I.T. Press, 1962.

Wagner, Serge, with the collaboration of Pierre Grenier. *Analphabétisme de minorité et alphabétisation d'affirmation nationale: à propos de l'Ontario français*. Toronto: Ministry of Education, 1990.

Wais, Bronislawa (Papuśa). "Gili Romanì—Phur Miri". *Lacio Drom* 5 (1987): 2–9.

Weber, Max. *The Religion of India: The Sociology of Hinduism and Buddhism*. Translated and edited by Hans H. Gerth and Don Martindale. New York: Free Press; London: Collier Macmillan, 1958.

Wellstood, Frederick C. "Some French Edicts against the Gypsies". *Journal of the Gypsy Lore Society* (2), 5 (1911–1912): 313–316.

Werbner, Pnina, and Tariq Modood, eds. *Debating Cultural Hybridity*. London: Zed Books, 1997.

Werbner, Pnina. "The Limits of Cultural Hybridity: On Ritual Monsters, Poetic License and Contested Postcolonial Purification". *Journal of the Royal Anthropological Institute* (N.S.) 7 (2001): 133–152.

Weyrauch, Walter O., ed. *Gypsy Law: Romani Legal Traditions and Culture*. Berkeley: University of California Press, 2001.

White, Hayden. *Tropics of Discourse: Essays on Cultural Criticism*. Baltimore and London: John Hopkins University Press, 1978.

Willems, Wim. *In Search of the True Gypsy: From Enlightenment to Final Solution*. Translated by D. Bloch. London: Frank Cass, 1997.

Williams, Patrick. "Storia del Manuš, del Pirdo e del porcospino". *Lacio Drom* 22, no. 1 (1986): 2–22.

Williams, Patrick. "'Noi non ne parliamo . . .' Le relazioni tra i vivi e i morti in una comunità "Manuš" della Francia". *La Ricerca Folklorica* 22 (1991): 75–87.

Williams, Patrick. *"Noi, non ne parliamo". I vivi e i morti tra i Manuš*. Translated by Fabio Viti. Rome: CISU, 1997.

Williams, Patrick. "La scrittura fra l'orale e lo scritto". In *Per iscritto: Antropologia delle scritture quotidiane*, edited by Daniel Fabre and translated by Anna Iuso, 79–99. Lecce: Argo, 1998.

Williams, Patrick. *Gypsy World: The Silence of the Living and the Voices of the Dead*. Chicago: University of Chicago Press, 2003.

Winstedt Eric O. "The Patteran". *Journal of the Gypsy Lore Society* (2), 2 (1911–12): 153–155.

Wlislocki, Heinrich von H. *Haideblüten. Volkslieder der transsilvanischen Zigeuner*. Leipzig: W. Friedrich, 1880.

Wlislocki, Heinrich von H. *Vier Märchen der transsilvanischen Zeltzigeuner*. Budapest, 1886.

Wlislocki, Heinrich von H. "Wanderzeichen der Zigeuner". *Ethnologische Mitteilungen aus Ungarn* 2, nos. 6–8 (1891–92): 133–139.

Wlislocki, Heinrich von H. *Zur Ethnographie der Zigeuner in Südosteuropa*. Frankfurt am Main: Peter Lang, 1994.

Wolf, Eric. "Aspects of Group Relations in a Complex Society". *American Anthropologist* 58 (1956): 1065–1078.

Woloch, Cecilia. *Tsigan: The Gypsy Poem*. Los Angeles: Cahuenga Press, 2002.

Womack, Craig S. *Red on Red: Native American Literary Separatism*. Minneapolis: University of Minnesota Press, 1999.

Young, James E. *Writing and Rewriting the Holocaust: Narrative and the Consequences of Interpretation*. Bloomington: Indiana University Press, 1988.

Young, Robert J. C. *Colonial Desire: Hybridity in Theory, Culture and Race*. London: Routledge, 1995.

Zabus, Chantal. *The African Palimpsest: Indigenization of Language in the West African Europhone Novel*. Amsterdam: Rodopi, 1991.

Zaniboni, Paola. "Itinerari per l'insegnamento della matematica". In *L'inserimento scolastico dei bambini rom e sinti*, edited by Sabrina Ignazi and Monica Napoli, 110–123. Milan: Franco Angeli, 2004.

Zarate, Geneviève, A. Gohard-Radenkovic, D. Lussier and H. Penz, eds. *Cultural Mediation in Language Learning and Teaching*. Strasbourg: Council of Europe, 2004.

Zuccon, Maria. "La legislazione degli Zingari negli Stati italiani prima della Rivoluzione". *Lacio Drom* 1–2 (1979): 1–68.

Index

A

Advić, Šemšo, 87–88, 166–167
Advisory Council for the Education of
    Romany and other Travellers
    (ACERT), 38
African-Americans. *See* Black Americans
alphabetic writing, 1, 52, 54, 64–65,
    67, 112, 139, 164
  instrumental use of, 62–64
  versus non-alphabetic writing, 3, 43
America (North), 64, 73, 85, 96, 115,
    121
America (South), 73, 84
American Rom, 47
Anderson, Benedict, 150
Andreas, Presbyter Ratisboniensis, 10
anti-Gypsism, 96, 146, 147, 197n17
  anti-Gypsy legislation, 8, 18, 20,
    184n37
appearance, Gypsies', 7, 11–13, 16,
    55, 99
assimilation, xiv–xv, 2, 7, 24, 29, 34, 75,
    79, 86, 108, 149, 161, 164, 168
  cultural, xv, 61, 64, 111, 115, 168
  policies of, xv, 29, 75, 79, 81, 86, 162
  through education, xiv, 2, 24, 28, 41
associations, 34–35, 38, 77, 78, 80, 81,
    86, 87, 90, 114, 142, 148, 172,
    198n31
Athinganoi. See names given to Gypsies
Auschwitz, 85, 86, 102, 103, 104
Australia, 84–85
Australian Aboriginals, xv, 126, 135
Austria, 9, 77, 85–86, 91, 158, 159
autoethnography, in Romani literature,
    191n4
  autoethnographic texts, 94, 191n4
Aventinus (Johann Thurmaier), 19

B

Bakhtin, Mikhail, 127, 129
  double consciousness, 129
  idea of the carnivalesque, 127
  notion of intentional hybridity, 129
  notion of linguistic hybridity, 127
Balkans, 59, 73, 74, 89
Balogh, Attila, 80
Banga, Dezider, 79, 107
bans, against Gypsies, 18–20, 148, 186n7
Barany, Zoltan, 74, 197n21
Bari, Károly, 46, 80, 117
Barth, Fredrik, 165, 194n12
Barthes, Roland, 64, 129
Barton, David, 64, 187n19
Basile Green, R., 120
Bastide, Roger, 12
Bavaria, 21
beggars
  Gypsies as, 14, 19, 55, 107, 187n28
  in medieval society, 9, 183n24
begging, 27, 29, 61, 64
Beier, A.L., 19
Belton, Brian, 196n14
Belugins, Alexander (Leksa Manuš), 76
Benjamin, Walter, 154
Berberski, Slobodan, 77, 142, 189n13
Bergen-Belsen, concentration camp,
    86, 158, 197n17
Berlin, 78
  Berlin Wall, 142
Bernal, Jorge M.F., 84, 151–152
Bhabha, Homi, 127–128
  notion of camouflage, 10
  notion of mimicry, 10, 128, 132,
    195n27
  Third Space, 127, 199n13
bilingualism
  bilingual education, 179
  bilingual texts, 132, 175
  of Romani authors, 122, 165
Black American(s), 96, 115
  Black American literature, 115

black colour/blackness of the Gypsies,
    11–13, 17, 96–97, 98–99,
    182n12, 182n14–15
Black diaspora, 152
(black)smiths, 79, 183n27
Bohémiens/Bohemians. *See* names
    given to Gypsies
Bologna, 11
Borrow, George, 56–57
borrowing
    in Romani literature, 4, 115, 132
    lexical/linguistic, 73, 156
boundaries, 71, 82, 119, 126, 128–
    129, 165–166
    between Roma and non-Roma, 49,
        59, 101, 164, 168
    between Romani groups, 4, 154
    notion of ethnic boundary (*see*
        Barth, Fredrik)
Bourdieu, Pierre, 194n15
bourgeois of Paris, journal of a, 11
bricolage, 128, 132–133, 135, 194n18
Britain. *See* United Kingdom

C
Canada, 85
cannibalism
    accusations of, 17
canon
    and Romani literature, 114, 116,
        118, 126, 132–135 (*see also*
        Romani literature, non-canonical
        features of)
    of world literature, 126
cant (jargon), 14, 190n34
caravan schools, 34
Caravan Sites Act (1968), 185n18
caravans, xv, 57, 131, 166, 176
Cardona, Raimondo, 53
carnival, as a site of subversion, 127
Centro studi zingari (Centre for Gypsy
    Studies), 148, 198n31
Césaire, Aimé, 97, 191n11
Charles III, Spanish King, 184n2–3
Charles University, 158, 198n32
child stealing, accusations of, 17
children
    assimilation policies of, xiv, 28, 29,
        30, 32, 86
    and hybrid literacy practices,
        173–180
    and non-Roma education, 3, 26, 30,
        31, 32, 33–41, 42–43, 67
    and the Romani approach to educa-
        tion, xv, 44–46

    and school mediators, 172–173
Children Act (1908), 184n4
chine (non-alphabetic signs), 59–61.
    See also graphic codes
Church attitudes to Roma/Gypsies,
    14–15, 30, 150
Cingani/*Cingari*. *See* names given to
    Gypsies
Cioabă, Luminiţa Mihai, 72, 81, 90,
    112, 189n19
Cirelli, Luigi, 72, 87, 88
Cohen, Anthony, 166
Cohen, Robin, 193n5
Colocci, Adriano, 16, 61–62
Cologne, 78, 90
Cologne Declaration, 90
colonisation
    of the Romani identity, 4, 7, 145
    self-colonisation, 132
Comité International Tsigane (CIT).
    See organisations
Common European Framework of
    Reference for Languages, 172
conciliation, 162
conflict resolution, through mediation,
    161, 196n2
contact zones, notion of. *See* Pratt,
    Mary Louise
Cornerus, Hermann, 9, 10, 11
Cotten, Rena, 47
Council of Europe, 35, 36, 37, 142,
    185n14–15, 199n14
Counter-Reformation, 14
Courthiade, Marcel, 157
Crabb, James, 31
criminalisation of the Roma/Gypsies,
    20, 62, 93, 183n22
cultural memory of the Roma/Gypsies,
    32, 117
Čvorović, Jelena, 47
Czech Republic, 37, 76, 79, 158
Czechoslovakia, 75, 79, 85, 186n7

D
dangerous classes, 18, 184n31
de Certeau, Michel, 194n10
decentralisation, in Romani literature,
    125–126
Declaration of a Nation. See Interna-
    tional Romani Union
Dekker, Thomas, 55–56
Deleuze, Gilles, 121, 122, 124–125
deterritorialisation, 121–122, 125,
    194n11
    linguistic, 4, 115, 122

dialect. *See* Romani language
dialogism, in Romani literature, 126
  dialogic structure of Romani texts,
    130–132
diaspora, 119, 128, 151–152, 193n5
  Black, 152
  diasporic literature, 119
  discourse among the Roma, 151,
    197n20
  Jewish, 152
  Romani, 151, 154
Dick-Zatta, Jane, 47, 49, 141, 164,
    177–178
displacement, 128, 152, 169, 194n11
  and migrant literature, 120, 121
  of Romani identity, 145
  and Romani literature, 122,
    125–126
Djélem Djélem (Romani anthem), 142,
    153, 197n26
Djurić, Rajko, 72, 77–78, 94, 107, 142,
    145, 146, 159
double consciousness. *See* Bakhtin,
    Mikhail
Doughty, Louise, 84, 85

E

Eagleton, Terry, 129
Eco, Umberto, 72
education. *See also* schooling
  formal, 43–44, 45, 46
  intercultural, 4, 36, 172, 179
  remedial, 35, 38
  special, 28, 38
  versus instruction, 34, 41, 44
Egypt, 10, 13, 19, 183n26
Egyptian Act (1530), 184n37
Egyptians. *See* names given to Gypsies
Elizabeth I, queen of England, 19
England, 19, 25, 30, 34, 38, 57, 72, 76,
    84, 85, 156
Enlightenment, 26
entertainers, 13
ethnic identity, 39, 88, 117, 118, 144,
    148, 156, 166, 171
  and Romani literature, 88, 115–118,
    124
  suppression of, 28, 29
ethnic literature(s), and Romani litera-
    ture, 115–118
ethnic minority, Roma as, 35, 140,
    196n16
ethnicity. *See* ethnic identity
ethnogenesis, 141
Ette, Ottmar, 125

European Charter for Regional or
    Minority Languages, 74, 157,
    188n2
European Charter on Roma Rights,
    142
European Commission, 35, 36, 37
European Parliament, 35, 36, 37
European Union (EU), 2, 26, 32, 35,
    36, 37, 73, 74, 142, 184n41
  Charter of Fundamental Rights, 32
  Copenhagen criteria, 37, 185n16
evangelical missionaries. *See*
    missionaries
evil nature of the Gypsies, 13, 96, 99
exile
  in contemporary society, 95, 193n6
  exilic literature, 119, 125
  of the Gypsies, 9, 10, 11, 19, 181n2

F

Fermo, 10
Ficowski, Jerzy, 75, 164
Finnegan, Ruth, 1, 187n17
Finland, 90, 158, 190n41
Florence, 89
folklore
  European, and the Gypsies, 15, 46,
    182n22
  of the Roma/Gypsies, 46, 78, 83
Forlì, 15
fortune telling, 13, 14, 61
Foucault, Michel, 8
France, 8, 20, 34, 37, 73, 82, 83, 91,
    110, 153
Franz, Philomena, 85–86, 111
Fraser, Angus, 9, 18
Frederick III, Emperor, 9
Freire, Paulo, xvi, 54, 171

G

Gaje/Gadže/Gorgio(s)
  meaning, 176, 181n1
  Roma's attitude towards, 50–51
genocide, xiii, 101–102, 104, 192n18
Germany, 8, 9, 11, 77, 83, 85, 106
Gheorghe, Nicolae, 141, 154, 195n1,
    196n13–14
Gitanos. See names given to Gypsies
Glissant, Edouard, 126, 191n11
Gomes, Ana Maria, 51
Graff, Harvey, 52, 53
Gramsci, Antonio, 54
graphic codes, non-alphabetic, 3, 43,
    55–62, 63, 67
Greece, 142

Grellmann, Heinrich, 27–28, 30, 31, 182n12, 191n3
Guattari, Félix, 121, 122, 124–125
Guillory, John, 114
"Gypsies", meaning, 181n1
Gypsiness, 118
Gypsy Council (UK), 34, 198n31

H
Hall, Stuart, 128
Hamilton, Mary, 64, 187n19
Hancock, Ian, 96, 144, 145, 147–148, 154, 159
Hava-Robbins, Nadia, 85, 101
hegemony, 54, 115
Heredia Maya, José, 84
heteroglossia. *See* Bakhtin, Mikhail
Holdosi, József, 80
Holocaust, 80, 85, 101, 104–105, 125, 145, 154. *See also* *Porrajmos*
    forgotten, 104, 148, 154, 192n18–19
    Jewish, 192n18
    Romani, 3, 79, 92, 101–105, 112, 158
Holy Roman Empire, 19
homelessness
    of the migrant writer, 119
    of the Romani people, 94, 109, 125, 197n21
homo viator, 9
Hortis, Samuel Augustini ab, 27
Hoyland, John, 30–31
Hübschmannová, Milena, 79, 198n32
Hungary, 11, 28, 37, 59, 76, 80, 186n7, 189n16
hybridity, 4, 65, 115, 119, 126, 127–129, 165, 194n17
    cultural, 120, 127, 164
    intentional, 129, 135
    (inter)textual, 129, 132, 134–135
    linguistic, 3, 127
    organic (*see* Bakhtin, Mikhail)

I
identity. *See also* ethnic identity
    common/shared, 4, 152, 155
    diaspora/diasporic, 128, 151–152
    displacement of, 145
    negotiation of, 66, 127, 128, 170
    textual construction of, 2, 7–8
identity-building, 141
    and Romani writing, 4, 66, 67, 118, 139, 140, 151, 159, 161

illiteracy, 1, 2, 30, 42, 50, 51, 165, 181n1, 187n12
illiteracy rate(s) among the Roma, 2, 35, 36, 38, 54, 187n16
in-betweeness, condition of, 119
India, 15, 73, 150, 156, 176
Indian origin(s)
    of the Roma, 27, 73, 76, 147, 150, 155–156, 197n29
    of the Romani language, 73, 177
intelligentsia, Romani, 77, 96, 139–141, 148, 149, 155, 156, 165
International Romani Day, 142
International Romani Union (IRU), 78, 142, 153, 155, 157
    Declaration of a Nation, 153–155
    Linguistics Commission of the, 157
International Romani Writers' Association (IRWA), 78, 81, 84, 90, 190n42
intertextuality, notion of, 4, 115, 129–130, 133, 134–135, 194n19
Italian-American literature, 115, 116
Italy, 25, 47, 51, 64, 72, 81, 87, 106, 109, 110, 141
    arrival of Gypsies in, 8, 10
    cultural mediators in, 172–173
    edicts against Gypsies in, 20
    education of Roma/Gypsies in, 33–34, 37

J
Jayat, Sandra, 83, 106, 109–112, 189n25
Jekhipè (oneness), 147
Jenische, 86, 108, 109, 190n34–35
Jews, 13, 18, 55, 101, 155, 181n3, 191n18
Joseph II, Emperor, 29
Journal of the Gypsy Lore Society, 83, 198n31
Jovanović, Ilija, 86, 99

K
Kafka, Franz, 122
Kalderaš Roma, 82, 152, 153
    dialect, 82
Kalinin, Valdemar, 76–77, 90, 188n10
Karpati, Mirella, 33–34, 185n8–9, 185n11
Kawczynski, Rudko, 197n17
Kerim, Usin, 82
King, Martin Luther, 155
King, Russell, 120

Klimová-Alexander, 196n3
Kochanowski, Vania de Gila (Jan), 83, 149–150, 159
Kosovo, 64, 77, 78
Krasnići, Alija, 77, 78
kris (stories of court trials), 47
Kristeva, Julia, 129, 194n19
Kwiek family, 197n29

L
Lacková, Elena (Ilona), 79
Lanciano, 142, 148
Lauret, Maria, 116
Le Bas, Damian, 194n14
Le Goff, Jacques, 183n24
Lee, Ronald, 85, 143
legislation, anti-Gypsy, 8, 14, 18–20, 23, 184n32, 184n37
Leland, Charles Godfrey, 57, 61
Lemon, Alaina, 96
Levacovich, Mansueto, 72, 88, 89, 99–100, 130, 131
Levakovich, Giuseppe (Tzigari), 58, 87, 89
Lévi-Strauss, 194n18
Liégeois, Jean-Pierre, 29, 32, 44, 46, 93, 185n22, 186n2
liminality, notion of, 165–166, 198n4
literacy
    alphabetic, 50, 52, 53, 55, 62, 144, 161, 164, 173
    critical, 54, 144
    hybrid, 4, 171, 173, 175, 179, 180, 199n13
    intellectuals' attitude towards, 4, 51, 71, 143–144
    intercultural, 161
    literate/non-literate divide, 1, 53
    mediating role of, 68, 170–180
    New Literacy Studies (NLS), 53–54
    restricted, 2, 4, 90
    Romani, 65, 68, 144, 151, 161, 170, 177, 179, 180
    Western model of, 52, 171
Little Egypt, 11, 19, 181n1
Lombroso, Cesare, 17
London, 142
Louis XII, king of France, 20
Louis XIV, king of France, 20
Luther, Martin, 14

M
Macedo, Donaldo, 54
Macedonia, 77, 158

Manuš (Romani group), 43, 67
    literacy practices among the, 43, 64–65
Manuš, Leksa, 76, 143, 196n14
marginalisation, 3, 23, 92, 97, 124, 143, 148
    politics of, 7
    of Roma/Gypsies within mainstream education, 171, 179
    and Romani literature, 92, 97, 124, 182n15
    Romani women's, 106–108
    self-marginalisation, 148, 149
Maria Theresa of Austria, Empress, 2, 26, 28, 186n7
Matras, Yaron, 49, 144, 158, 159
Maximoff, Matéo, 46, 82–83, 193n4
Mead, Margaret, 68
mediation
    as conflict resolution, 162, 163, 196n2
    cultural, 162, 167, 172
    mediating role of Romani literature, 67, 164–170
mediators
    Roma and Sinti, 170, 171, 172–173, 176, 199n14
    Romani women as, 168–170, 172
    traditional, 141, 195n2
    writers as, 164, 166
Mehr, Mariella, 82, 86–87, 90, 106, 108–109, 190n36
memory, xiv, 52, 83, 101
    collective, 2, 41, 151
    cultural, 32, 44, 117, 154
    Holocaust, 101–103, 148, 158
metalworking, 13, 156
migrant literature(s), 118–121, 194n7
    and Romani literature, 120, 122, 135
migration(s), 82, 120, 121
    forced, 122
    and the Romani language, 73, 156
    theory of Gypsy, 150
Milan, 15, 172
    State of, 20, 184n39
mimicry, 10, 128, 132, 195n27
minor literature, 122, 124, 170
    Romani literature as, 125, 127
minority
    languages, 72, 73, 74, 122, 157, 188n2
    national, 80, 184n7, 188n6
    status, 35, 74, 188n6, 196n16
Mirga, Andrzej, 154, 196n13–14
missionaries, 2, 30–31, 41

Modena, Duchy of, 20
Morley, David, 84–85
Moscow, 76
multilingualism, 119, 158
  multilingual texts by Romani
    authors, 72, 87, 91
Münster, Sebastian, 9, 10, 19
music, 84, 85, 110, 183n29. *See also*
    songs
  Romani musicians, 13, 29, 79, 85,
    88, 148, 156, 189n16, 189n23
myths, concerning Gypsies, 13, 145,
    183n28

N

Naficy, Hamid, 193n6
names given to Gypsies, 19, 123, 147
  Athinganoi, 123
  Bohémiens/Bohemians, 19, 20
  Cingani/*Cingari*, 14, 20, 184n40
  Egyptians, 8, 11, 19, 20, 55, 123–
    124, 181n1, 184n32, 184n37
  Gitanos, 84, 147
  Saracen(s), 14
  Tsigan/*Tsygani*, 123, 167
  Új Magyár (new Hungarians), 28
  Zigeuner, 19, 123
  Zingari, 147
nation, Romani/Gypsy, 139, 152–155.
    See also Romanestan
  national anthem, 142, 155, 197n26
  non-territorial, 142, 153
National Association of Teachers and
    Travellers (NATT), 38
National Gypsy Education Council
    (NGEC), 34, 38
Native American/American Indian
    literature, 115, 135
Nazis
  and Roma and Sinti, 75, 83, 85, 96,
    123, 197n17
Nedich, Jorge Emilio, 84, 193n4
negotiation, 115, 128, 161–162, 164,
    166
Négritude, 97, 191n11
Nikolić, Jovan, 77, 78
nomadism. *See also* travelling
  criminalisation of, 14, 23, 29, 62,
    81, 93
  and Gypsies' racial identity, 191n3
  and Romani literature, 3, 92–95,
    121, 131–132, 167
  non-Gypsies' perception of, 9, 29, 62
  versus migration, 121

non-alphabetic writing, 3, 43, 55–62,
    65, 67, 68
Nuremberg trials, 191n18
Nurse, Keith, 127

O

occupations, 7, 13, 14, 16, 18, 28, 29,
    183n24
Okely, Judith, 8, 51, 59, 168
Ong, Walter, 48, 193n2
Open Society Institute, 77, 185n15
Opera Nomadi (pro-Roma associa-
    tion), 34, 87, 172, 190n38
Opre Roma Report, 37–38
orality
  oral features of Romani language,
    43, 48–49
  oral mode of communication, 3, 43,
    46, 55, 67, 130, 158, 174
  oral tradition, 43, 46–48, 50, 75, 129–
    130, 132, 134, 177, 179, 180
Organisation for Security and Coopera-
    tion in Europe (OSCE), 37, 142
organisations
  All-Russian Union of Gypsies, 76
  Comité International Tsigane (CIT),
    142, 153
  European Roma and Travellers
    Forum (ERTF), 196n8
  Phralipe, 80
  Roma National Congress (RNC),
    142, 155, 196n7
  Zentralrat Deutscher Sinti und
    Roma, 196n8
origin(s) of the Roma, 7, 150, 154, 155,
    156, 183n26, 197n21. *See also*
    Indian origin(s)

P

Papuśa/Papusza (Bronislawa Wajs),
    75–76, 164, 195n29
  Songs of Papusza, 75
pariah group
  Gypsies as, 23, 122, 125, 150, 194n12
Paris, 10, 11, 83, 109
patrin (non-alphabetic signs), 55–59,
    61–62, 67
periodicals in Romani, 81, 150, 158,
    198n31
peripatetic practices/strategies, 50, 59,
    62, 93
peripatetics, notion of, 190n2
persecution, 83, 84, 89, 100, 147, 148,
    149–150, 154, 155

in the former Czechoslovakia, 85
on racial grounds, 196n17
in sixteenth-century Europe, 7, 20
in twentieth-century Europe, 17, 79
Philip IV, king of Spain, 28
Phralipe. See organisations
Piasere, Leonardo, 58, 66, 93
pilgrims, xiii, 9, 14, 15, 19
Plowden Report, 38
Poland, 59, 75, 83, 142, 157
politics, 139, 144. *See also* Romani
   activists
   and identity-building, 139, 140, 141,
      151, 159, 161
   diaspora, 151, 197n20–22
   World Romani Congress (WRC), 78,
      142, 153, 156, 157
pollution taboos, 106
Polska Roma, 75, 164
polyglottism, 126
"polyphonic" text, 169. *See also* Bakthin,
   Mikhail
Pope, the, and the Gypsies, 10, 15
Porrajmos, 101, 102, 154, 192n19. *See
   also* Holocaust
postcolonial theory, 127, 163
Prague, 142, 158
   Prague Spring, 79
Pralipe (theatre company). *See* theatre,
   Romani/Gypsy
Pratt, Mary Louise, 115, 199n8
   notion of autoethnography, 191n4
   notion of contact zones, 115
Predari, Francesco, 16, 28
primitive nature of the Gypsies, 16–17,
   18. *See also* stereotypes
primitivism, 16, 24, 184n30
   and Gypsy education, 27, 33, 40
Pro Juventute (welfare organisation), 86
punishment for Gypsies, 14, 18, 21, 30
Pushkin, Alexander, 76, 146
   Tsygany, 167, 199n7

R

Rabelais, François, 127
racism, 96, 165, 170
   against Romani children, 38, 41
   and Romani literature, 96–98, 112
Reformation, 14, 15
reformation of the Gypsies, 26, 30–31
Reilly, John, 117
religion
   apparent lack of religion among
      Gypsies 15, 30

of the Roma, 150, 187n22
representation(s)
   cultural, 23, 118, 180
   of Gypsies as wild, 15–17, 55, 56
   self-representations, 93, 95, 96, 111,
      166
   textual, 7, 17, 23, 27, 146, 163
rogues, 14, 19, 21. *See also* vagrants
Rom, Roma, Romani, as self-definitions, 147, 181n1
Romanes, 49, 176, 179. *See also*
   Romani language
Romanès, Alexandre, 83, 189n27
Romanestan (the Romani nation), 142,
   153
Romani activists, 4, 77, 78, 80, 84,
   140, 141, 149, 151, 153, 161
   attitude towards schooling, 143–144,
      196n13
   notion of nationhood, 155–156
   and the Romani Holocaust, 154–155
   and writing, 139, 140, 150, 151–152,
      157, 159
Romani authors, 3–4, 65, 71–72, 74–91,
      93, 94, 100, 112–113, 118, 120,
      122, 124, 125, 126, 134–136,
      139, 140, 161, 165, 179
   as mediators, 164–168
   female, xvi, 3, 64, 92, 106–112, 161,
      165, 168–170
   Italian, 87, 132–134
Romani language (Romani, *Romani
   chib*), 43, 48–49, 72, 78, 85,
      139, 143, 144, 148, 176, 177
   dialectal variation in, 73
   and Indian origins, 27, 147, 156, 157
   and Romani literature, 73–74
   periodicals in, 76, 79, 81, 150, 158,
      198n31
   standardisation of, 71, 157
Romani Library, 90, 190n42
Romani literature
   autonomy of, 89, 124, 194n15
   as decentralised writing, 125–126, 135
   as deterritorialised literature, 122,
      125–126, 135
   mediating function of (*see* mediation)
   non-canonical features of, 90, 114,
      117
   themes in, 3, 88, 92–106, 131–133,
      135, 190n1
   vis-à-vis world literature, 126, 135
Romani studies, 4, 139, 144, 149, 159,
      196n14, 198n32

Romania, 59, 76, 81, 82, 83, 96, 142, 158
Romanichal Gypsies, 64, 148
Romanipe, 93. *See also* Gypsiness
Romantic authors/period
 and the idealisation of Gypsies, 27, 93, 146, 184n30
Rome, 15, 89, 198n31
Romen (theatre company). *See* theatre, Romani/Gypsy
Rose, Romani, 197n17
Rosenberg, Karen, 102
Rosenberg, Otto, 85, 190n31
Rotaru, Ionel, 153
Rushdie, Salman, 128
Russia, 73, 76, 82, 83, 96, 140, 188n6, 188n9

S
Šaban, Iliaz, 94, 97, 107, 188n12
safe-conducts, 9–10, 11, 20, 23, 181n4
Safran, William, 151, 197n21
Salo, Matt, and Salo, Sheila, 64
Sampson, John, 198n30
Sandland, Ralph, 145
Sanskrit, and the Romani language, 73
savage Gypsy, image of the, 8, 15–16, 28, 184n30. *See also* stereotypes
school provision for Roma/Gypsies
 and the EU, 32, 35–36
 failure of, 2, 26, 39, 41
 in the UK, 38–39
schooling, 3, 36, 44, 68
 attitude of the Roma/Gypsies towards, 25, 41, 50, 51, 67–68, 143
 compulsory, xiv, 41, 68, 75
 Decade of Roma Inclusion, 185n15
 exclusion of Romani children, 39
 INSETRom programme, 199n14
Schöpf, Paula, 106–108, 112, 169
Ščuka, Emil, 79, 142
sedentarisation, 28, 32, 73
 forced, 30, 31, 75, 164
sedentary societies, 7, 59
 perception of nomadism and migration among, 9, 119, 122
segregated education, 37
Sejdić, Rasim, 87–88, 186n4, 195n29
Serbia, 59, 64, 77, 158
Serbian Roma/Gypsies, 47, 86
Sibley, David, 23
Sigismund, king of Hungary, and Emperor, 9, 10, 11, 181n6
Simson, Walter, 16

Sinti
 cultural mediators, 172
 in Germany, 57, 85, 158, 196n8, 196n13
 in Italy, 25, 33, 39, 51, 87, 88, 106, 109, 185n8, 186n9, 191n3
 self-definition, 181n1
slavery, 83, 96, 154, 182n18, 189n24
Slovak Republic, 79
Slovak Roma, 79
Slovakia, 76, 79
Slovenian-Croatian Roma, 58, 87, 89, 112, 141
 alphabetic writing among, 64, 67
 women as cultural mediators, 172
Smith, Anthony, 155
Smith, Charles (Charlie), 84, 90, 130
Smith, Ray, 84
smithery, 29
songs (oral tradition), 46, 80, 88, 120, 186n6
Soravia, Giulio, 88, 186n4, 193n1
sorcery, 13, 15, 150
Soros Foundation, 37
Soviet Union, 76, 142
space
 exclusionary, 23
 liminal, 165, 179
 perception of, 121–122
 social, 17, 50, 165
 Third Space, 127, 199n13
 versus place, 121–122, 194n10
Spain, 84, 156, 186n7
 Roma education in, 34, 37
Spinelli, Santino, 72, 84, 88, 98, 104, 107, 133–134, 148–149, 159
Spivak, Gayatri, 128
Stankiewicz, Stanisław, 142
stealing, 11, 19, 31, 47, 182n19
 child stealing, allegation of, 17
 Gypsies' alleged propensity to steal, 30
stereotypes, 7, 23, 24, 135, 145–146, 170, 180
 anti-Gypsy, 112, 139, 146–147, 159, 165
 of Gypsies as primitive/savage, 1, 2, 8, 23, 26, 29, 30, 33, 114
 of the Gypsy as illiterate/uncivilised, 17, 26, 27, 28, 180
 manipulation of, 10, 116
 about Romani women, 168
 romantic, 94, 131, 132
Stojka, Ceija, 82, 86, 102–103, 111
Stojka, Mongo, 86

Storey, Jimmy, 85
Strasbourg, 14
Strasbourg Declaration on Roma, 199n14
Street, Brian, xiii, 52, 171
Šuto Orizari, 77, 188n11
Swann Report, 39
Sweden, 73, 87, 158
Switzerland, 85, 86, 190n34–35
Symons, Arthur, 16

T
Tamburri, Anthony, 116, 117
Tauber, Elisabeth, 51, 186n11
teachers, Romani
  as intellectuals, 140
  role of, 143, 144
theatre, Romani/Gypsy, 76, 81, 188n6, 189n21
  Pralipe (Yugoslavia), 77
  Romen (Russia), 76
theft, 14, 60. *See also* stealing
Tipler, Derek, 46
Tong, Diane, 46
trail-signs, 56–57. See also *patrin* signs
translation, 72, 88, 120, 126, 162, 164, 167, 168, 172, 176, 178
  cultural, 120, 126, 163, 166
  as mediation, 163, 164
  self-translation, 163, 164, 166, 168
  theories of, 162–163
transnational literature, 124. *See also* world literature
transnationalism, 119
Transylvania, 59
Traveller-Gypsies, 25, 51, 59, 194n18
travelling, 93, 95, 110, 167, 190n1. *See also* nomadism
Turner, Victor, 165, 166

U
United Kingdom (UK), xv, 38, 79, 91
United Nations (UN), 37, 142, 153
United States of America (USA). *See* America
universities
  and Romani studies, 148, 158–159, 196n13

V
vagabonds, 14, 19, 20. *See also* vagrants

Vagrancy Act (1597), 184n36
vagrants, Gypsies labelled as, 14, 19, 27, 187n28
Van Gennep, Arnold, 165, 198n4
van Kappen, O., 9
Venice, 20, 176
Vienna, 86
violence, in Romani literature, 96, 98–100, 104, 108–109, 112, 130, 133
visual representations of Gypsies, 12, 145

W
Wanderzeichen (nomadic signs), 59
warning signs for Gypsies, 20–23
Weber, Max, 194n12
White, Hayden, 17
Wiernicki, Krzystztof, 46
wildness, 15, 17
Williams, Patrick, 61, 64, 65
Wlislocki, Heinrich von, 59
Woloch, Cecilia, 85
women
  mediating function of, 172
  in Romani society, 106, 111, 168–170
  violence against, 108–109
world literature, 90, 124, 125, 126
World Romani Congress (WRC). *See* politics
World War II, 79, 82, 83, 142
writing
  instrumental use of, 3, 10, 43, 62–64, 67, 68, 161, 195n30
  non-alphabetic writing/graphic systems, 3, 43, 55, 59, 63, 65, 67
  political, 139–140, 144, 150–151

Y
Yugoslavia, 76, 77–78, 82, 87, 88, 188n12
Yusuf, Šaip, 77

Z
Zaniboni, Paola, 179
Zigeuner. See names given to Gypsies
Zigeunerwarntafel, 21, 23. *See also* warning signs for Gypsies
Zingari. See names given to Gypsies

For Product Safety Concerns and Information please contact our EU
representative GPSR@taylorandfrancis.com
Taylor & Francis Verlag GmbH, Kaufingerstraße 24, 80331 München, Germany